The
Total CISSP® Exam
Prep Book

Practice Questions, Answers,
and Test Taking Tips and Techniques

OTHER AUERBACH PUBLICATIONS

ABCs of IP Addressing
Gilbert Held
ISBN: 0-8493-1144-6

Application Servers for E-Business
Lisa M. Lindgren
ISBN: 0-8493-0827-5

Architectures for E-Business Systems
Sanjiv Purba, Editor
ISBN: 0-8493-1161-6

A Technical Guide to IPSec Virtual Private Networks
James S. Tiller
ISBN: 0-8493-0876-3

Building an Information Security Awareness Program
Mark B. Desman
ISBN: 0-8493-0116-5

Computer Telephony Integration
William Yarberry, Jr.
ISBN: 0-8493-9995-5

Cyber Crime Investigator's Field Guide
Bruce Middleton
ISBN: 0-8493-1192-6

**Cyber Forensics:
A Field Manual for Collecting, Examining, and Preserving Evidence of Computer Crimes**
Albert J. Marcella and Robert S. Greenfield, Editors
ISBN: 0-8493-0955-7

Information Security Architecture
Jan Killmeyer Tudor
ISBN: 0-8493-9988-2

Information Security Management Handbook, 4th Edition, Volume 1
Harold F. Tipton and Micki Krause, Editors
ISBN: 0-8493-9829-0

Information Security Management Handbook, 4th Edition, Volume 2
Harold F. Tipton and Micki Krause, Editors
ISBN: 0-8493-0800-3

Information Security Management Handbook, 4th Edition, Volume 3
Harold F. Tipton and Micki Krause, Editors
ISBN: 0-8493-1127-6

**Information Security Policies, Procedures, and Standards:
Guidelines for Effective Information Security Management**
Thomas R. Peltier
ISBN: 0-8493-1137-3

Information Security Risk Analysis
Thomas R. Peltier
ISBN: 0-8493-0880-1

Information Technology Control and Audit
Frederick Gallegos, Sandra Allen-Senft, and Daniel P. Manson
ISBN: 0-8493-9994-7

New Directions in Internet Management
Sanjiv Purba, Editor
ISBN: 0-8493-1160-8

New Directions in Project Management
Paul C. Tinnirello, Editor
ISBN: 0-8493-1190-X

A Practical Guide to Security Engineering and Information Assurance
Debra Herrmann
ISBN: 0-8493-1163-2

**The Privacy Papers:
Managing Technology and Consumers, Employee, and Legislative Action**
Rebecca Herold
ISBN: 0-8493-1248-5

**Secure Internet Practices:
Best Practices for Securing Systems in the Internet and e-Business Age**
Patrick McBride, Joday Patilla, Craig Robinson, Peter Thermos, and Edward P. Moser
ISBN: 0-8493-1239-6

Securing and Controlling Cisco Routers
Peter T. Davis
ISBN: 0-8493-1290-6

Securing E-Business Applications and Communications
Jonathan S. Held and John R. Bowers
ISBN: 0-8493-0963-8

**Securing Windows NT/2000:
From Policies to Firewalls**
Michael A. Simonyi
ISBN: 0-8493-1261-2

TCP/IP Professional Reference Guide
Gilbert Held
ISBN: 0-8493-0824-0

The Complete Book of Middleware
Judith Myerson
ISBN: 0-8493-1272-8

AUERBACH PUBLICATIONS

www.auerbach-publications.com
To Order Call: 1-800-272-7737 • Fax: 1-800-374-3401
E-mail: orders@crcpress.com

The
Total CISSP® Exam
Prep Book

Practice Questions, Answers, and Test Taking Tips and Techniques

THOMAS R. PELTIER
PATRICK D. HOWARD

AUERBACH PUBLICATIONS

A CRC Press Company
Boca Raton   London   New York   Washington, D.C.

Library of Congress Cataloging-in-Publication Data

Peltier, Thomas R.
    The total CISSP exam prep book : practice questions, answers, and test taking tips and techniques / Thomas R. Peltier, Patrick D. Howard.
        p. cm.
    Includes bibliographical references and index.
    ISBN 0-8493-1350-3
        1. Computer networks--Security measures--Examinations--Study guides. 2. Electronic data processing personnel--Certification. I. Howard, Patrick D. II. Title.

TK5105.59 .P454 2002
005.8--dc21

2002066436

Visit the Auerbach Publications Web site at www.auerbach-publications.com

© 2002 by CRC Press LLC
Auerbach is an imprint of CRC Press LLC

No claim to original U.S. Government works
International Standard Book Number 0-8493-1350-3
Library of Congress Card Number 2002066436

Contributors

John A. Blackley, CISSP, a native of Scotland, completed his Bachelor's degree in electrical engineering at Glasgow University in 1974. Since moving to the United States in 1982, his career has included 18 years in information security. John took his first information security position with a financial services company in Louisville, Kentucky. Starting with security administration, he gained the experience and breadth of knowledge to become the Director of Information Security and Business Contingency Planning. During that time, John also became a member of the faculty at Eastern Kentucky University — advising on the loss prevention program. Moving to Texas in 1992, John filled a similar position for one of the nation's Fortune 100 corporations. He developed that organization's Business Contingency Planning program and organized and was responsible for the development of every aspect of its comprehensive information security program. In 1995, John became Senior Consultant for Europe's largest dedicated information security consultancy and carried out engagements for national and multi-national organizations in such locations as Seoul, Mauritius, Brussels, London, Lisbon, and Dublin. Returning to Texas in 1998, John is now Principal Security Architect for ThruPoint's information security practice. As such, John provides direction and support to the salesforce and the engineers in information protection and availability matters, as well as undertaking significant security-related projects in his own right. John has published a number of articles in the business press and has been a speaker at conferences and seminars around the world. He teaches elements of preparation courses for the CISSP certification exam and addresses organization and management issues relating to the practice of information security.

Bob Cartwright, CISSP, is president of Enterprise Security Solutions. He has more than 15 years of information systems security experience and a comprehensive investment of 22 years within information systems. He has referential expertise in information security program development, management, and hands-on implementation. He holds a bachelor's degree in business administration, an MBA in information systems, and is a Certified Information Systems Security Professional (CISSP). His experience in and dedication to information security has resulted in a member seat of the Computer Security Institute (CSI) Advisory Board, an internationally recognized name in virus response, and a permanent speaking invitation for a number of security conferences. Before starting his own security consulting firm, Bob was recruited into the Netigy Corporation to assume responsibility for the entire security life cycle as the regional practice manager. He was responsible for developing client relationships, identifying roles and appropriate security solutions for each client, and negotiating the terms and obligations and providing the delivery oversight to ensure on-time/on-budget projects. This required him to utilize his skills as a trusted security advisor, facilitator, and educator. Bob's success as the regional practice manager relied heavily on his ability to build the proper team utilizing client and consultant resources, to maintain a presence as mentor to the team, and to operate within the dynamics of a diverse group of information technology personnel. Information security is a matter of trust. Bob has demonstrated his ability to establish trust with clients by using his international reputation as a subject matter expert. He consistently provides superior projects and timely confidential responses to sensitive client issues. Bob has built this trust with leadership and personal reputation and continues to seek the opportunity to increase that trust and presence with new clients.

Terri Curran, CISSP, of QinetiQ TIM, has more than 26 years of information security and systems operations experience. Terri has been involved with information security consulting during the past several years in practice management and development capacities. In her consulting career, Terri has developed and deployed security solutions for manufacturing, consumer goods, financial, and other Fortune 200-level companies. She provides industry-leading expertise in information security policies and awareness programs. Terri has provided extensive knowledge transfer to international companies in the areas of ISO/IEC 17799 and other international codes and regulations; security training; security change control integration; business recovery; incident management; emergency response capabilities; and investigation management. She is an experienced facilitator in the areas of information security problem identification, scope clarification, project planning, executive management briefings, and measured success workshops. Prior to her consulting career, Terri was the Corporate Information Security Officer for The Gillette Company in Boston. She developed and implemented the framework for international information security deployment during nearly 20 years with the Company. Prior to joining Gillette, she held systems operations positions of increasing responsibility at Stride-Rite, Call-Data Systems (Grumman Aircraft), and Boston University. Terri is a frequent speaker at industry conferences, briefings, and meetings, and has authored for, and been quoted in, industry-leading journals and publications. She assisted with the development of the original Computer Crime and Security Certificate program at Northeastern University and has lectured at the collegiate level on computer privacy and security. Terri is CISSP (Certified Information Systems Security Professional)-certified (June 1992). She additionally holds membership in the HTCIA (High Tech Crime Investigation Association), CFE (Certified Fraud Examiners), CSI (Computer Security Institute, former charter member of the CSI Peer Group), ISSA (Information Systems Security Association), and ASIS (American Society for Industrial Security). Terri anticipates acquiring the ASIS CPP (Certified Protection Professional) designation in 2002.

Rebecca Herold, CISSP, CISA, FLMI, of QinetiQ TIM, has more than 13 years of information security experience. Rebecca is currently a trusted advisor for HIPAA compliance and remediation for a large international organization. Rebecca was the Global Security Practice SME for the Central Region for Netigy Corporation for almost two years. Prior to joining Netigy, Rebecca was Senior Systems Security Consultant at Principal Financial Group (PFG) where she was instrumental in developing the corporate information protection department. Some of her accomplishments there included creating the company's information protection awareness program; creating the corporate anti-virus strategy and heading the first virus SWAT team; creating and maintaining information protection policies and procedures; and creating and implementing a Computer Incident Response Team (CIRT). Rebecca's program received the CSI Outstanding Information Protection Program of the Year award in 1997. Rebecca has performed numerous information security projects for large and multinational organizations. She has also published numerous information security journal, magazine, and newsletter articles and has written a book on privacy entitled *The Privacy Papers,* (Auerbach Publications, 2001). Rebecca has given many presentations at conferences and seminars. She has a B.S. in math and computer science and an M.A. in computer science and education. Rebecca is a Certified Information Systems Security Professional (CISSP), a Certified Information Systems Auditor (CISA), and a Fellow of the Life Management Institute (FLMI). Rebecca has been a member of the Information Systems Audit and Control Association (ISACA) since 1990 and has held all board positions throughout her membership in the Iowa chapter. Rebecca is a charter member of the Iowa Infragard chapter.

Patrick D. Howard, CISSP, is a senior information security consultant with QinetiQ TIM. He has more than 20 years of experience in information security. A former military police officer, Pat successful served in military positions in law enforcement, operations, physical security, and security management, retiring from the U.S. Army in 1992. Since then he has served as an information security consultant with several government contracting firms in the Washington, D.C., area, including Comis Corp., PRC, and Troy Systems, supporting the Nuclear Regulatory Commission, U.S. Coast Guard, House of Representatives, and Departments of Agriculture, Labor, and Defense among others. Pat was formerly employed as a senior manager for Ernst & Young where he developed E&Y security consulting methodologies and created policies and standards for BankBoston, John Hancock Insurance, Textron, and Sprint. Most recently, he was manager for Netigy Corporation, where he performed risk analysis and policy/procedure development engagements with eSylvan, Aramark, Black & Decker, and other firms and government agencies. At Netigy, he was also charged with developing an innovative corporate security consultant certification (QeSA) program; he developed and delivered CISSP preparatory training to consultant and client personnel, and created corporate security consulting methodologies. Pat currently serves as an instructor for the Computer Security Institute, where he leads a team of subject matter experts conducting CISSP Prep for Success Workshops across the United States. He has recently written articles on the security policy life cycles that have been published in *Data Security* and in the *Handbook for Information Security Management*. Pat has a B.A. degree from the University of Oklahoma and an M.A. from Boston University.

Carl Jackson, CISSP, is a Certified Information Systems Security Professional (CISSP) and brings more than 25 years of experience in the areas of information security, continuity planning, and information technology internal control reviews and audits. As the Vice President–Business Continuity Planning for QinetiQ Trusted Information Management Corporation, he is responsible for the continued development and oversight of QinetiQ Trusted Information Management methodologies and tools in the enterprisewide business continuity planning arena, including network and E-business availability and recovery as well as for continuity planning practice management and oversight.

Before joining QinetiQ-TIM, Mr. Jackson was a partner with Ernst & Young LLP where he served as the firm's BCP Service Line Leader. Mr. Jackson has extensive consulting experience with numerous major organizations in multiple industries, including manufacturing, financial services, transportation, health care, technology, pharmaceutical, retail, aerospace, insurance, and professional sports management. He also has extensive business continuity planning experience as an information security practitioner, manager in the field of information security and business continuity planning, and as a university-level professor.

Mr. Jackson was a founding board member and past-president of the Information Systems Security Association (ISSA) and is currently serving as the chairman of the International ISSA Board of Directors. Mr. Jackson is a past member and past Emeritus member of the Computer Security Institute (CSI) Advisory Council and is the recipient of the 1997 CSI Lifetime Achievement Award. He has also served on the editorial and advisory boards of both the Contingency Planning Management (CPM) magazine and Datapro Reports on Information Security and is a frequent public speaker on these topics.

Cheryl Jackson, CISSP, CBCP, is an information systems security professional with more than 20 years of progressive experience in information services. She is a Certified Information Systems Security Professional (CISSP), and her career includes experience in operations, systems administration, analysis, design, and implementation of end-to-end information security solutions. These comprehensive information security programs effectively combine personnel, management and technology to assure confidentiality, integrity and availability of mission-critical business information. She is also a Certified

Business Continuity Planner (CBCP), and in this role has been responsible for every aspect of business continuity planning, including risk analysis, business impact analysis, and the design, testing, and implementation of business continuity plans, disaster recovery procedures, and crisis management plans. She has extensive consulting experience with major organizations in multiple industries, including investment banking, oil and gas, manufacturing, energy, transportation, and communication.

She recently joined the ThruPoint Security Practice as an information protection subject matter expert and principal consultant. Cheryl was formerly part of the Netigy Global Security Practice as a manager on the team responsible for the continued development of methodologies and tools in the security management process arena. Her career also includes Perot Systems, as part of the Information Security and Business Continuity Teams, where she led a number of engagements for major clients to develop information security solutions and business continuity/crisis management/disaster recovery plans. Prior to that, she worked for The MinuteMaid Company, a division of the Coca-Cola Company, for ten years as a member of the Information Security team, responsible for design, implementation, and management of information security controls on all of the company computing platforms. Among her accomplishments at MinuteMaid, Jackson designed and implemented the company's first corporatewide information security program.

She is currently serving on the board of directors for the South Texas ISSA Chapter. She is a former chairperson and emeritus member of the Computer Security Institute Advisory Council, past-president of the Southwest CA-ACF2 Users Group, and a frequent speaker at professional conferences and meetings. She is currently one of the tag team of experts serving as an instructor for the CISSP Prep for Success class.

David Lynas, CISSP, is recognized one of the world's leading authorities on information security strategy and architecture. He is a globally respected information security professional with a proven record of success and more than 20 years of practical experience in delivering some of the world's most high-profile security solutions across almost every aspect of that multidisciplined profession. David was the first European ever to present a keynote address to the annual Computer Security Institute conference and he was among the first Europeans to be accredited as a Certified Information Systems Security Professional (CISSP) by the International Information Systems Security Certification Consortium (ISC)². He now personally sponsors CISSP examinations each year in Ireland. He is also the founder and chairman of the highly prestigious COSAC Information Security Symposium (http://www.cosac.net), now in its ninth year of providing a highly participative and interactive thought-leadership forum for experienced InfoSec managers and professionals. David has owned and directed successful information security consulting businesses for more than ten years. Originally responsible for information security at one of Ireland's largest clearing banks, he founded the consulting company AKA Associates in 1991. Through a process of international mergers and acquisitions, he became operations director at Sherwood Associates Limited and director of security architecture for Netigy Corporation's Global Security Practice, where he led the development of the SABSA methodology — rapidly becoming the *de facto* standard approach to designing, deploying, and operating security architecture. Using this architectural approach, David has led many successful global-scale engagements with up to nine-figure budgets for companies in the finance, health care, aeronautics, telecommunications, chemicals, manufacturing, government, and technology sectors.

Justin Peltier is a Senior Security Consultant with Clover Technologies with over seven years of experience in firewall and security technologies. As a consultant, Mr. Peltier has been involved in implementing, supporting, and developing security solutions, and has taught courses on many facets including vulnerability assessment and CISSP preparation. Formerly with Suntel Services, Justin directed the security practice development. Prior to that he was with Netigy where he was involved with the corporate training effort. Mr. Peltier has lead classes for MIS, Netigy, Suntel Services, and Sherwood Associates. Justin currently holds 10 certifications in an array of technical products.

Thomas R. Peltier, CISSP, is in his fourth decade of computer technology experience as an operator, an applications and systems programmer, a systems analyst, and an information systems security officer. Currently, he is the president of Peltier & Associates, a security training and consulting company. Prior to that, he was director of policies and administration for Netigy Corporation's Global Security Practice, the national director for consulting services for CyberSafe Corporation, the and corporate information protection coordinator for Detroit Edison. This program has been recognized for excellence in the field of computer and information security by winning the Computer Security Institute's Information Security Program of the Year for 1996. Tom previously was the information security specialist for General Motors Corporation, and was responsible for implementing an information security program for GM's worldwide activities.

Tom has had a number of articles published on various computer and information security issues, including developing policies and procedures, disaster recovery planning, copyright compliance, virus management, and security controls. He has published several books, including *Information Security Risk Analysis, Information System Security Policies and Procedures: A Practitioners' Reference, Information Security Risk Analysis, The Complete Manual of Policies and Procedures for Data Security,* and was a contributing author to the *Computer Security Handbook, third and fifth editions* and *Data Security Management.* Tom has been the technical advisor on a number of security films from Commonwealth Films. He is the past chairman of the Computer Security Institute (CSI) advisory council, the chairman of the 18th Annual CSI Conference, founder and past-president of the Southeast Michigan Computer Security Special Interest Group and a former member of the board of directors for (ISC)[2], the security professional certification organization. He was the 1993 Lifetime Award recipient at the 20th Annual CSI Conference. He received the 1999 Information Systems Security Association's Individual Contribution to the

Profession Award and the CSI Lifetime Emeritus Membership Award. In 2001, he was inducted into the ISSA Hall of Fame. He conducts numerous seminars and workshops on various security topics and has led seminars for CSI, Crisis Management, the American Institute of Banking, the American Institute of Certified Public Accountants, the Institute of Internal Auditors, ISACA, and Sungard Planning Solutions. Tom was also an associate professor at the graduate level for Eastern Michigan University.

Dedication

To Mike Corby, the Global Security Practice,
and spirit of what we tried to accomplish.

Contents

Acknowledgments

The development of this study guide for the security professional was truly a team effort. Pat Howard laid out the form, and the team members worked to achieve that vision. Pat and I had the opportunity to play "good cop, bad cop" when it came to deadlines. The team rose to the occasion and met the deadlines.

First in our list of acknowledgements is the team of authors: John Blackley, Bob Cartwright, Terri Curran, Becky Herold, Pat Howard, Carl Jackson, Cheryl Jackson, David Lynas, Justin Peltier, and me, Tom Peltier. Each person completed their assigned task during a period of great personal change and uncertainty.

The next group that needs addressing is the founding members of the certification process. No effort can succeed without the managing director, and Rick Koenig worked day and night to see that this process was successful. Most CISSPs do not know of the personal sacrifices that Rick made to see this project through. Our deep gratitude goes to you, Rick.

The original board should also be acknowledged. This group includes Hal Tipton, William H. Murray, Mike Corby, Micki Krause, Corey Schou, Sally Meglathery, Tom Peltier, Jim Wade, and Ralph Spencer Poore. This group of directors established the professional and ethical standards that are the foundation of the CISSP certification.

Who can leave out their publisher? Certainly not us! Rich O'Hanley has taken the time to discuss security certification with numerous organizations to understand what their needs are and then present these findings to the writing team. Rich O'Hanley, not only the world's best editor and task master, but a good friend and source of knowledge. How he keeps his sanity while working with writers is totally beyond me. Thanks Rich!

Preface

People are the most important component of a company's information security program. Managers must rely on their assigned security personnel to develop, implement, manage, and maintain security controls according to industry-standard practices and standards. These controls protect an organization's most critical information resources, and in most respects are the "keys to the kingdom." Because of the critical responsibilities with which they are tasked, and because they can bypass or render security controls ineffective, security personnel must have knowledge of leading security practices and concepts, and must have a commitment to the highest ethical standards. Certification as a Certified Information Systems Security Professional, or CISSP, provides managers with a high level of assurance that the holder of such certification has a broad knowledge of information security principles and meets high standards of integrity.

Additionally, the growing complexity of the information systems security field has made professional certification a highly desirable qualification. Security practitioners who have been awarded the CISSP certification are viewed across the industry as having the credibility to perform standard information security functions with professionalism and integrity. Therefore, those who can meet the qualifications necessary to sit for the CISSP Examination, and who elect to adhere to the International Information Systems Security Certification Consortium's (ISC)² code of ethics, should prepare themselves to take the examination as soon as possible. However, unlike many other professional certifications, studying for the CISSP Examination is much more difficult. The Common Body of Knowledge (CBK), on which the CISSP examination is based is expansive, and requires broad knowledge of information in the following ten discrete security disciplines:

1. Access Control Systems and Methodology
2. Telecommunications and Network Security
3. Security Management Practices

4. Applications and System Development Security
5. Cryptography
6. Security Architecture and Models
7. Computer Operations Security
8. Business Continuity Planning and Disaster Recovery Planning
9. Law, Investigations, and Ethics
10. Physical Security

Until now, personnel preparing to sit for the CISSP Examination were not afforded the luxury of studying a single, easy-to-use study manual. This new study guide allows the CISSP candidate to test his or her current knowledge in each of the domains. Along with the testing, the candidate has the reference material identified for each question. In addition, the Bibliography is divided by domains and lists all of the references used to create this study guide. This book will help you, the candidate, become intimately familiar with the references covering these ten security domains.

This book is divided into three sections. The first section consists of 250 sample questions with the correct answers and the references. Appendix B is another, all-new set of 250 questions set in random order just as you will see when you are ready to sit for the exam. We recommend that you treat Appendix A as a test exam and give yourself six hours to complete the 250 questions. The third section, Appendix C, contains the answers to the sample exam.

Introduction

Preparing for the CISSP Exam

There is really nothing magical about preparing for the CISSP exam, just organization and perseverance. Many people have successfully completed the exam and over time have shared many tips, tricks, and strategies that they used to master the exam. To help you get organized for the task ahead, and to lessen your anxiety about the exam, this section documents some of the suggestions of CISSPs who have gone before you. The section covers key points you need to know to properly prepare yourself to take the examination, from the twinkling in your eye to the receipt of the certificate designating you as a Certified Information Systems Security Professional.

Find Out What You Need to Know

Once you have decided to investigate the CISSP certification and think that certification might be right for you at this stage of your career, then you need to find out what it is that you are expected to know in order to become certified. To be a CISSP you must demonstrate a mastery of the Common Body of Knowledge (CBK) by successfully completing a 250 question examination administered by the (ISC)². You can quickly determine what subjects are contained in the CBK by reviewing the *CISSP Study Guide* that (ISC)² offers via its Web site. This reference guide provides an outline of the subjects, topics, and sub-topics contained within each domain in the CBK, and with it you can readily identify terms and concepts that you need to know for the exam.

Find Out if You Meet Certification Requirements

There is no need to proceed further on your path to certification if you are not qualified to take the exam or to be a CISSP. Because of the stipulations placed on the certification by (ISC)², you need not peruse the CISSP reading list, attend CISSP preparation classes, or create a study plan unless you can meet the qualifications for applying for the examination. Go to the (ISC)² Web site (http://www.isc2.org) and review the examination application form to ensure that you are aware of and can comply with the requirements for taking the exam. These include:

- **Experience.** First, you must have three years of direct experience in at least one of the ten CBK domains. This experience must be through performance of duties as a practitioner, auditor, consultant, vendor, investigator, or instructor, and extends only to actual time worked. Required experience is cumulative. That is, if 50 percent of your job performance was directly related to a particular CBK domain, and you had worked in that capacity for four years, then you would have accumulated two years of direct work experience for the purpose of certification. You should also be aware that experience is a better teacher than study, and those with broad working experience in the CBK will have a much easier time passing the exam than those who do not.
- **Code of Ethics.** Also, to apply for the examination, you have to agree to read the (ISC)² Code of Ethics, to confirm that you have not in the past violated any of its provisions, and to confirm that you will adhere to the (ISC)² Code of Ethics in the future. Read the Code of Ethics; and if you find you cannot abide by them, then stop here and go back; the CISSP certification is not for you.
- **Background.** Finally, upon application, you must provide background information that could result in the rejection of your application. You must report to the (ISC)² if you have been convicted of a felony or if you currently have such a charge pending against you; you may be disqualified. Or if you have every been involved or publicly identified with hackers or hacking, you must explain this on your application, and it could lead to your application being rejected if your background with hackers/hacking does not comport with the Code of Ethics. Your application must also stipulate whether or not you have ever had a professional license, certification, membership, or registration revoked, or if you have been censured or disciplined by a professional organization or government agency. Reporting information of this nature will not automatically result in the rejection of your application, but it must be reviewed by the (ISC)² to determine if your conduct is consistent with the Code of Ethics.

Find Out What You Know and Do Not Know

When you have determined that you can meet the requirements for applying for the examination, and have a good idea of the kind of knowledge that you are expected to know to be certified, then you need to get a rough idea of what you know now, so that you can pinpoint your strengths and weaknesses by domain. By taking a practice examination such as the one provided in this book, you can identify which domains you need to improve your knowledge, and which ones you do not need to worry about (or at least not have to spend too much time studying for). Because you only need to score 70 percent to pass the exam, that percentage is a good benchmark to apply to your expertise in each domain. If can score 70 percent or above in a given domain on a practice exam, that is a good indicator that you are in fairly good shape to take the exam. Likewise, in domains where you fail to score 70 percent, then you should have a pretty strong indication that you need to do some work. Knowing where you need to concentrate your study efforts is the most important element in developing a plan for mastering the CISSP examination.

Build a Study Plan

Now that you know and have confirmed the domains on which you need to focus the majority of your time, you can build a study plan that permits you enough time to prepare for the exam. How much time is enough? Because even the best-laid plans go awry, you should expect to spend one month for every domain in which you fail to score 70 percent on a practice exam. Because of the need to anticipate distracters such as work, vacation, and family obligations, one month per domain is a good rule of thumb. Once you have calculated how much time you need to prepare, you can go the (ISC)² Web site once again and identify an examination date and location that is consistent with this schedule. You should plan on applying for the exam at least six months prior to the exam date to ensure that you reserve a seat. Spaces go particularly fast for examinations offered in larger cities.

Reference Materials

Unlike several other certifications, there is no single reference work that you can purchase and cover the entire CBK to the depth necessary to pass the examination. Therefore, you need to build time into your study plan to locate, obtain, purchase, and use reference materials. The bibliography in this book is a good starting place for identifying by domain references that might be helpful to you. The (ISC)² Web site also provides an up-to-date reading list that you should consider in preparing for the examination. Many of the references can be readily purchased over the Internet and, in the case of many U.S. Government publications, can be downloaded cost-free. If you are fortunate, your organization or co-workers may already have many of the references that you need, or your company may be willing to purchase them if they are judged to be of long-term value.

Study Courses

If you are particularly weak (a score of 40 percent or lower) in several domains, your plan should include time for a formal CISSP preparation course. The

(ISC)² offers an intensive eight-day course over two weeks that provides comprehensive training in all ten domains. The Computer Security Institute and other firms offer shorter versions of the CISSP preparation instruction, focusing on students who desire refresher training in all ten domains. Also, the (ISC)² offers a one-day overview to familiarize potential CISSPs with the CBK. If you have the need, and can afford the time and expense, these courses can significantly improve your chances for passing the examination. The security professionals who teach such classes are CISSPs themselves and can help you learn how to understand the intent of the questions and how to best answer them. These courses cover a lot of important material that you need to know for the exam. However, because they cover so much, it is virtually impossible to retain it all for a long period of time. Therefore, if you take one of these courses, schedule yourself for an exam two to six weeks following the course.

Group Study

Your plan should also build in opportunities for collective study. If you can find someone to study with in your company or organization, in your local chapter of a professional security organization, or in your neighborhood, then you can prepare for the examination together. Dividing study tasks and responsibilities among two or more students is an effective means of expanding knowledge of the CBK, in reducing the amount of time required to prepare, and in providing a sounding board to discuss difficult concepts and ideas. Do not overlook online study groups either. They can provide you with an outlet for asking those peculiar but important questions that you cannot find the answer for in your reference materials. Typically, CISSPs belong to these study groups and can help you based on their actual experience.

What to Study

You will find it most productive if you concentrate on procedures rather than on the specifics of particular security technologies. The examination is designed to assess your grasp of terms and concepts at a high level across a broad collection of subjects. The proper perspective for approaching the examination is that of a corporate- or department-level information security officer who is required to perform various tasks that require having broad knowledge across the entire spectrum of the CBK. This would include knowledge of industry-standard procedures and standards, as well as a working knowledge of security technologies and the problems they are designed to counter. Knowledge of platform-specific vulnerabilities and controls is not required.

Confirmation Letter

Once you have applied for the examination, you will receive a confirmation letter from the (ISC)² stating the time, date, and location of the examination, as well as other information you will need to take the exam. Be sure to bring this letter with you to the examination, along with a photo ID card to verify your identity. Without them you will not be allowed access to the exam site.

The Night Before

The night before the examination you should concentrate on getting a good night's rest, not in cramming for the examination. This is not the kind of exam that you can or should pull an "all-nighter" for. You should anticipate the need to memorize some material well before the exam. The CBK contains lists of information that you need to have at your fingertips — the OSI Model for example. Set aside time in your plan for memory drills to ensure you have this information down rote on the day of the examination. Consider using note cards, acrostics, or whatever it takes to help you remember information such as this. The evening prior to the exam you should not spend more than two or three hours making your final preparations. Use the remainder of the evening to relax and prepare for a good night's sleep.

The Morning Of

Make sure that you know how to get to the examination site so that you can get there in leisurely fashion, keeping your stress level as low as possible. Build in enough time to eat breakfast. It will help you get through a long examination. At least have a cup of coffee and read the newspaper to help you relax. Do whatever is necessary for you to remain calm going into the exam. You should plan on getting to the exam site at least 30 minutes prior to the time you are advised to arrive, just in case something goes wrong. It is advisable to take a bio break before going into the examination room because stringent procedures for leaving the room will be in effect once the exam starts.

At the Exam Site

You can anticipate producing your photo ID and confirmation letter to gain access to the examination site. The proctors are all security professionals and will check you in by the numbers. You will be required to take a seat at a standard writing table. You can expect to have sufficient space to work comfortably. Once the head proctor begins, you will be given verbal instructions, which will take about 30 minutes. During that time, the proctor will describe procedures in effect for the exam (restroom breaks, refreshments, scratch paper, asking questions, etc.). Each examinee will be provided a sealed examination booklet and an answer sheet, along with a pencil.

Multiple versions of the examination will be issued so that students sitting side-by-side will each have a different version. You will not be allowed to talk, and may be disqualified if you do. Upon the proctors' direction, all examinees will break the seal of their test booklets at the same time, and the exam will begin. Once the exam starts, the head proctor will function as the official timekeeper and will periodically inform you of the time remaining, either verbally or by posting it in writing.

What to Bring Along/Leave Behind

It might be a good idea to bring along bottles of water or other refreshments, and also some snacks. However, be considerate of others taking the exam and do not bring anything that might cause noise when opening or unwrapping it. When you check in, show the proctor what you have brought along so that he or she can see that your bag only contains refreshments. You should also attempt to find out what the rules are on getting to your bag once the examination has started. Avoid bringing phones, pagers, calculators, PDAs, and other electronics with you to the exam. If you do, you will not be allowed to use them or even to have them within arm's length. You will be required to turn them off and stow them in the back of the room. If you have alarms on any of these devices (or on your watch), be sure to deactivate them to avoid distracting others.

Your Objective

The test will consist of 250 multiple-choice questions, each having four possible answers. Your task is to select the best answer from the four answers provided. The questions are arrayed in no particular order, and it is not obvious how many questions there are for each domain. You will only be graded on your answers to 225 of the examination questions. The remaining 25 questions are included in the examination as part of the vetting process for new questions. You will have no way of knowing which questions will be graded and which ones will not. Remember, you must attain a score of 70 percent to pass the examination. That should be your goal. You get no bonus points if you score above 70 percent. In fact, if you pass, you will never know your passing score. Hence, from your point of view, a score of 71 is the same as a score of 98.

About the Questions

There are a few generalizations that can be made about examination questions without revealing their content. Negative questions — those that ask you to identify an answer that is an exception — are avoided on the exam as much as possible. Also, the examination avoids the use of acronyms. The CISSP exam is international in scope and attempts to minimize U.S.-specific questions. The examination is given in English only. However, if English is not your first language and you need to use a dictionary to translate from your native language to English and vice versa, then bring one with you and ask the proctor if you might be permitted to use it.

Manage Your Time

You will have six hours to complete the examination, and will have plenty of time to complete it. You have a total of 360 minutes to complete 250 questions. In other words, you have 1¾ minutes for each question. That amounts to about 40 questions per hour. An effective strategy that has worked for many is to go through the exam three times. Go through the first time with the objective of answering the questions you know well, or those that you feel 90 percent certain of the answer. Make the second pass looking to answer all the questions that you feel 50 percent certain of the answer. With these, re-read the choices given, try to eliminate incorrect choices, and reconsider the remaining answers. That leaves the third time through to simply guess the answers if necessary. Perhaps by the time you get to this final pass, you will be mainly dealing with the 25 sample questions that will not be graded anyway.

Take Breaks

Plan to take breaks throughout the examination. Take brief eye/mind/stretch breaks where you are seated every few questions. Perhaps at the 60- or 90-minute mark, stand up and quietly go to the back of the room and take a stretch break, drink something, and eat a snack. Remember that the most common cause of headache is insufficient fluid intake. Try to get your mind off of the exam for a few minutes. This will help maintain your level of alertness. No more than one examinee at a time may go to the restroom, and must be escorted by a proctor while outside the exam room. This, of course, takes time and can lead to delays, so it is best to plan ahead.

Keep Moving

It is advisable not to spend too much time on any single question. Getting bogged down leads to frustration and loss of confidence. Whereas, looking for questions that you feel certain of the answer provides positive reinforcement and builds confidence. A good rule of thumb is that if you cannot answer a question in two minutes, then move on to the next one. Be sure to read each question carefully in as generic a manner as possible. Do not read into any question specifics that you may be familiar with from your experience. This leads to trouble and confusion. Simply read what the question asks, as well as the answers provided. One effective approach is to mask the answers and carefully read the question before uncovering the answers. You should always be aware of the time remaining so that you can pace yourself accordingly. Be sure to leave yourself enough time at the end to be able to treat the last questions with the level of attention they require. Answer all 250 questions. There is no penalty for guessing. So, if you hear the proctor say that you have five minutes remaining, then you will know that you should go through and guess an answer for each remaining question. You should also be aware that any question in the exam might provide you with a clue to answering another question somewhere else in the exam. This is another reason why it is important to go completely through the examination at least twice.

Comments Regarding Poor Questions

You will be provided with an opportunity to comment on specific questions after you have completed the examination. The proctor will provide you with instructions on how to do this before the exam begins. If you have a question that you want to contest or comment on, be sure you can identify the "questionable" question once you have finished. In many cases, those that you will want to comment on will be from the group of 25 sample questions that are not graded. It is important for you to take the time to comment on such questions, not only for yourself but also for others who will take the test after you.

Decompress

After you have completed the examination, take as much time as you need to decompress, relax, and try to get back to normal after months of eating, breathing, and living CISSP. Enjoy life again. However, do not forget to record some general notes and impressions about those parts of the test that gave you trouble. It may come in handy if you discover that you did not pass. Do not, however, record specific question information — remember the Code of Ethics. Nor should you provide information about specific questions to others, either voluntarily or when asked. You will receive your exam results two to three weeks after you take the exam via normal mail. If you passed the exam, your notification letter will address you as a CISSP and will indicate your CISSP number. Later on, you will receive a CISSP lapel pin and certificate through the mail.

If You're Not Successful

If you unfortunately do not pass the exam, the letter from the (ISC)² containing your exam results will provide your overall score as a percentage, as well as a breakdown of results by domain. This is valuable information that allows you to concentrate on those domains in which you did poorly, and is a great benefit in preparing to take the exam a second time, with hopefully a better result.

PRACTICE STUDY QUESTIONS

Chapter 1

Access Control Systems and Methodology Domain

The Access Control domain addresses the collection of mechanisms that permits system managers to exercise a directing or restraining influence over the behavior, use, and content of a system. Access control permits management to specify what users can do, what resources they can access, and what operations they can perform on a system.

Given the realization that information is valuable and must be secured against misuse, disclosure, and destruction, organizations implement access controls to ensure the integrity and security of the information which they use to make critical business decisions. Controlling access to computing resources and information can take on many forms. However, regardless of the method utilized, whether technical or administrative, access controls are fundamental to a well-developed and well-managed information security program.

This domain addresses user identification and authentication, access control techniques and the administration of those techniques, and the evolving and innovative methods of attack against implemented controls.

Biometrics are used to identify and authenticate individuals and are rapidly becoming a popular approach for imposing control over access to information because they provide the ability to positively identify someone by their personal attributes, typically a person's voice, handprint, fingerprint, or retinal pattern. Although biometric devices have been around for years, new innovations continue to emerge. Understanding the potential as well as the limitations of these important tools is necessary so that the technology can be applied appropriately and most effectively. We will lay the foundation here and follow up with more detail in Domain 10, Physical Security.

Nowhere is the use of access controls more apparently important than in protecting the privacy, confidentiality, and security of patient healthcare information. Outside North America, especially in European countries, privacy has been a visible priority for years. More recently, American consumers have come to demand an assurance that their personal privacy is protected, a demand which demonstrates awareness that their medical information is becoming increasingly widespread and potentially subject to exposure. The Health Insurance Portability and Accountability Act (HIPAA) of 1996 and the Gramm-Leach-Bliley Act of 1999, which governs disclosure of personal financial information, just to name two regulations, are definitive evidence that the U.S. Government has heeded the mandate of the American citizens.

Malicious hacking has been a successful means of undermining information controls and an increasing challenge to the security of information. Hackers tend to chip away at an organization's defenses and have been successful on far too many occasions. In this domain, we learn about the advancing state-of-the-art attack tools that have led to highly publicized scenarios; for example, the recent defacement of the U.S. Justice Department's Web site and denial-of-service attacks on many commercial sites.

Social engineering techniques are another of many ways to undercut the installed controls while taking advantage of human nature. In social engineering, unscrupulous persons use devious means to obtain information that can be applied to defeat implemented controls. For example, envision a call to an unsuspecting user by someone masquerading as a desktop technician, wherein the caller says he needs the user's network password to diagnose a technical problem and then uses that password to compromise the system.

Key Discussion Terms

- Access control list
- Accountability
- Brute-force attack
- Custodian
- Data owner
- Denial of service
- Dictionary attack
- Discretionary access control
- Lattice-based access control
- Layers of control
  - Administrative
  - Physical
  - Technical
- Man-in-the-middle attack

- Mandatory access control
- Network spoofing
- Radius
- Rule-based access control
- Role-based access control
- Security domains
- Single sign-on
- Social engineering
- Spamming
- Sniffers
- TACACS
- TACACS+
- Trust
- Trust relationship

Practice Study Questions

1. Typical one-time password implementations represent:

   a. Limited authentication for a set period of time (initial log-in using the same password for a period of a week or month).
   b. Two-factor authentication (initial log-in with userid and password and the one-time password entered as secondary authentication).
   c. Single-factor authentication with passwords stored on the target machine.
   d. Single-factor authentication (log-in with userid and the one-time password entered).

   Explanation Answer b is correct because it is generally implemented via password generation software that is common on the initiating and target machine. Answer a is incorrect because it infers that a password is issued once and then used repeatedly for a set time frame. Answer c is incorrect because passwords are not stored in a one-time authentication technique. Answer d is incorrect because it only is using one layer of authentication.

   Reference Tudor (2001), pages 225–226.[6]

2. When planning a token-based authentication methodology, which of the following must *primarily* be taken into consideration?

   a. Costs relative to the use of human-based or electrical-based tokens
   b. Acceptance of extended authentication techniques by clients
   c. Evaluation of whether all access is token based or only subsets of access (such as remote access)
   d. Implementation planning and integration with applications and remote access services

   Explanation All the answers factor into a token-based authentication technique. However, answer c is the *most* appropriate. Risk must be evaluated to determine the most critical information to be protected by this authentication technique.

   Reference Ford and Baum (1997), pages 133–134.[2]

3. Which of the following is *not* within the scope of a single sign-on (SSO) implementation?

   a. SSOs will not impact system performance or cause significant system overhead.
   b. SSOs will not support access to systems or applications that a client would not have normal access to.
   c. SSOs will support selection of alternative user profiles in client sign-on.

d. SSOs will support audit trails and will log events that do not support security policy.

Explanation   Answer c is correct. Single sign-on is applicable to one user, one account name, and one password. Multiple account names should not be linked together. Answers a, b, and d are all applicable within an SSO implementation.

Reference   Tipton and Krause (2000), pages 27–43.[5]

4. Which of the following is *not* considered an active attack method?

   a. Planting
   b. Tampering
   c. Penetration
   d. Denial of service

Explanation   Answer a is correct. Planting occurs when an intruder has already penetrated a system and left behind some type of malicious code (e.g., a Trojan horse or time-seeded virus). All the other answers can be considered active attack methods. Tampering is an active attack in which information transmitted during communications sessions is altered. Penetration is accomplished by masquerade or by exploiting system flaws. Denial-of-service attacks occur when a system is flooded with requests that overload the system's resources.

Reference   Ford and Baum (1997), pages 95–97.[2]

5. What is the main characteristic of a dictionary attack?

   a. A program attempts to use well-known passwords on specific operating system accounts.
   b. A social engineering process is used to obtain information through company directories.
   c. Special words pertinent to a company's business are attempted to be matched.
   d. Encrypting each word in a dictionary to see if it matches an encrypted password.

Explanation   Answer d is correct. Because many operating systems encrypt passwords, a match is attempted on a one-for-one basis. Answer a is incorrect because, although pure guessing is an effective method of attack, it does not use a dictionary-based format. Answer b is incorrect, although social engineering is frequently used to obtain password information. Answer c is incorrect because, although special words can be added to a dictionary, the use of special words alone does not constitute a dictionary attack.

Reference   Summers (1997), pages 84 and 342.[4]

6. What is the closest definition of a spam attack?

   a. Sending threatening electronic mail to users via distribution lists
   b. Sending personal electronic mail to users via distribution lists
   c. Sending unsolicited junk electronic mail to users via distribution lists
   d. Sending product or service surveys to users via distribution lists

Explanation   Answer c is correct. A spam attack can be delivered to one or many users. Answers a, b, and d are incorrect; although incorrect use of electronic mail systems, they do not constitute spam attacks (although a spam message may contain threatening, personal, or survey-type information).

Reference   Tipton and Krause (2000), pages 649–650.[5]

7. Under certain circumstances, original audit trails can:

   a. Be modified to isolate a certain incident for research.
   b. Be used to proactively protect against a network attack.
   c. Enable and support criminal or civil legal remedies.
   d. Gather information from multiple sources about a series of attacks on different networks.

Explanation   Answer c is correct. Intrusion detection systems can generate audit trails that can legally be used to verify threats against a network. Answer a is incorrect because audit trails should never be modified; copies of audit trail logs can be edited for research and investigation. Answer b is incorrect because audit trails contain information that occurred in the past (this is a trick question because audit trails can be used to *predict* behavior, but not stop an action). Answer d is incorrect because audit trails are generated from different sources, but the correlation of information from audit trails is done in a different phase of the investigation.

Reference   King, Dalton, and Osmanoglu (2001), page 297.[3]

8. In a log-structured file system, all data is stored in the form of:

   a. Checkpoint files
   b. Recovery journals
   c. Mirrored files
   d. Incremental backups

Explanation   Answer b is correct. All data is stored in this manner. *Log* is synonymous with *journal* in this context. Answers a, c, and d are different types of backup techniques.

Reference   Summers (1997), pages 361–364.[4]

9. Access control enforces what basic security principle?

    a. Authorization
    b. Integrity
    c. Confidentiality
    d. Availability

Explanation Answer a is correct. Access control policies, procedures, and processes support the authorization of clients to information. Answers b, c, and d are basic security principles as well, but not directly applicable to the access control category.

Reference Summers (1997), page 116.[4]

10. The access matrix model of access control is characterized by which of the following?

    a. Mathematical structure that represents security levels
    b. Constrained data items and transformation procedures
    c. Information flow control
    d. Subjects, objects, and rights

Explanation Answer d is correct. In this model, objects are the resources to be controlled, subjects are the active entities, and rights are the accesses subjects have to objects. Answer a is characteristic of the lattice structure access model. Answer b is characteristic of the Clark–Wilson access control model. Answer c is characteristic of the Bell–LaPadula access model.

Reference Summers (1997), pages 116–119.[4]

11. How could a PIN (personal identification number) typically be compromised?

    a. Session hijacking
    b. Social engineering and theft
    c. Personal knowledge of a client or user
    d. Use of commonly known or dictionary passwords

Explanation Answer b is correct. A PIN is associated with a physical device, such as an ATM card. This relies on the principle of "something you know, something you have." Answer a is incorrect because session hijacking assumes that a session has already been established and that information can be obtained through packet sniffing or inspection. Answer c is incorrect because theft of the device (ATM card, for example) would be essential in addition to the personal knowledge of a person's habits, likes, and dislikes. Answer d is incorrect because a dictionary attack is used as a password cracking mechanism.

Reference Ford and Baum (1997), pages 133–134.[2]

12. What is *not* a disadvantage of a token-based authentication system?

    a. There is no opportunity for a brute-force attack.
    b. Token hardware and software can be costly to maintain.
    c. The token can be lost or stolen.
    d. The client must always have the token.

Explanation Answer a is correct. The fact that a brute-force attack cannot be executed against a token is a clear advantage. The other answers are disadvantages of using a token-based authentication system and must be taken into consideration when evaluating this type of implementation.

Reference Summers (1997), pages 346–347.[4]

13. The closest definition of a callback system is:

    a. A client dials into a mainframe and the mainframe issues remote program calls.
    b. A client dials into a remote access server, enters a password, and a return call is initiated by the remote access server.
    c. A client dials into a toll-free VPN number and establishes a call to an application.
    d. A client dials into a modem pool and the first available number answers the call.

Explanation Answer b is correct. There are other implementations of callback systems, but the most common is through the use of an RAS (remote access server). Answer a is a reference to RPC (remote procedure call) a programming technique. Answer c is a viable access technique but is an incorrect definition of callback, as is answer d.

Reference Summers (1997), pages 548–550.[4]

14. What is the purpose of an intrusion detection system (IDS)?

    a. To develop attack signatures and build these signatures into an alert system
    b. To determine if ACLs are being properly employed in a networked environment
    c. To automatically collect traces of client activity and analyze them, trying to identify instances of misuse
    d. To interpret network traffic from encrypted sources

Explanation Answer c is correct. An IDS collects evidence of prior activity. It is not a proactive prevention mechanism, although results obtained from an IDS can be used to statistically predict an event or incident. Answer a is incorrect because attack signatures are usually part of the software and services provided from a vendor — much like a virus signature update. Answer b is incorrect because, although an IDS will eventually lead to the determination of access flaws, it will not normally inspect ACL information. Answer d is incorrect because IDSs may not be able to interpret or correlate information from encrypted sessions.

Reference   Summers (1997), pages 637–646.[4]

15. Which of the following defines an intrusion?

   a. Any set of actions that a client executes due to poorly defined access controls
   b. Any set of actions that attempt to compromise the integrity, confidentiality, or availability of a resource
   c. Any set of actions that overlays or bypasses system audit trails
   d. Any set of actions that provides an intruder with the means to bypass a firewall or DMZ

Explanation   Answer b is correct. An intrusion can violate any of these security requirements, internally or externally. Answer a is incorrect because, although poor design can lead to an incident, this is not a direct definition of intrusion. Answer c is incorrect because these actions may be part of an attack or intrusion, but not the whole intrusion pattern. Answer d is incorrect because this is a method of intrusion, not a definition of intrusion.

Reference   King, Dalton, and Osmanoglu (2001), pages 286–287.[3]

16. Which of the following is *not* an intrusion technique?

   a. IP spoofing
   b. DNS spoofing
   c. Network spoofing
   d. SET spoofing

Explanation   Answer d is correct. SET (Secure Electronic Transaction) is a special protocol developed by financial institutions and is used for multi-party transactions across networks. It is not an intrusion technique. Answer a is a significant technique because an intruder intercepts packet sequences and then turns fabricated packets back to the originator. Answer b is a viable technique because intruders set up machines to function as legitimate domain name servers. Answer c is another example of intrusion (also called passive intrusion), in which information is gathered covertly and then used at a later time to gain unauthorized access to a system.

Reference   Tipton and Krause (2000), pages 73–75.[5]

17. To prevent attacks, the methods of attack must be understood. Which of the following are the stages of an attack?

a. Planting stage, activation stage, and mission stage
b. Social engineering phase, information gathering stage, and execution stage
c. Identification phase, propagation phase, and scanning phase
d. Scanning phase, authentication phase, and announcement phase

Explanation Answer a is correct. The planting stage indicates the method of attack. The activation stage is how the attack is executed (date or time trigger). The mission stage is the *payload*, or what the attacker is trying to accomplish. Answer b is incorrect because social engineering is a component of the planting phase. Answer c is incorrect because scanning is only one component of an attack. Answer d is incorrect because it is just incorrect.

Reference Summers (1997), pages 79–80.[4]

18. Which of the following is *not* an access control policy that supports information integrity?

a. Constrained change policy
b. Operation sequencing policy
c. Reference validation policy
d. Supervisory control policy

Explanation Answer c is correct. The term "reference validation" pertains to security architecture within specific models. All the other answers are correct.

Reference Summers (1997), pages 109–110, 253.[4]

19. The industry best practice for review of client accounts and access rights is:

a. Six months for all accounts.
b. Three months for all accounts.
c. Three months for privileged accounts and six months for all others.
d. Regular intervals, according to the confidentiality of the information.

Explanation Answer c is correct. Answers a and b do not take into consideration that some accesses will be more sensitive than others. Answer d, although appropriate in certain instances, is not an industry best practice.

Reference ISO/IEC 17799:2000, page 35.[1]

20. Within industry best practice, which of the following roles has responsibility for authorizing access control maintenance?

   a. Information owner
   b. Information user
   c. Information custodian
   d. Information administrator

Explanation   Answer a is correct. Only the owner of information should authorize access to a resource. Answer b is incorrect because the user of information is restricted by the owner's determination of business need. Answer c is incorrect because the custodian supports changes to a resource based on the owner's approval. Answer d is incorrect because, although a custodian and administrators may share job roles, the owner ultimately decides access to a resource.

Reference   ISO/IEC 17799:2000, page 20.[1]

21. There are three major types of authentication techniques available. What are they?

   a. Control, executable, and cleansing
   b. Filtering, access, and logging
   c. Password, key, and token
   d. Static, robust, and continuous

Explanation   Answer d is correct. Static authentication includes passwords and other techniques that can be compromised through relay attacks. Robust authentication involves the use of cryptography or other controls to create one-time passwords. Continuous authentication prevents hijacking. Answers a, b, and c are just interchangeable security terms.

Reference   Tipton and Krause (2000), pages 51–53.[5]

22. When clients are expected to select passwords that meet an organization's security requirements, what is an appropriate control measure to take?

   a. Require that clients sign a statement to keep passwords confidential and that this statement constitutes a condition of employment.
   b. Initiate timeout requirements for new password selection.
   c. Inform clients that access to systems is dependent on secure password selection.
   d. Keep password notification messages in a locked, secured area.

Explanation   Answer a is correct. Management must ensure that employees are aware that security is a function of their job/role responsibilities.

Answer b is incorrect because timeout access controls usually pertain to password/PIN response. Answer c is incorrect because access to systems is defined by information owners, not password selection criteria. Answer d is incorrect because password notification messages should be in a two-factor notification method (get a notification, call a new number).

Reference ISO/IEC 17799:2000, page 35.[1]

23. The definition of an audit trail most closely matches which of the following definition?

    a. A summary of attack signatures that can be applied to a network
    b. A list of all changes to revenue-generating programs that external auditors can reference
    c. A list of change control activities that support modifications to an existing production system
    d. A record of all actions that supports a later reconstruction of who did what to information

Explanation Answer d is correct. An audit trail is intended to collect information that will support an investigation, remediation effort, or process improvement. Answer a is incorrect because attack signatures are associated with intrusion detection (including anti-virus signatures). Answer b is incorrect because, although an audit trail is essential to internal audit activities, a detailed reference to specific programs is inappropriate here. Answer c is incorrect because, although change control proceedings are important to control risk, this definition does not support the question.

Reference Summers (1997), page 106.[4]

24. Within intrusion detection methodology, the term signature is defined as:

    a. A piece of information that is encrypted to authenticate a client or process.
    b. An attack pattern that repeats itself once introduced into an environment.
    c. A pattern of events of an attack based on past intrusions.
    d. A key that is attached to a message in the form of a digital certificate.

Explanation Answer c is correct. Signatures are commonly distributed by IDS vendors as part of ongoing support to a software IDS component. Answer a is incorrect because it refers to the use of digital signatures within authentication to a network or application. Answer b is incorrect because an attack pattern can be something unidentified and not assigned a signature designation at the time of the attack.

Answer d is incorrect because the use of digital certificates is yet another authentication technique.

Reference Summers (1997), page 638.[4]

25. Which of the following are appropriate activities during response to an intrusion?

a. Analysis, evaluation, investigation, integration, and operations
b. Challenge, analyze, form response team, management notification, and scanning
c. Detection, evaluation, notification, containment, and eradication
d. Assessment, design, deployment, implementation, and management

Explanation Answer c is correct. Incidents must be accurately detected, evaluated by trained people, communicated properly to management, contained efficiently and in a controlled manner, and removed where applicable. The other answers contain facets of a coordinated response effort, but have overlap or operational support implications.

Reference Summers (1997), pages 602–605.[4]

Chapter 2

Telecommunications and Network Security Domain

The Telecommunications and Network Security domain encompasses the structures, transmission methods, transport formats, and security measures used to provide integrity, availability, authentication, and confidentiality for transmissions over private and public communications networks and media.

Information technology has become ubiquitous, due in large part to the extent of network connectivity. Telecommunication methodologies allow for the timely transport of information — from corner to corner, across the country, and around the globe. It is no surprise that this domain is one of the largest, because it encompasses the security of communications technologies as well as the ever-expanding realms of the intranet, Internet, and extranet.

Firewalls, which continue to play an important role in protecting an organization's perimeter, are explored in this domain. Firewalls are basically barriers between two networks that screen traffic, both inbound and outbound, and through a set of rules, allow or deny transmission connections. In this domain, we compare the multiple aspects of filtering devices.

While perimeter firewalls provide some level of protection, an organization's information (e.g., electronic mail), must still flow into and outside the organization. Unfortunately, keeping these communication channels open allows for potential compromise. This domain covers the potential vulnerabilities of the free flow of information as well as the protection mechanisms and services available. The computer viruses of the late 1980s appear tame compared with the rogue code that is rampant today. The networked globe allows for speedy replication. Malicious programs that take advantage of the weaknesses (or functionality) of vendor systems traverse the Internet at a dizzying speed. While companies are implementing defensive postures as fast as they can, in many instances, internal organizations lack the capacity or the tools to fortify their own infrastructures. In some cases, such as is documented in this domain, niche messaging vendors offer services to augment internal security, addressing threats such as e-mail spamming and malicious viruses. They also offer a 24-hour/7-day monitoring capability and, in many instances, a pre-emptive notification capability that many organizations cannot accommodate with internal resources.

One of the most successful means of protecting data in transit is the use of encapsulation and encryption employed in virtual private networking. In this domain, we explore the concepts and principles of virtual private networks (VPNs), which allow for the transfer of private information across the public networks while maintaining the security of the data. With benefits that include the ability to do secure business with partners, offer new channels for goods and service delivery, and reach new markets at reduced costs, VPNs hold great promise. In this domain, we look at ways to evaluate, deploy, and leverage VPN technologies, as well as divulge the potential vulnerabilities inherent in those technologies.

Computer and communication technologies are rapidly evolving; devices are growing smaller and more functional at the same time, allowing the consumer more mobility, flexibility, and agility. Nowhere is this more true than in the wireless space. Moreover, wireless networks are more cost-effective because installing and configuring cable and connected devices are not required. The desire to have access to information without the need to tether someone to a wired device is becoming a corporate mandate. And yet, the wireless world has its own set of vulnerabilities. In this domain, we address securing the wireless environment, at the physical layer, on the local area network and over the Internet.

Key Discussion Terms

- Encrypted/signed e-mail
- Message retention
- Sender
- Receiver
- Relay
- Subnetting
- DHCP
- ICMP
- SNMP
- SMTP
- ARP
- DNS

- Firewalls
- Packet filtering
- Proxies
- Stateful inspection
- Network address translation (NAT)
- Transparency
- Integrated functions
- Gateways and routers
- ACLs
- Traffic modification
- Disabled services

Practice Study Questions

1. What is the most common network security vulnerability?

    a. Excessive trust relationships
    b. Inadequate border router access control
    c. Hosts running unnecessary services
    d. Inadequate logging at network and host levels

Explanation   Answer b is the correct answer. Misconfigured router's ACLs can allow information leakage through ICMP, IP NetBIOS, and lead to unauthorized access to services on your DMZ network.

Reference   Scambray, McClure, and Kurtz (2001), page 662.[72]

2. Brute force is most commonly used to:

    a. Crack passwords.
    b. Spam e-mail addresses.
    c. Eradicate viruses.
    d. Propagate viruses.

Explanation   Answer a is correct. An encrypted password is compared to encrypted guesses until a match is found.

Reference   Scambray, McClure, and Kurtz (2001), page 341.[72]

3. Which is *not* part of a DDoS attack?

    a. An attack is launched from multiple systems.
    b. Systems have a remote control that launches the attack on order.
    c. DDoS attacker gains admin rights on remote systems.
    d. DDoS attacks are not Internet based.

Explanation   Answer d is the correct answer. DDoS attacks are always Internet based.

Reference   Scambray, McClure, and Kurtz (2001), page 501.[72]

4. PBX hacking is often successful because:

    a. Managing the PBX requires it to be unsecured.
    b. PBX vendors require remote access.
    c. Many companies never turn off the remote access connection.
    d. Hacking PBXs requires special tools.

Explanation   Answer c is the correct answer. Many vendors require remote access and the PBX is set up as default; many companies turn it on only when it is being used.

Reference   Scambray, McClure, and Kurtz (2001), page 404.[72]

5. Which of the following is a stand-alone program?

    a. Virus
    b. Worm
    c. Trojan horse
    d. Bomb

Explanation   Answer b is the correct answer. A worm is an independent program; it reproduces by copying itself from one computer to another, usually over a network. Answer a is incorrect; a virus is a code fragment that copies itself into a larger program, modifying that program. Answer c is incorrect; a Trojan horse is a code fragment that hides inside a program and performs a disguised function. Answer d is incorrect; a bomb is a form of Trojan horse used to release a virus, worm, or some other system attack.

Reference   Russell and Gangemi (1991), page 79.[7]

6. NAT (Network Address Translation) is *not* used to:

    a. Hide internal addressing scheme
    b. Provide increased productivity to internal network
    c. Translate internal addresses to external addresses
    d. Translate external addresses to internal addresses

Explanation   Answer b is the correct answer. NAT does not provide increased productivity. It is used at the firewall or router to translate the internal addresses to one exterior address when it sends information to the Internet and translates the external address to the correct internal address when a packet is sent to the internal network.

Reference   Cassidy and Dries (2000).[69]

7. Which of the following is *not* a component of the TCB (Trusted Computer Base)?

    a. There must be an explicit and well-defined security policy enforced by the system.
    b. Individual subjects are not identified.
    c. Audit information must be kept and protected so that actions affecting security can be traced to the responsible subject.
    d. The computer systems must contain hardware and software mechanisms that can be evaluated independently to provide sufficient assurance that the system enforces the security policy.

Explanation   Answer b is the correct answer. Individual subjects must be identifiable.

Reference   Fites and Kratz (1996), page 206.[70]

8. Footprinting (the gathering of target information) is the first step of the hacker attacking a company. Which is *not* an example of footprinting?

   a. Open source search
   b. Scanning
   c. Network enumeration
   d. DNS interrogation

   Explanation Answer b is the correct answer. Scanning is the use of the information obtained in footprinting to look for potential vulnerabilities.

   Reference Scambray, McClure, and Kurtz (2001), page 6.[72]

9. An example of a network layer protocol is:

   a. IPSec.
   b. POP.
   c. SKIP.
   d. SWIPE.

   Explanation Answer b is the correct answer. POP is an acronym for Post Office Protocol; it defines how e-mail is picked up across a network.

   Reference Tipton and Krause (2000), Vol. 2, page 70.[73]

10. Which is *not* a type of DoS (denial-of-service) attack?

   a. Bandwidth consumption
   b. Resource starvation
   c. Spoofing
   d. Routing and DNS attacks

   Explanation Answer c is the correct answer. Spoofing is pretending to be someone else, not denying service.

   Reference Scambray, McClure, and Kurtz (2001), page 485.[72]

11. Which is *not* a common DoS attack?

   a. Syn flood
   b. Smurf
   c. Mickey
   c. Bonk

   Explanation Answer c is the correct answer. There is no attack named Mickey.

   Reference Scambray, McClure, and Kurtz (2001), chapter 12.[72]

12. Scanning (determining which systems are alive and reachable) is the next step after footprinting by the "would-be attacker." Which is *not* an example of scanning?

   a. Ping sweeps
   b. Nmap
   c. Port scans
   d. TCP scans

Explanation   Answer b is the correct answer. Nmap is a tool used for port scanning.

Reference   Scambray, McClure, and Kurtz (2001), page 48.[72]

13. Which is *not* a security goal for remote access?

   a. Reliable authentication of users and systems
   b. Protection of confidential data
   c. Automatic log-in (no action by user required)
   d. Logging and auditing of system utilization

Explanation   Answer c is the correct answer. If no action by user is required, that means that there is no reliable identification and authentication and the password is hard-coded.

Reference   Tipton and Krause (2000), Vol. 2, page 100.[73]

14. Which is *not* a common remote access architecture?

   a. Remote access via modems and the public telephone network
   b. Access via dedicated network connections (dedicated circuits or Frame Relay)
   c. Intranet-based remote access
   d. Internet-based remote access

Explanation   Answer c is the correct answer. To access an intranet, one must first have access to the network via modem, direct connect, or a public network.

Reference   Tipton and Krause (2000), Vol. 2, page 106.[73]

15. Which is *not* a type of firewall (a device used to prevent outsiders from gaining access to your network, usually a combination of software and hardware)?

   a. Stateful inspections
   b. Disabled services
   c. Proxies
   d. Packet filtering

Explanation   Answer b is the correct answer. Disabled services takes place on a host, which means that the user already has access to the network.

Reference   Anonymous (1998), page 638.[68]

16.   Intrusion detections systems are:

   a. Actively searching for vulnerabilities.
   b. Passively listening for attacks.
   c. Both actively searching for vulnerabilities and passively listening for attacks.
   d. Passively listening for vulnerabilities.

Explanation   Answer b is the correct answer. IDSs sit on the network or host and passively monitor the host or network for attacks.

Reference   Tipton and Krause (2000), Vol. 2, page 583.[73]

17.   The *most* secure way of transferring a file is:

   a. To transfer via FTP.
   b. To encrypt the file before transferring.
   c. By tunneling.
   d. To send it over the Internet.

Explanation   Answer b is the most correct answer. By encrypting the file first, one does not have to worry if the transfer mechanism is secure.

Reference   Russell and Gangemi (1991), page 165.[71]

18.   The third step in attacking a company's network after footprinting and scanning is enumeration (extracting valid account or exported resource names from systems). The type of information *not* enumerated by intruders is:

   a. IP address range.
   b. Network resources and shares.
   c. Users and groups.
   d. Application and banners.

Explanation   Answer a is the correct answer. IP address ranges are found out during the footprinting and scanning steps.

Reference   Scambray, McClure, and Kurtz (2001), page 72.[72]

19.   A common attack that is *not* an enumeration attack is:

   a. DNS zone transfers.
   b. Telnet.

    c. Keystroke logging.

    d. Banner grabbing.

Explanation   Answer c is the correct answer. Keystroke logging is used to capture and replay all the keystrokes on a machine. It is software that sits between the operating system and the keyboard and records all the keystrokes.

Reference   Scambray, McClure, and Kurtz (2001), chapter 3.[72]

20. Which is *not* a consideration for an IPSec VPN implementation?

    a. System requirements

    b. Application performance

    c. Non-TCP/IP protocols

    d. Cost

Explanation   Answer c is the correct answer. IPSec can only be applied to the TCP/IP protocol. Therefore, multi-protocol networks and environments that employ IPX/SPX, NetBEUI, and others will not take direct advantage of the IPSec VPN.

Reference   Tipton and Krause (2000), Vol. 2, page 194.[73]

21. An advantage of link encryption over end-to-end encryption is:

    a. It makes key management and distribution easier.

    b. It is more efficient; the network does not need to have any special encryption facilities.

    c. It is easier; the user does not need to take any action.

    d. It protects data from start to finish, through the entire network.

Explanation   Answer c is the correct answer. Answers a, b, and d all are advantages of end-to-end encryption.

Reference   Tipton and Krause (2000), Vol. 2, page 224.[73]

22. Which of the following information obtained by a sniffer is *not* important in launching a DoS attack?

    a. Addresses of key hosts

    b. Traffic flow

    c. Network services

    d. The presence of server software known to be vulnerable to DoS attacks

Explanation   Answer b is the correct answer. Answers a, c, and d all provide valuable information to the attacker. The attacker can use this information to mount a successful DoS attack against the resource, compromising its availability.

Reference   Tipton and Krause (2000), Vol. 2, page 130.[73]

23. Network passwords are the entry point into the network and thus should be strong. A password is *not* strong if:

 a. It contains alpha, numeric, and special characters
 b. It has a minimum of eight characters.
 c. It is in the dictionary.
 d. It is a one-time password.

Explanation   Answer c is the correct answer. Answers a, b, and d are all examples of strong passwords. If the password is in the dictionary, then password crackers will crack it very quickly.

Reference   Russell and Gangemi (1991), page 48.[71]

24. Which is *not* a DDoS (distributed denial-of-service) attack?

 a. TFN (tribe flood network)
 b. Trinoo
 c. Stacheldraht
 d. SubSeven

Explanation   Answer d is the correct answer. Answers a, b, and c are all DDoS attacks. Answer d, SubSeven, is a backdoor program in the Windows environment.

Reference   Scambray, McClure, and Kurtz (2001), chapter 12.[72]

25. Which of the following is *not* true regarding IPSec?

 a. Operates at layer 5 of OSI Model
 b. Defines two headers in IP packets to handle authentication and encryption
 c. Defines security on top of standard IP networking
 d. Allows multiple, simultaneous tunnels

Explanation   Answer a is the correct answer. IPSec operates at layer 3 of the OSI model.

Reference   Tipton and Krause (2000), Vol. 2, chapter 8.[73]

Chapter 3

Security Management Practices Domain

Security management entails the identification of an organization's information assets and the development, documentation, and implementation of policies, standards, procedures, and guidelines. It also includes management tools such as data classification and risk assessment (risk analysis) that are used to identify threats, classify assets, and to rate their vulnerabilities so that effective security controls can be implemented.

This domain addresses the importance of establishing the foundation for the security program with policies that reflect the organization's philosophy about information asset protection. Among the practices discussed are how to deal with risk and how a practitioner manages risk to develop the trust and assurance required from information systems.

The organization's users are a critical component in achieving and maintaining information assurance. The best information security policy will sit dormant on a shelf unless the security manager has an effective, enterprise-wide, ongoing security awareness campaign. Training experts agree that a well-developed communication plan can spell the difference between the success or failure of a security program.

Key Discussion Terms

- Annual loss expectancy
- Asset
- Availability
- Awareness
- Background investigation
- Classification
- Confidentiality
- Configuration management
- Countermeasure
- Criticality
- Guideline
- Integrity

- Owner
- Policy
- Procedure
- Residual risk
- Return on investment
- Risk
- Risk analysis
- Risk management
- Sensitivity
- Standard
- Threat
- Vulnerability

Practice Study Questions

1. Conducting a Business Impact Analysis to determine which application or system is most essential to meet the business process will determine the maximum amount of downtime. To determine the downtime availability requirement is to identify the application or system what?

   a. Confidentiality
   b. Threats
   c. Integrity
   d. Criticality

   Explanation   The correct answer is d and can be found in the cited reference. Answer a is one of the tenets of information security and deals with sensitivity. Answer b is part of the risk analysis process, and answer c deals with the quality of the information.

   Reference   Tipton and Krause (2000), page 118.[67]

2. The security level of an object, or more properly the process used to determine this level, is known as:

   a. Classification.
   b. Public.
   c. Restricted.
   d. Secret.

   Explanation   The correct answer is a and can be found in the cited reference. Answers b, c, and d are classification levels that can be affixed to information resources.

   Reference   Jackson and Hruska (1992), page 899.[59]

3. The process by which authorized modifications are made to operating systems is called:

   a. Promotion to production.
   b. Emergency response.
   c. Change control management.
   d. Quality assurance.

   Explanation   Answer c is the correct answer and can be found in the cited reference. Answer a is the process used to move applications from development into production. Answer b is the process organizations use to respond to emergency situations. Answer d is the process used to ensure that products and services meet client expectations.

   Reference   Tipton and Krause (2000), pages 261–262.[67]

4. The process of dividing the management or execution of certain activities of responsibility, in order to reduce opportunities for unauthorized modification or misuse or services, is termed:

   a. Rotation of assignments.
   b. Separation of duties.
   c. Package removal.
   d. Access control.

   Explanation Answer b is the correct answer. Answer a is used to ensure that each function has a trained backup. Answer c is a process that tracks organization or personal property being removed from the campus environment. Answer d is the process that allows authorized users access to the resources they need to complete their assigned tasks.

   Reference ISO/IEC 17799:2000, Section 8.1.4, page 21.[58]

5. In an information classification policy, information that is disclosed outside the company and would not harm the organization, its employees, customers, or business partners would be classified as what?

   a. Top secret
   b. Confidential
   c. Restricted
   d. Public

   Explanation Answer d is the correct answer and can be found in the cited reference. Answers a, b, and c are other levels of information classification and are generally more restricted in access than public information.

   Reference Tipton and Krause (1999), page 342.

6. This principle requires that each subject be granted the most restrictive level of access needed for the performance of authorized tasks. The application of this principle limits the damage that can result from accident, error, or unauthorized use. This principle is known as:

   a. Least privilege.
   b. License.
   c. Log file.
   d. Separation of duties.

   Explanation The correct answer is a and can be found in the cited reference. Answer b is an agreement under which the owner of the function can provide use to others. Answer c is a file that contains copies of transactions for various resources. Answer d is the process of ensuring that one individual cannot do all of the functions of a process.

Reference   Hutt, Bosworth, and Hoyt (1995), page G-14.[8]

7. Any employees, contractors, or vendors of the company who use information systems resources as part of their job are known as:

   a. Owners.
   b. Custodians.
   c. Stewards.
   d. End users.

Explanation   The correct answer is d and can be found in the cited reference. Answer a is the business executive or business manager who is responsible for a company business information asset. Answers b and c are the entities designated by the owner to keep and protect information resources as prescribed by the owner.

Reference   Tipton and Krause (1999), page 344.

8. When considering security, a process is done through risk assessment that examines the assets, threats, and vulnerabilities of the system to determine the most appropriate, cost-effective safeguards. This process is known as:

   a. Cost-benefit analysis.
   b. System development life cycle.
   c. Standards.
   d. Budgeting.

Explanation   The correct answer is answer a and can be found in the cited reference. Answer b is the process that takes a project from inception to production. Answer c are the mandatory actions or devices that support policies, and answer d is the process of projecting revenues and expenses for some period of time.

Reference   National Institute of Standards and Technology (1995), page 78.[60]

9. Information systems and the security of information systems should be provided and used in such a manner that the rights and legitimate interests of others are respected. This principle is known as the:

   a. Accountability principle.
   b. Awareness principle.
   c. Ethics principle.
   d. Integration principle.

Explanation   Answer c is the correct answer and can be found in the cited reference. Answer a is the principle that anyone responsible for protecting information should have these responsibilities stated explicitly. Answer b is the principle that those held responsible must be made aware of these responsibilities. Answer d is the philosophy that measures, practices, and procedures should be coordinated throughout the enterprise.

Reference   International Information Security Foundation, *GASSP*, (1997), Appendix B, page 43.[57]

10. The task that includes the qualitative identification of susceptibility that could increase the frequency or impact of threat events affecting a specific target environment is called:

   a. Risk evaluation.
   b. Project sizing.
   c. Threat analysis.
   d. Vulnerability analysis.

   Explanation   The correct answer is d and can be found in the cited reference. Answer a involves prioritizing identified threats. Answer b is the task that identifies scope, constraints, objectives, and responsibilities for a given project. Answer c is the process used to identify potential threats to information resources.

   Reference   Tipton and Krause (1999), page 432.

11. When sending or responding to a reference request during the employment process, it is necessary to have a reference authorization waiver. This document should contain the job applicant's signature, a statement releasing the former employer from liability, and clearly specify the type of information that may be divulged. This waiver form is also known as a(an):

   a. Hold harmless agreement.
   b. Employment agreement.
   c. Patent release form.
   d. Resumé.

   Explanation   The correct answer is a and can be found in the cited reference. Answer b is a document to prevent personnel from working for competitors for a period of time after leaving their employer. Answer c is used in the hiring process to spell out patent ownership, and answer d is the employee's curriculum vitae (CV).

   Reference   Tipton and Krause (1999), page 733.

12. The form of risk analysis that attempts to assign independently objective numeric values to the components of the risk analysis and to the level of potential losses is known as:

a. Value analysis.
b. Annual loss exposure.
c. Quantitative risk analysis.
d. Qualitative risk analysis.

Explanation The correct answer is c and can be found in the cited reference. Answer a is a form of qualitative risk analysis, and answer b is a form of quantitative risk analysis. Answer d is the subjective form of risk analysis.

Reference Peltier (2001b), page 19.[65]

13. Management controls designed to prevent security breaches are based on three well-established business principles. Which of the following is *not* one of those principles?

a. Individual accountability
b. Separation of duties
c. Auditing
d. Rotation of assignments

Explanation Answer d is the correct answer and is *not* one of the founding business principles of information security. It is an element used in training employees to be able to back up other employees.

Reference Tipton and Krause (2000), page 7.[67]

14. The process dealing with procedures for making and communicating decisions about how data is to be handled is called:

a. Top secret.
b. Data classification.
c. Access level.
d. Restricted.

Explanation The correct answer is b and can be found in the cited reference. Answers a and d are normally classification levels found with a classification policy. Answer c is used to identify the clearance and authorization of users.

Reference Fites and Kratz (1996), page 113.[54]

15. The access principle that ensures that management is not granted access simply because of their position or that an entry-level clerk is denied access because of his or her position is known as the:

    a. Need-to-know principle.
    b. Dual control principle.
    c. Right of succession.
    d. Personnel security.

Explanation The correct answer is a and can be found in the cited reference. Answer b is the principle in which some function is so important to the security and safety of the information that it must be performed by two or more competent individuals. Answer c is the process of ascending to the throne of a monarchy. Answer d is the general heading that data classification and handling fall under.

Reference Jackson and Hruska (1992), pages 423–424.[59]

16. Not everyone needs the same degree or type of information security awareness to do their jobs. An awareness program that distinguishes between groups of people and presents only information that is relevant to that particular audience will have the best results. The process of dividing the audience into logical groupings is known as:

    a. Level of awareness.
    b. Job category.
    c. Technology used.
    d. Segmenting the audience.

Explanation The correct answer is d and can be found in the cited reference. Answers a, b, and c are categories into which an audience can be divided when preparing an awareness program.

Reference Peltier (2000), pages 26–27.[63]

17. Individual systems and resources may be determined to be unclassified and to be of a specific sensitivity level. When those elements are combined with other resources, the totality of the information may be classified or in a higher sensitivity category, with higher protection requirements. This process is known as:

    a. Access type.
    b. Aggregation.
    c. Asset granularity.
    d. Authorization.

Explanation The correct answer is b and can be found in the cited reference. Answer a is the nature of an access to a particular device, program, or file (such as read-only). Answer c is the degree to which assets are considered as individual assets or as a class. Answer d is the granting to a user, program, or process the right of access.

Reference   Fites and Kratz (1996), page 114.[54]

18. Who has the ultimate responsibility for the security of an organization's information systems?

    a. System administrators
    b. Information systems security officer
    c. Senior management
    d. Help desk

Explanation   The correct answer is c and can be found in the cited reference. Answer a are the employees who design and operate information systems. Answer b are the personnel responsible for the day-to-day security implementation/administration duties. Answer d are the personnel tasked with incident handling.

Reference   National Institute of Standards and Technology (1995), Special Publication 800-12, Section 3.1, Introduction and Overview, pages 16–17.[60]

19. Information security is a business responsibility shared by all members of the management team. A management forum to ensure that there is clear direction and visible management support for security initiatives should be established. Typically, such a forum undertakes all but one of the following. Which activity is *not* undertaken?

    a. Approving information security policy
    b. Establishing security personnel responsibilities
    c. Auditing compliance to security policies
    d. Approving security initiatives

Explanation   The correct answer is c and can be found in the cited reference. Only auditors can audit. This is a legal term and is reserved for the formal process of conducting an audit of a specific process or set of processes within an enterprise.

Reference   ISO/IEC 17799:2000, Section 4.1.1, page 3.[58]

20. The procedure established to ensure that all personnel who have access to any sensitive information have the required authorities as well as all appropriate clearances is known as:

    a. Personnel security.
    b. Secure working area.
    c. Security perimeter.
    d. Secure configuration management.

Explanation   Answer a is correct and can be found in the cited reference. Answer b is an accredited facility that is used for handling, discussing, or processing sensitive defense information. Answer c is the boundary where security controls are in effect to protect assets. Answer d is the use of procedures to control the changes to a system's hardware or software.

Reference   Fites and Kratz (1996), page 377.[54]

21.   An accidental or intentionally caused event that prevents a system from fulfilling its requirements is known as:

   a. Computer abuse.
   b. Copy protection.
   c. Compromise.
   d. Countermeasure.

Explanation   The correct answer is c and can be found in the cited reference. Answer a is the use of a computer in a non-authorized manner. Answer b is a method that makes it difficult to make copies of electronic media. Answer d is a mechanism that reduces the vulnerability of a threat to a system.

Reference   Jackson and Hruska (1992), page 900.[59]

22.   An access policy that restricts access to files and other objects based on the identity of users or groups of users to which they belong and can be applied by the owner at their judgment is known as:

   a. Read access.
   b. Write access.
   c. Mandatory access control.
   d. Discretionary access control.

Explanation   Answer d is the correct answer and can be found in the cited reference. Answer a is a form of access that allows a user to only read a file. Answer b is a form of access that allows a user to read and update a file. Answer c is an access policy supported for systems that process especially sensitive data.

Reference   Russell and Gangemi (1991), page 67.[66]

23.   The Model Business Corporation Act reflects that a corporation acts through the individuals who act on its behalf. In the event of a security breach, corporate officers must be able to show that reasonable care was taken to protect corporate assets. This reasonable care doctrine is also known as:

   a. Duty of care.
   b. Due diligence.

c. Duty of loyalty.
d. Fiduciary responsibility.

Explanation   Answer b is correct and can be found in the cited reference. Answer a is an element of due diligence and requires that senior management make informed business decisions using effective business techniques such as risk analysis. Answer c is also an element of due diligence, in that decisions made by senior management must be made in the best interest of the corporation. Answer d establishes that management is charged with a trust to properly protect the assets of the enterprise.

Reference   Bryson (1995), page 1, 7 and 8.[52]

24. The statutory authority responsible for a particular type or category of information or the individual or organization responsible for the actual data contained therein is known as:

a. The data owner.
b. The data custodian.
c. The data user.
d. Accountability.

Explanation   The correct answer is a and can be found in the cited reference. Answer b is the individual or group entrusted with the possession of, and responsibility for, the security of the specified data. Answer c is the individual or group granted access to the data. Answer d is the property that ensures that the actions of an entity can be traced uniquely to the entity.

Reference   Fites and Kratz (1996), page 1–2.[54]

25. The protection afforded an automated information system in order to attain the applicable objectives of preserving the integrity, availability, and confidentiality of information resources is known as:

a. Operational control.
b. Technical control.
c. Computer security.
d. Management control.

Explanation   The correct answer is c and can be found in the cited reference. Answer a addresses security controls that focus on controls implemented and executed by people as opposed to systems. Answer b refers to controls implemented by systems. Answer d relates to controls implemented and supported by management.

Reference   National Institute of Standards and Technology (1995), NIST Special Publication 800-12, Section 1.4, Important Terminology, page 5.[60]

Chapter 4

Applications and System Development Security Domain

Applications and system development security refers to the controls that are included within systems and applications software, and the steps used in their development. Applications are agents, applets, software, databases, data warehouses, and knowledge-based systems. These applications can be used in distributed or centralized environments.

The professional should fully understand the security and controls of the system development life cycle process. Included in this domain are application controls, change controls, data warehousing, data mining, knowledge-based systems, program interfaces, and concepts used to ensure data and application integrity, confidentiality, and availability. The security and controls that should be included within systems and application software are discussed, as are the steps and security controls in the software life cycle and change control process, and the concepts used to ensure data and software integrity, confidentiality, and availability.

Key Discussion Terms

- Acceptance
- Aggregation
- Applet
- Buffer overflow
- Covert channel
- Change control
- Data hiding
- Data mining
- Data warehousing
- DBMS
- Encapsulation
- Expert system
- Granularity
- Inference
- Inheritance
- Logic bomb
- Mobile code
- Object-oriented programming
- Object reuse
- Polyinstantiation
- SDLC
- Trojan horse
- Virus
- Worm

Practice Study Questions

1. What is the a method used by service providers to formally establish the quality of computing services they provide?

    a. Total Quality Management
    b. Service level agreement
    c. Performance monitoring
    d. Auditing

Explanation   Answer b is the correct answer. Service level agreements establish contractual guarantees regarding the quality of a particular service provided. Answer a is partially correct but is too generic and therefore not the best answer available. Answers c and d are also partially correct in that performance monitoring and auditing assess the quality of services provided; however, their purpose is not to establish a formal level of quality of services that will be provided to a customer.

Reference   Vallabhaneni (2000), page 237.[12]

2. In software development, the process used to determine if the implementation is consistent with the specifications is known as:

    a. Validation.
    b. Verification.
    c. Certification.
    d. Testing.

Explanation   Answer b is the correct answer. Verification is concerned with determining if the implementation of a system is consistent with system specifications. Answer a is incorrect because validation is concerned with predicting how well a system will meet real-world needs. Answer c is incorrect because certification is the process for producing a statement that specifies the extent to which security measures meet specifications. Answer d is too vague to be correct.

Reference   Summers (1997), page 238.[11]

3. The programming technique that employs barriers to prevent access to the procedures and data of a component is known as:

    a. Information hiding.
    b. Abstraction.
    c. Encapsulation.
    d. Confinement.

Explanation   Answer c is the correct answer. Encapsulation is a design technique used to shield a program component to prevent unwanted access from the outside to limit the effects of interference from outside the component. Answer a is incorrect because information hiding aims only to conceal the way a module performs its task. Answer b is incorrect because abstraction is merely a means of reducing the complexity in specifications and designs to make them easier to understand. Answer d is incorrect because confinement is a technique used by an operating system to limit resources that an untrusted program can access.

Reference   Summers (1997), page 240.[11]

4. What is the term used to describe validation errors, domain errors, serialization errors, and boundary-condition errors?

   a. Program flaws
   b. Vulnerabilities
   c. Bugs
   d. Security flaws

Explanation   Answer d is the correct answer. Security flaws refer to any part of a program that can cause the program to violate its security requirements, and include validation errors, domain errors, serialization errors, and boundary-condition errors. Answer a in incorrect because program flaws relate to all unexpected program behavior, including security flaws. Answer b is incorrect because vulnerabilities is a generic term that is too broad to be acceptable. Answer c is incorrect because it is an informal term for program flaws.

Reference   Summers (1997), page 245.[11]

5. An unattended communication path that can be used to violate a system's security policy is known as a:

   a. Covert channel.
   b. Data leak.
   c. Timing channel.
   d. Storage channel.

Explanation   Answer a is the correct answer. A covert channel is a communications channel that permits two cooperating processes to transfer information in violation of a security policy, but without violation of access controls. Answer b is incorrect because it is a distracter. Answers c and d are incorrect because each one is a type of covert channel.

Reference   Summers (1997), page 246.[11]

6. Complete mediation, separation of privilege, and open design are examples of principles of:

a. System development.
b. System design for security.
c. Security controls.
d. Implementation.

Explanation Answer b is the correct answer. The examples given are specified in Saltzer and Schroeder's principles for system design for security. Systems designed using these principles are more likely to meet their security goals. Answer a is incorrect because system development is too broad to be correct. Answer c is incorrect because the examples given are not necessarily security controls (i.e., open design). Answer d is incorrect because these principles relate to system design rather than system implementation.

Reference Summers (1997), page 250.[11]

7. Ensuring that two independent mechanisms agree before allowing an action to take place is an example of which of the following design principles?

a. Complete mediation
b. Economy of mechanism
c. Separation of privilege
d. Least privilege

Explanation Answer c is the correct answer. Separation of privilege requires that access to an object should depend on more than a single condition being met. Answer a is incorrect because complete mediation refers to a design requirement for checking all access attempts. Answer b is incorrect because economy of mechanism relates to the design principle calling for the design to be as simple and small as possible. Answer d is incorrect because least privilege relates to the design principle that specifies that each program (and each user) should operate using the minimum number of privileges possible.

Reference Summers (1997), page 251.[11]

8. The design principle that states a system should produce evidence that can be reviewed to determine how effectively it enforces its security policy is called:

a. Explicitness.
b. Documentation.
c. Verifiability.
d. Auditability.

Explanation   Answer d is the correct answer. Auditability is the feature that allows verification of the accuracy of processing transactions and results, and the adequacy of procedures and controls through the generation of audit information. Answer a is incorrect because it relates to the design principle that specifies that a design should make required system properties explicit. Answer b is incorrect because documentation refers to the process of describing security services and how to use them, but is not a design principle. Answer c is a distracter.

Reference   Summers (1997), page 252.[11]

9. The purpose of polyinstantiation is to counter the problem of:

    a. Inference.
    b. Leakage.
    c. Overclassification.
    d. Need-to-know.

Explanation   Answer a is the correct answer. The purpose of creating multiple *tuples* at different classification levels having the same primary key value is to prevent low-level users from inferring the existence of higher-classified data. Answer b is incorrect because leakage relates to the problem of confinement on a multilevel secure network in which a host can leak information to another host. Answer c is incorrect because it relates only to the problem of inappropriately classifying low-level information at a higher classification level than necessary, and the purpose of polyinstantiation is not to solve this problem. Although polyinstantiation implements the principle of need-to-know, answer d is incorrect because it relates to a security principle, the purpose of which is to limit access to information based on the need-to-know.

Reference   Summers (1997), page 421.[11]

10. A situation in which a user retrieves many data items of the same type to discover sensitive information not revealed by just a few of the items is an example of the problem of:

    a. Scavenging.
    b. Aggregation.
    c. Inference.
    d. Browsing.

Explanation   Answer b is the correct answer. When non-sensitive data elements are combined or aggregated with other data, the totality of the information is actually sensitive. Answer a is incorrect because scavenging relates to a type of attack in which file storage space is searched to gain access to sensitive data. Answer c is incorrect because inference is the ability to infer or derive sensitive data from non-sensitive data; that is, the non-sensitive data accessed is not actually sensitive data. Answer d is incorrect because browsing is the search through available information without knowing in advance what is being sought or that it exists at all.

Reference Summers (1997), page 449.[11]

11. War-dialing is an example of what type of attack?

    a. Flooding.
    b. Sniffer.
    c. Scanning.
    d. Masquerading.

Explanation Answer c is the correct answer. The purpose of war-dialing is to automatically dial all telephone numbers in a range to determine which might provide system access. It is a type of scanning because it presents sequentially changing information to a computer to find values that result in a positive response. Answer a is incorrect because flooding is a type of network attack in which spurious messages are transmitted in an attempt to degrade service. Answer b is incorrect because the aim of a sniffer attack relates to the penetration of a system's security mechanisms in order to install software to collect information from network sessions. Answer d is incorrect because masquerading is a type of attack in which the attacker pretends to be an authorized user in order to obtain that user's access rights to a system.

Reference Summers (1997), page 81.[11]

12. Masquerading is synonymous with which one of the following terms?

    a. Browsing
    b. Scanning
    c. Sniffing
    d. Spoofing

Explanation Answer d is the correct answer. Spoofing and masquerading are synonymous terms for an attacker pretending to be an authorized user to attempt to obtain that user's access rights to a system. Answer a is incorrect because browsing refers to a search through available information without knowing ahead of time what is being searched for, or that it even exists. Answer b is incorrect because scanning is a type of attack in which a computer is presented sequential information in order to find values that result in a positive response. Answer c is incorrect because sniffing is a type of attack in which a system's security mechanisms are penetrated and software is installed to collect information from network sessions.

Reference Summers (1997), page 80.[11]

13. Which of the following is *not* an example of passive misuse?

   a. Data diddling
   b. Shoulder-surfing
   c. Eavesdropping
   d. Sniffing

Explanation   Answer a is the correct answer. Because it results in data alteration, data diddling affects the integrity of data and is a form of active misuse. Active misuse is defined as an attack on the integrity or availability of information. Shoulder-surfing, eavesdropping, and sniffing can result in violation of the confidentiality of data without affecting the state of the system or information, and are examples of passive misuse.

Reference   Summers (1997), page 82.[11]

14. An attack to defeat a safeguard by attacking below the level of the safeguard is known as what type of attack?

   a. Backdoor.
   b. Tunneling.
   c. Covert channel.
   d. Brute force.

Explanation   Answer b is the correct answer. The aim of a tunneling attack is to breach system security controls by attacking at a level beneath the control. System utilities (e.g., Superzap) are often designed to bypass security controls under special circumstances and can be used to perform a tunneling attack. Answer a is incorrect because a backdoor is a hidden mechanism designed into a program to permit system security controls to be bypassed. Answer c is incorrect because a covert channel is a communications channel that permits two cooperating processes to transfer information in violation of a security policy, but without violation of access controls. Answer d is incorrect because a brute-force or exhaustive attack attempts to breach system security controls by trying every possible combination of passwords or keys.

Reference   Summers (1997), page 85.[11]

15. Baselines and checksums are normally associated with which one of the following concepts?

   a. Recovery
   b. Prevention
   c. Detection
   d. Assurance

Explanation Answer c is the correct answer. At a point when files are considered to be intact, automated change detection systems compute a baseline, and a baseline table containing file names and corresponding checksums is generated. This information provides a point of reference in detecting when changes to files documented in the baseline table have taken place. Answer a is incorrect because recovery places more reliance on the availability of files, whereas baselines and checksums focus on the integrity of files. Answer b is incorrect because prevention relates to controls implemented to prevent an adverse event from occurring. Answer d is incorrect because assurance relates to steps taken to ensure that appropriate actions are taken to reduce or eliminate vulnerabilities in controls.

Reference Summers (1997), page 93.[11]

16. Breaking activities into sufficiently small segments that individual pieces are understandable and can be reasonably subjected to correctness proofs or exhaustive testing is known as the principle of:

   a. Layering.
   b. Simplicity.
   c. Coupling.
   d. Modularity.

   Explanation Answer d is the correct answer. Modularity relates to the development of software with attributes (i.e., unity, smallness, simplicity, independence, etc.) that result in highly independent modules. Answer a is incorrect because layering is a principle for constructing processes in layers so that at each layer a different activity is performed. Answer b is incorrect because simplicity is merely an attribute of a module. Answer c is incorrect because coupling relates to the degree of independence that a module has in relation to other routines in a program.

   Reference Fites and Kratz (1996), page 318.[7]

17. A change control process does *not* need to ensure:

   a. That changes are reasonable.
   b. That changes are authorized.
   c. That changes are tested.
   d. That changes are recorded.

   Explanation Answer a is the correct answer. Whether or not changes are reasonable is not a function of the change control process. However, the process must ensure that all changes are authorized, tested, and recorded. Changes that have been appropriately authorized are assumed to be reasonable.

   Reference Fites and Kratz (1996), page 321.[7]

18. An attack in which the contents of a file are changed between the time the system security functions check the access permissions to a file and the time the file is actually used in an operation is called a:

   a. Covert channel attack.
   b. TOC/TOU attack.
   c. Scavenging attack.
   d. Timing channel attack.

   Explanation   Answer b is the correct answer. A "Time of Check versus Time of Use" (TOC/TOU) attack exploits a flaw whereby controls that carefully validate parameters validated by system controls are changed before the parameters are used. Answer a is incorrect because a covert channel attack refers to the use of an undetected communications channel that permits two cooperating processes to transfer information in violation of a security policy, but without violation of access controls. Answer c is incorrect because a scavenging attack relates to a type of attack in which file storage space is searched to gain access to sensitive data. Answer d is incorrect because a timing channel attack is a form of covert channel attack.

   Reference   Fites and Kratz (1996), page 444.[7]

19. A storage facility in which data from multiple heterogeneous databases is brought together to facilitate user queries is called:

   a. A database management system.
   b. A data mart.
   c. A data warehouse.
   d. An expert system.

   Explanation   Answer c is the correct answer. A data warehouse is a collection of data designed to support decision making, and generally refers to the combination of many different databases across an entire enterprise. Answer a is incorrect because a database management system is used to manage a single database. Answer b is incorrect because a data mart focuses on a particular subject or department, rather than on an entire enterprise. Answer d is incorrect because an expert system is an application program that supports decision making using a subject-specific knowledge base and rules.

   Reference   Vallabhaneni (2000), page 210.[12]

20. An automated tool used to convert data in a data warehouse into useful information is referred to as:

   a. Structured Query Language (SQL).
   b. DBMS.
   c. An inference engine.
   d. A data mining tool.

Explanation Answer d is the correct answer. Because a data warehouse itself does not extract information, data mining tools are used for this purpose to search for hidden patterns and other useful information. Answer a is incorrect because SQL statements are used to request information from a database rather than a data warehouse. Answer b is incorrect because, similar to answer a, a database management system (DBMS) is used to request information from a database. Answer c is incorrect because an inference engine is used to evaluate knowledge base data against rules in an expert system.

Reference Vallabhaneni (2000), page 211.[12]

21. What is a mechanism called that allows objects of a class to acquire part of their definition from another class?

    a. Inheritance
    b. Cohesion
    c. Coupling
    d. Polymorphism

Explanation Answer a is the correct answer. Inheritance refers to a relationship among classes of objects in which one class shares the structure and behavior defined in another class. Answer b is incorrect because cohesion relates to the degree to which functions or processing elements of a module are related or bound together. Answer c is incorrect because coupling is the degree to which program modules depend on each other. Answer d is incorrect because polymorphism refers to an object's behavior in response to a command being determined by the class to which the object belongs.

Reference Vallabhaneni (2000), page 217.[12]

22. The major concern in interrupt handling is how to avoid:

    a. Disclosure of sensitive data.
    b. Deadlocks and endless loops.
    c. Breach of security mechanisms.
    d. Loss of data integrity.

Explanation Answer b is the correct answer. Interrupt handling is an important aspect of real-time systems because of the demand for operating efficiency. When a process is suspended due to an interrupt, it must be handled by the operating system according to established priorities to permit the process to be resumed as quickly as possible. Deadlocks and endless loops resulting from poor interrupt handling can delay the resumption of processing and are therefore of major concern. Answers a and d are incorrect because interrupt handling relates primarily to data availability rather than data confidentiality and data integrity. Answer c is not correct because interrupt handling focuses on system performance rather than on the reliability of security controls.

Reference   Vallabhaneni (2000), page 220.[12]

23. The form of artificial intelligence that has the ability to learn and to utilize accumulated experience for decision making is known as:

    a. Fuzzy logic.
    b. Expert systems.
    c. Neural networks.
    d. Parsing.

    Explanation   Answer c is the correct answer. Neural networks are characterized by their ability to decide and to learn to improve performance through trial-and-error decision making. Answer a is incorrect because the purpose of fuzzy logic is to recognize more than simple true and false values, but does not learn from accumulated experience. Answer b is incorrect because expert systems rely on knowledge bases, rules, and inference engines to support decision making, but are incapable of learning from experience. Answer d is incorrect because parsing is the form of artificial intelligence that breaks program code into logical parts and then explains the form, function, and interaction of these parts (e.g., compilers parse source code to be able to translate it into object code).

    Reference   Vallabhaneni (2000), page 223.[12]

24. The user interface, inference engine, and knowledge base are integral parts of the:

    a. Neural network.
    b. Data warehouse.
    c. Reference monitor.
    d. Expert system.

    Explanation   Answer d is the correct answer. Expert systems are designed to consist of a user interface, inference engine, and knowledge base, all of which interact with each other. Answers a, b, and c are incorrect because neural networks, data warehouses, and reference monitors do not implement all three of these distinct components.

    Reference   Vallabhaneni (2000), page 226.[12]

25. What is the primary risk associated with applets such as Java and ActiveX?

    a. The user must trust that what is downloaded will do what has been promised.
    b. Applets cannot be scanned to determine if they are safe.

c. Browsers cannot restrict the execution of applets.

d. It is difficult to configure firewalls to block the reception of applets.

Explanation   Answer a is the correct answer. Applets are small applications that a server automatically downloads onto a user's computer. When users execute these applets using applet-enabled Web browsers, they trust that the source server permits only trustworthy applets to be downloaded, and they trust that the applet itself will do what has been promised and nothing more. Answer b is incorrect because applets can be scanned to determine whether or not they should be trusted. Answer c is incorrect because browsers can be configured to accept applets only from trusted servers, or not at all. Answer d is incorrect because firewalls can be readily instructed to block the reception of applets from external sources unless they have been authenticated.

Reference   Vallabhaneni (2000), pages 191–192.[12]

Chapter 5

Cryptography Domain

The Cryptography domain addresses the principles, means, and methods of disguising information to ensure its integrity, confidentiality, and authenticity. Unlike the other domains, cryptography does not support the standard of availability.

The professional should fully understand the basic concepts within cryptography. This would include public and private key algorithms in terms of their applications and uses. Cryptography algorithm construction, key distribution, key management, and methods of attack are also important. The applications, construction, and use of digital signatures are discussed and compared to the elements of cryptography. The principles of authenticity of electronic transactions and non-repudiation are also included in this domain.

Key Discussion Terms

- Cryptanalysis
- Cryptology
- Plaintext, cleartext, ciphertext
- Encipher
- Decipher
- Cryptanalysis key
- Key clustering
- Work factor algorithm
- Digital signatures
- Digital certificates
- Kerberos
- SSL

- Adaptive chosen ciphertext attack
- Man-in-the-middle attack
- Timing attacks
- Brute-force attack
- Birthday attack
- Symmetric (private) key cryptography
- Hash functions
- Electronic document authorization (EDA)
- Public key
- PKI

Practice Study Questions

1. An encapsulated secure payload always provides which one of the following security functions?

    a. Availability
    b. Confidentiality
    c. Authentication
    d. Integrity

    Explanation   Answer b is the correct answer. Answer a is incorrect because encryption does not handle any availability functions. Answers c and d are incorrect because they are part of the function of the authentication header.

    Reference   Atkinson (1995), RFC 1825.[19]

2. A message authentication code provides which one of the following security functions?

    a. Availability
    b. Confidentiality
    c. Authentication
    d. Integrity

    Explanation   Answer d is the correct answer. Answer a is incorrect because encryption does not handle any availability functions. Answer b is incorrect because it is a function of the encapsulated secure payload; and answer c is incorrect because it is a function of the authentication header, which is broader than the message authentication code.

    Reference   Krawczyk, Bellare, and Canetti (1997), RFC 2104.[23]

3. ISAKMP is a type of:

    a. Key management protocol.
    b. Hash algorithm.
    c. Encryption scheme.
    d. Private key cryptography.

    Explanation   Answer a is the correct answer. Answers b, c, and d are all encryption concepts but unrelated to ISAKMP.

    Reference   Piper (1998), RFC 2407.[24]

4. Which of the following is an example of a symmetric algorithm?

    a. DES
    b. RSA

c. SSL
d. SHA1

Explanation   Answer a is the correct answer. Answer b is incorrect because RSA uses a public key or asymmetric algorithm. Answer c is incorrect because SSL uses RSA for encryption. Answer d is not an encryption algorithm at all.

Reference   Fites and Kratz (1996), page 33.[20]

5. Which of the following is an example of an asymmetric algorithm?

   a. DES
   b. 3DES
   c. SSL
   d. SHA1

Explanation   Answer c is the correct answer because SSL uses RSA encryption. Answers a and b are incorrect because they are symmetric algorithms. Answer d is incorrect because it is not an encryption algorithm.

Reference   Fites and Kratz (1996), page 43.[20]

6. Which one of the following is an application for encrypting remote access to a server?

   a. SSL
   b. PGP
   c. S/MIME
   d. SSH

Explanation   Answer d is the correct answer. Answer a is incorrect because SSL encrypts Web traffic. Answers b and c are incorrect because PGP and S/MIME deal with e-mail.

Reference   Guttman, Leong, and Malkin (1999), RFC 2504.[21]

7. Which one of the following examples illustrates the use of a one-way function?

   a. DES and SHA1
   b. 3DES and MD5
   c. MD5 and SHA1
   d. 3DES and SHA1

Explanation   Answer c is correct. Answers a, b, and d are all incorrect because they contain DES or 3DES, which are symmetric algorithms that can be reversed.

Reference   Schneier (1996), page 28.[26]

8. Which of the following is not a component of key management?

 a. Generation
 b. Storage
 c. Assessment
 d. Distribution

Explanation Answer c is the correct answer. Answers a, b, and d are all components of creating and managing a public key infrastructure.

Reference Fites and Kratz (1996), page 23.[20]

9. A remote user using VPN software attached to the file server that then terminates the VPN connection is an example of?

 a. Link encryption.
 b. Asymmetric encryption.
 c. Symmetric encryption.
 d. End-to-end encryption.

Explanation Answer d is correct. Answer a is incorrect because it is the opposite of answer d. Answers b and c are incorrect because they deal with the key exchange mechanism and not the encrypted spans of networks the data will traverse.

Reference Fites and Kratz (1996), page 23.[20]

10. Which one of the following terms can be defined as "the hardware, software, and procedures associated with generating, distributing, and using encryption keys"?

 a. Public key cryptography
 b. Key management
 c. Private key cryptography
 d. Diffie–Hellman

Explanation Answer b is the correct answer and is taken verbatim from the reference. Answer a is incorrect because it is too broad in scope. Answer c is incorrect because it is also too broad in scope. Answer d is incorrect because it is a component of key exchange.

Reference Fites and Kratz (1996), page 27.[20]

11. Which of the following is true about DES?

 a. DES uses public key cryptography.
 b. DES is a block cipher.
 c. DES is an asymmetric encryption algorithm.
 d. DES is a stream cipher.

Explanation   Answer b is the correct answer. Answer a is incorrect because DES uses private key cryptography. Answer c is incorrect because DES is a symmetric algorithm. Answer d is incorrect because it is opposite to answer a.

Reference   Fites and Kratz (1996), page 33.[20]

12. What is the greatest potential disadvantage to encryption?

    a. Performance degradation
    b. Difficulty to implement
    c. The lack of standards
    d. There is no potential disadvantage to encryption

Explanation   Answer a is the correct answer. Answer b can be true but is not the *most* correct answer. Answer c is incorrect because standards such as IPSec exist. Answer d is incorrect because there are trade-offs when implementing encryption.

Reference   Schneier (1996), page 285.[26]

13. *Password cracking* an encrypted password file is which of the following types of attack?

    a. Known plaintext
    b. Chosen plaintext
    c. Timing attack
    d. Known ciphertext

Explanation   Answer d is the correct answer. Answer a is incorrect because in this example you would already have the password and would be looking to find the ciphertext. Answer b is incorrect because in this example you would have both the password and the encrypted password and would be looking for the encrypting key. Answer c is incorrect because in this example you would have neither the password nor the encrypted password — only the time it took the system to generate the encrypted password.

Reference   Fites and Kratz (1996), page 438.[20]

14. Which of the following is true about IDEA?

    a. IDEA is a based on a 56-bit key.
    b. IDEA is an asymmetric encryption algorithm.
    c. IDEA is a block cipher.
    d. IDEA cannot be exported outside the United States.

Explanation   Answer c is the correct answer. Answer a is incorrect because IDEA is based on a 128-bit key. Answer b is incorrect because

IDEA is a symmetric algorithm. Answer d is incorrect because export restrictions have been relaxed.

Reference Schneier (1996), page 261.[26]

15. What is the disadvantage of public key cryptography when compared to private key cryptography?

   a. Public key cryptography is slower.
   b. Public key cryptography is based on a shorter encryption key.
   c. Public key cryptography has no key exchange mechanism.
   d. Public key cryptography cannot be exported outside the United States.

Explanation Answer a is the correct answer. Answer b is incorrect because public key can be based on a longer key than private key. Answer c is incorrect because PKI, by definition, is a public key exchange. Answer d is incorrect because export restrictions have been relaxed.

Reference Schneier (1996), page 285.[26]

16. Which of the following is true about the El Gamal encryption algorithm?

   a. It is a symmetric algorithm.
   b. It is patented by RSA.
   c. It was developed by the NSA.
   d. It is a public key algorithm.

Explanation Answer d is the correct answer. Answer a is incorrect because El Gamal is an asymmetric algorithm. Answer b is incorrect because RSA patented its own public key algorithm. Answer c is incorrect because El Gamal was not developed by any branch of the U.S. Government.

Reference Schneier (1996), page 300.[26]

17. Which of the following is true about IDEA?

   a. IDEA is a based on a 56-bit key.
   b. IDEA is a symmetric encryption algorithm.
   c. IDEA is a stream cipher.
   d. IDEA cannot be exported outside the United States.

Explanation Answer b is correct. Answer a is incorrect because IDEA is based on a 128-bit key. Answer c is incorrect because IDEA is a block cipher. Answer d is incorrect because current export restrictions have been relaxed.

Reference Schneier (1996), page 261.[26]

18. Whitfield Diffie and Martin Hellman invented the first:

a. Symmetric key algorithm.
b. Block cipher algorithm.
c. Stream cipher algorithm.
d. Asymmetric key algorithm.

Explanation   Answer d is the correct answer. Answers a, b, and c were invented by other people.

Reference   Schneier (1996), page 275.[26]

19. Which one of the following is defined in the digital signature standard?

a. DES
b. DSA
c. MD5
d. HMAC

Explanation   Answer b is the correct answer. Answer a is incorrect because DES is an encryption algorithm. Answer c is incorrect because MD5 is a message hash algorithm. Answer d is incorrect because HMAC is a message authentication code.

Reference   Schneier (1996), page 304.[26]

20. Which one of the following is not a key distribution method?

a. MD5
b. Kerberos
c. ISAKMP
d. Manual

Explanation   Answer a is the correct answer. Answer b is incorrect because Kerberos is a key distribution method. Answer c, ISAKMP, is an acronym for Internet Security Association Key Management Protocol. Answer d is a common answer for symmetric encryption algorithms.

Reference   Schneier (1996), page 329.[26]

21. Which of the following is *not* a message digest?

a. SHA1
b. MD5
c. El Gamal
d. HMAC

Explanation   Answer c is correct. Answers a, b, and d are all message digests.

Reference   Schneier (1996), page 300.[26]

22. Which one of the following cryptographic attacks looks for pairs of identical hashes?

    a. Chosen plaintext
    b. Known plaintext
    c. Birthday attack
    d. Clipper Chip

Explanation Answer c is the correct answer. Answer a is incorrect because, in chosen plaintext attacks, the plaintext and the corresponding ciphertext can be obtained. Answer b is incorrect because, in a known plaintext attack, certain ciphertext/plaintext pairs are known. Answer d is incorrect because it has nothing to do with attacks on cryptography.

Reference Fites and Kratz (1996), page 438.[20]

23. How large are the blocks that DES uses during encryption?

    a. 56 bits
    b. 64 bits
    c. 128 bits
    d. 168 bits

Explanation Answer b is the correct answer. Answer a is incorrect because DES uses a 56-bit key, but the block is 64 bits. Answer c is incorrect because that is the key length for IDEA. Answer d is incorrect because 168 is the number of bits for a 3DES key.

Reference Fites and Kratz (1996), page 33.[20]

24. What is the act of converting plaintext to ciphertext?

    a. Encrypting
    b. Decrypting
    c. Public key cryptography
    d. Man-in-the-middle attack

Explanation Answer a is the correct answer. Answer b is incorrect because it is opposite to answer a. Answer c is incorrect because it is too general a term. Answer d is incorrect because it is a specific type of attack on cryptography, and is too narrow in focus. While answers c and d are somewhat correct, answer a is the *best* answer.

Reference Fites and Kratz (1996), page 21.[20]

25. Which of the following application does *not* use cryptography?

    a. SSL
    b. SSH

c. PGP
d. FTP

Explanation   Answer d is the correct answer. Answer a uses RSA asymmetric cryptography; answer b uses encryption to secure a Telnet-like session; answer c uses DES and IDEA for encryption.

Reference   Postel and Reynolds (1985), RFC 959.[25]

Chapter 6

Security Architecture and Models Domain

The Security Architecture and Models domain contains the concepts, principles, structures, and standards used to design, implement, monitor, and secure operating systems, equipment, networks, applications, as well as those controls used to enforce various levels of confidentiality, integrity, and availability.

The professional should fully understand security models in terms of confidentiality, integrity, and information flow. The successful candidate will be able to identify the differences between the commercial and government security requirements. While system security evaluation criteria are in a state of flux, the material presented in this domain includes the international (ITSEC), U.S. Department of Defense (TCSEC) concepts. Security practices such as Internet (IETF IPSec) are discussed. The technical platforms and their security requirements are examined in terms of hardware, firmware, and software. The key security architecture for protecting information assets is presented in three of the four layers and includes preventative, detective, and corrective aspects.

Key Discussion Terms

- Trust
- Secure operating system
- Software engineering
- System software
- Protected security-relevant functions
- Resource access control
- Process of limiting access to resources of a system
- Process isolation
- Enforcement of least privilege
- Hardware segmentation
- Protection mechanism
- Compiler
- Interpreter
- Security policy
- Trusted Computing Base (TCB)
- MAC
- DAC

Practice Study Questions

1. Hardware and software that correspond to hardware and software in a different system at the same OSI layer are known as:

    a. Peer components.
    b. Peer services.
    c. Peer protocols.
    d. Peer entities.

    Explanation   Answer d is correct. Hardware and software at the same layer of the OSI model in different systems are referred to as peer entities. Answer a is a distracter. Although hardware and software provide a service at a given OSI layer, answer b is incorrect because services are not entities as are hardware and software. Answer c is incorrect because hardware and software are not protocols.

    Reference   Summers (1997), page 470.[49]

2. Within an access control model, the object is:

    a. The entity that performs an action.
    b. The entity that is acted upon.
    c. The data.
    d. The program.

    Explanation   Answer b is correct because it is an object that is the entity in an access control model that is acted upon. Answer a relates to a subject. Answer c may be true but objects are not limited to data entities. Answer d may be true but objects are not limited to program entities.

    Reference   Fites and Kratz (1996), page 117.[46]

3. The Biba access control model addresses the goal of:

    a. Integrity.
    b. Availability.
    c. Non-repudiation.
    d. Auditability.

    Explanation   Answer a is correct. Answers b, c, and d are not addressed by Biba.

    Reference   Summers (1997), page 142.[49]

4. The protection mechanisms within a computing system that collectively enforce security policy are known as the TCB. What does this acronym represent?

   a. Terminal Connection Board
   b. Trusted Computing Base
   c. Trusted Connection Boundary
   d. Trusted Cipher Base

Explanation   Answer b is correct. Answers a, c, and d are fictitious terms.

Reference   Fites and Kratz (1996), page 163.[46]

5. Which one of the following memory storage mechanisms is volatile?

   a. ROM
   b. RAM
   c. Secondary
   d. Sequential

Explanation   Answer b is correct because RAM is volatile. Answer a is not volatile. Answer c is a term for a nonvolatile medium such as a disk drive. Answer d relates to the structure of the storage, not its medium.

Reference   Fites and Kratz (1996), page 147.[46]

6. Where would one least expect to find security vulnerabilities in a well-architected system?

   a. The security kernel
   b. Maintenance hooks
   c. State changes
   d. Timing (TOC/TOU)

Explanation   Answer a is correct — this should be the most secure component of the system. Answer b is notorious for backdoor exposures. State changes (answer c) are vulnerable to interference (e.g., initialization and failure states). Answer d is vulnerable due to the disconnect in time between authorization and action.

Reference   Fites and Kratz (1996), page 158.[46]

7. Discretionary access control relates to:

   a. Permanent and irreversible access rules defined within an operating system.
   b. Access rules that can be circumvented at the discretion of the user.
   c. Control capabilities defined within an operating system, which the security administrator or his or her policy may opt to utilize.

    d. Access control lists maintained discretely from one another in a policy file.

Explanation   Answer c is correct. Answer a is mandatory access control. Answer b is not a valid control. Answer d may be possible but the means of ACL storage is not relevant to the term "discretionary access control."

Reference   Fites and Kratz (1996), page 152.[46]

8. In the Clark–Wilson access control model, an *access triple* binds together which pairs of entity types?

    a. Subjects to Programs and Subjects to Objects
    b. Subjects to Programs and Programs to Objects
    c. Objects to Subjects and Subjects to Programs
    d. Objects to Programs and Objects to Subjects

Explanation   Answer b is correct — subject access to objects is controlled via programs. Answer a would represent two separate access tuples not bound into a triple. Answer c would theoretically be an access triple but would be inconsistent with the model and would not function correctly. Answer d would represent two separate access tuples not bound into a triple.

Reference   Fites and Kratz (1996), page 334.[46]

9. Which one of the following most fully describes the *certification* process of a system for security purposes?

    a. Analysis of the extent to which security requirements are satisfied by the system
    b. A management judgment to operate the system in a target operational environment
    c. A security audit of system functionality
    d. Issuance of a clearance certificate

Explanation   Answer a is correct. Answer b is the definition of *accreditation*. Answer c is not enough; the system must be reviewed within the context of requirements. Answer d is not enough; the system must be reviewed prior to the paperwork being issued.

Reference   Fites and Kratz (1996), page 163.[46]

10. Which one of the following operating system components and functions is normally the least well protected?

    a. Execution domain
    b. User mode

c. Reference monitor

d. Process isolation

Explanation   Answers a, c, and d are all normally associated with operating system kernel code and its privileged functionality. Answer b is correct because it is the remaining functionality deliberately made available to users outside the protected kernel.

Reference   Fites and Kratz (1996), page 169.[46]

11.   If a CPU is in *supervisor state,* it will:

a. Access both privileged and non-privileged instructions.

b. Access only privileged instructions.

c. Access only non-privileged instructions.

d. Accept interruptions but not execute instructions.

Explanation   Answer a is correct. Answer b is a false statement. Answer c is a condition of *problem state.* Answer d is a condition of *wait state.*

Reference   Fites and Kratz (1996), page 169.[46]

12.   TCSEC is the acronym for:

a. Tested Computer Security Evaluation Certificate.

b. Trusted Computer Security Evaluation Criteria.

c. Tested Computer System Evaluation Certificate.

d. Trusted Computer System Evaluation Criteria.

Explanation   Answer d is correct. Answers a, b, and c are fictitious terms.

Reference   Fites and Kratz (1996), page 163.[46]

13.   The risk incurred by time elapsing between an access permission being checked and the object being accessed is usually referred to as:

a. Access latency.

b. Trusted timestamp.

c. TOC/TOU.

d. Strong typing.

Explanation   Answer c is correct — Time Of Check versus Time Of Use. Answer a is a fictitious term. Answer b is a valid term but relates to a means of authenticating time. Answer d is the string enforcement of abstract data types.

Reference   Fites and Kratz (1996), page 172.

14. Which of the following most fully describes the *accreditation* process of a system for security purposes?

    a. Analysis of the extent to which security requirements are satisfied by the system

    b. A management judgment to operate the system in a target operational environment

    c. A security audit of system functionality

    d. Issuance of a clearance certificate

Explanation Answer b is correct because it provides the best description of accreditation. Answer a is the definition of *certification*. Answer c is insufficient because the system must be reviewed within the context of requirements and then approved by management of the target environment. Answer d is insufficient because the system must be reviewed and approved by management of the target environment prior to the paperwork being issued.

Reference Fites and Kratz (1996), page 163.[46]

15. In terms of access control system architecture, limiting the independent activity of subjects by attaching them to each other or to objects is usually referred to as:

    a. Security associations.

    b. Binding.

    c. Bridging.

    d. Handshaking.

Explanation Answer b is correct. Answer a refers to the relationship between two entities in terms of a shared security attribute. Answer c is a fictitious term. Answer d is the dialogue between two entities to mutually identify and authenticate each other and is therefore incorrect.

Reference Fites and Kratz (1996), page 147.[46]

16. Which one of the following TCSEC classes requires mandatory access control?

    a. D

    b. C1

    c. C2

    d. B1

Explanation Answer d is correct. Mandatory access control (as defined by Bell–LaPadula) is a requirement of all Division B classes under TCSEC. Answer a is incorrect because Class D requires only minimal protection. Answer b is incorrect because Class C1 requires discretionary controlled access protection. Answer c is incorrect because Class C2 requires controlled access protection.

Reference   Fites and Kratz (1996), page 163.[46]

17.   Which one of the following system architecture features or functions is *least likely* to contribute to the continuous availability of the system?

  a. Discretionary access control
  b. Process isolation
  c. Enforcement of least privilege
  d. Hardware segmentation

Explanation   Answer a is correct because control capability may not be fully implemented. Answer b reduces the probability of system failure by ensuring that processes cannot interfere with each other's memory space. Answer c reduces the probability of system failure by ensuring that processes cannot access privileged code when it is not necessary to do so. Answer d reduces the probability of system failure by ensuring that user processes cannot access segments restricted for operating system use.

Reference   Fites and Kratz (1996), page 152.[46]

18.   Which one of the following is assumed to be already in place by the Trusted Network Interpretation (TNI) that provides Orange Book interpretations for trusted computer network systems?

  a. Procedural protection measures
  b. Communications integrity measures
  c. Measures to protect against denial-of-service
  d. Transmission security measures

Explanation   Answer a is correct because procedural protection measures are not included in the Trusted Network Interpretation. Answers b, c, and d are included in the TNI and are therefore incorrect.

Reference   Fites and Kratz (1996), page 207.[46]

19.   Which one of the following is a function of the reference monitor?

  a. Mediate access of all subjects to all objects
  b. Perform integrity checks on objects
  c. Provide a common interface between platforms and applications
  d. Perform integrity checks on subjects

Explanation   Answer a is correct because the primary function of a reference monitor is to mediate access of all subjects to all objects it manages. Answer b is a valid control but is not performed by the reference monitor. Answer c is a function of an API. Answer d is a valid control but is not performed by the reference monitor.

Reference   Fites and Kratz (1996), page 157.[46]

20. Which one of the following is *not* required to achieve a C2 certification under TCSEC criteria?

    a. A security policy
    b. Subject sensitivity labels
    c. A protected audit trail
    d. A security features user guide

Explanation   Answer b is correct because these are required only for Classes B2 and above. Answer a is incorrect because a security policy is required for Classes C1 and above. Answer c is incorrect because a protected audit trail is required for Classes C2 and above. Answer d is incorrect because a security features users guide is required by Classes C1 and above.

Reference   Fites and Kratz (1996), page 163.[46]

21. A computer's ability to simultaneously execute two or more programs is known as:

    a. Multi-tasking.
    b. Multi-programming.
    c. Multi-processing.
    d. Multi-processor.

Explanation   Answer c is correct because multi-processing is the term used to refer to a computer's ability to execute multiple programs at the same time. Answer a is the concurrent or interleaved execution of two or more tasks. Answer b is the interleaved execution of two or more programs by a single processor. Answer d is a computer with two or more processors with common access to main storage.

Reference   Fites and Kratz (1996), page 147.[46]

22. Which one of the following is *not* defined by the Bell–LaPadula model?

    a. The concept of a secure state of system operation
    b. Rules for giving subjects access to objects
    c. Fundamental modes of access
    d. The three goals of integrity

Explanation   Answer d is correct because it is defined by the Clark–Wilson model. Answers a, b, and c are defined by Bell–LaPadula.

Reference   Fites and Kratz (1996), page 411.[46]

23. In an operating system, the *abstraction* security principle can be defined as:

   a. Operating system processes are constructed in layers.
   b. User identities are clustered into groups.
   c. Sets of permissible values and operations are established for each class of object.
   d. Data handled by one operating system layer is hidden from the other layers.

Explanation   Answer c provides the correct definition of abstraction. Answer a is the definition of *layering*. Answer b is incorrect because it is relevant to user administration, not operating systems. Answer d is the definition of *data hiding* and is therefore incorrect.

Reference   Fites and Kratz (1996), page 235.[46]

24. Which of the following security evaluation standards measures both functionality and assurance levels?

   a. TCSEC and ITSEC
   b. Common Criteria and TCSEC
   c. Common Criteria and ITSEC
   d. TCSEC alone

Explanation   Answer c is correct because the Common Criteria and ITSEC both measure functionality and assurance levels. Answer a includes TCSEC, which evaluates functionality only; answer b includes TCSEC, which evaluates functionality only; and answer d TCSEC also evaluates functionality only.

Reference   Fites and Kratz (1996), page 163.[46]

25. Which one of the following functions would you *not* expect to see as a capability of a non-government operating system?

   a. It isolates one process from another in memory.
   b. It recognizes different protection layers in the same process.
   c. It enforces mandatory access control.
   d. It segregates user-controlled segments from system-controlled segments.

Explanation   Answer a is incorrect because address management would be expected. Answer b, segregation of privileged and non-privileged routines, would be expected and is therefore incorrect. Answer c is correct because mandatory access control is typically used in classified government or defense systems. Answer d is incorrect because segregation of privileged and non-privileged routines would be expected.

Reference   Fites and Kratz (1996), page 163.[46]

Chapter 7

Operations Security Domain

Operations security is used to identify the controls over hardware, media, and the operators with access privileges to any of these resources. Operations security involves the administrative management of all types of information processing operations, the concepts of security of centralized as well as distributed operations, the various choices for operations controls, resource protection requirements, auditing operations, monitoring, and intrusion detection.

Key Discussion Terms

- Job requirements and specifications
- Background checking
- Separation of duties and responsibilities
- Job rotation
- Terminations
- Handling disgruntled/former employees

- Need-to-know
- Least privilege
- Audit logging
- Audit trails
- Monitoring
- Intrusion detection

Practice Study Questions

1. The overall information protection program of an organization addresses the entire spectrum of computer security, whereas *system-level security programs* ensure appropriate and cost-effective security for each system. In regard to a *system-level security program* when addressing operations security, it should have all except which one of the following?

   a. System-specific security policy
   b. Life cycle management
   c. Published mission and functions statement
   d. Appropriate integration with system operations

   Explanation The correct answer is c because a published mission and functions statement is an element of a *central security program*. Each of the other answers is part of a *system-level security program*, as follows. Answer a, a system-specific security policy, documents the system security rules for operating or developing the system; answer b, life cycle management, helps to ensure that security is authorized by appropriate management and that changes to the system are made with attention to security; and answer d, appropriate integration with system operations, integrates effective security management into the management of the system to help ensure that the people who run the system security program understand the system, its mission, its technology, and its operating environment.

   Reference National Institute of Standards and Technology (1996), Section 3.2.2 (System-Level Program).[35]

2. Which one of the following is *not* a characteristic of a computer virus?

   a. A program that copies itself into host programs or into special executable bootstrap areas of disks.
   b. It spreads by replicating, then inserting itself into other programs, thus spreading the infection.
   c. Except for the ones that overwrite code, few viruses deliberately damage the program they infect.
   d. A freestanding program that replicates itself, usually in networks, but does not integrate its code into host programs.

   Explanation Answer d is the correct answer because this is a characteristic of a worm, not a virus.

   Reference Kabay (1999), chapter 3.[33]

3. Which of the following is ineffective against computer viruses?

   a. Diagnosis
   b. Disinfection
   c. Inoculation
   d. Antibiotics

Explanation   Answer d is the correct answer because there is no such thing as an antibiotic for computer viruses. Answer a, diagnosis, is effective in locating virus-infected files and boot sectors after the fact. Answer b, disinfection, is effective in getting rid of the damage and restoring the intact files and sectors. Answer c, inoculation, is effective in preventing damage.

Resource   Kabay (1999), chapter 3.[33]

4. There are six stages of activity in incident response. Each stage is critical, and overlooking one or more of the stages can result in time-consuming and costly incident mitigation efforts. These steps have a logical order to them. Which of the following is out of order?

   a. Preparation
   b. Detection
   c. Eradication
   d. Containment

Explanation   Answer d, containment, is out of order. It should occur after detection as the third stage. Answer a, preparation, is the first stage. Answer b, detection, is the second stage. Answer c, eradication, is the fourth stage (after containment). Restoration and follow-up are the fifth and sixth stages, respectively.

Reference   Tipton and Krause, 1996–97 Yearbook, Part 1, 1–4.[38]

5. It is a good practice to purge media before submitting it for destruction. Some methods of purging data are more effective than others, depending on the type of media. Which one of the following is an *ineffective* method based on the type of media?

   a. Degaussing magnetic tapes
   b. Clearing read-only memory (ROM)
   c. Ultraviolet light to clear erasable programmable read-only memory (UVPROM)
   d. Overwriting CD-ROM (read-only)

Explanation   Answer b is correct because data is permanently stored in read-only memory; clearing and purging this media has no relevance. Answer a, degaussing magnetic tapes, is a preferred method to clear data because overwriting, which is also effective, is time-consuming. Answer d, overwriting CD-ROM (read-only), is a preferred method to clear data, and is also effective on WORM (write-once-read-many) and magneto-optical (read-many-write-many) disks.

Reference   Vallabhaneni (2000), page 324.[42]

6. Good separation of duty is difficult to implement in computer operations, costly, and often possible only for a large operations staff. In an ideal situation, which of the following would be an operator responsibility?

 a. Setting the system configuration parameters
 b. Adjusting resource quotas
 c. Setting parameters for covert channel handling
 d. Verifying the system configuration

Explanation   Answer b is correct. Answer a is the responsibility of the system programmer. Answer c is the responsibility of the auditor. Answer d is the responsibility of the security administrator.

Reference   Summers (1997), chapter 12.[37]

7. After storage media is erased, there may be some physical characteristics that allow data to be reconstructed, which represents a security threat. Which one of the following is the correct term for this condition?

 a. Object reuse
 b. Data clearing
 c. Data purging
 d. Data remanence

Explanation   Answer d is correct because data remanence is the residual physical representation of data that has been in some way erased. Answer a, object reuse, is the reassignment to some subject of a medium (e.g., page frame, disk sector, or magnetic tape) that contained one or more objects. To be securely reassigned, no residual data from the previously contained object(s) can be available to the new subject through standard system mechanisms. Answers b and c, clearing and purging, involve a potential risk of reconstruction of data if the clearing and purging operations are not performed properly.

Reference   Vallabhaneni (2000), chapter 7.[42]

8. Periodic system backups support the ability to recover and restart after a failure or disaster and prevent destruction of information. Backup

requirements differ between online and batch systems. Which one of the following is a requirement for batch system backups?

a. More damage can be done quickly due to errors
b. Have long backup intervals
c. Require stringent backup procedures
d. Highly technical and complex

Explanation   Answer b is correct. The other answers are characteristic of online and database system backups.

Reference   Vallabhaneni (2000), chapter 7.[42]

9. According to the Yellow Book, operating system response to failures can be classified into three general categories. Which one of the following does *not* belong?

a. System reboot
b. Emergency system restart
c. Power failure
d. System cold start

Explanation   Answer c is correct because it is a *cause* of failure, rather than a classification of failure.

Reference   U.S. Department of Defense (1985a), guidance for applying the TCSEC to specific environments.[39]

10. The Orange Book contains criteria for building systems that provide specific sets of security features and assurances. The classes recognized under the trusted computer systems evaluation criteria (TCSEC) range from D to A1, in order of increasing desirability from a computer security point of view, with A1 being the highest level of security. Which one of the following is out of order?

a. Discretionary Security Protection
b. Structured Protection
c. Labeled Security Protection
d. Security Domains

Explanation   Answer b — Structured Protection, Class (B2) — is out of order. The correct order is as follows: Class (D) Minimal Protection; Class (C1) Discretionary Security Protection; Class (C2) Controlled Access Protection; Class (B1) Labeled Security Protection; Class (B2) Structured Protection; Class (B3) Security Domains; Class (A1) Verified Design.

Reference   U.S. Department of Defense (1985b), or Orange Book;[40] National Research Council (1991).[36]

11. Physical and environment protection are used to prevent unauthorized individuals from accessing media. Which one of the following is *not* considered a media control?

a. Integrity verification
b. Marking
c. Logging
d. Backups

Explanation Answer d is correct because this is not considered a media control. Answer a, integrity verification, is a necessary media control to determine whether the media has been read correctly or subject to any modification. Answer b, marking, is necessary to control media by identifying media with special handling instructions, to locate needed information or to log media to support accountability. Answer c, logging, is used to support accountability. Logs can include control numbers (or other tracking data), time and date of transfers, names and signatures of individuals involved, and other relevant information.

Reference National Institute of Standards and Technology (1995), Special Publication 800-12, chapter 14 (Media Controls).[34]

12. When disposing of media, it may be important to ensure that information is not improperly disclosed. The process of removing information from media is called sanitization. Which one of the following is *not* a commonly used technique for effective sanitization?

a. Overwriting
b. Deletion
c. Degaussing
d. Destruction

Explanation The correct answer is b because deletion only deletes the pointer to a file; thus, it is not an effective means of sanitization. Answer a, overwriting, uses a program to write 1s, 0s, or a combination onto the media. Answer c, degaussing, utilizes strong permanent magnets or electric degaussers to magnetically erase data from magnetic media. Answer d, destruction, sanitizes the media by shredding or burning.

Reference National Institute of Standards and Technology (1995), Special Publication 800-12, chapter 14 (Media Disposition).[34]

13. In the Orange Book, the classes of systems recognized under the trusted computer systems evaluation criteria for Class (B) systems include all but one of the following. Which one?

a. (B1) Labeled Security Protection
b. (B2) Structured Protection

c. (B3) Security Domains
d. (B4) Minimal Protection

Explanation   The correct answer is d because there is no Class (B4) evaluation criteria. Answer d refers to Controlled Access Protection, which is Class (C2). The remainder of the answers are correctly labeled.

References   National Research Council (1991), appendix A, page 244;[36] U.S. Department of Defense (1985b), or Orange Book.[40]

14. There are compelling reasons to have criteria for evaluating the security of computer systems and products. The reasons include all but one of the following. Which one?

   a. They provide a common terminology for describing security services and degrees of security.
   b. Vendors are guided by the criteria in deciding what features to develop and what development practices to follow to use them.
   c. Users, in selecting and acquiring products, rely upon them.
   d. They are mandated under U.S. federal law as prescribed in NIST publications.

Explanation   The correct answer is d because there is no mandated compliance with criteria for evaluating security set forth by NIST. These are recommendations only. Answers a through c are correct reasons.

References   Summers (1997), page 258:[37] National Institute of Standards and Technology (1995)[34] and (1996).[35]

15. The primary goal of computer support and operations is the continued and correct operation of a computer system. The important security considerations within some of the major categories of support and operations include all but one of the following. Which one?

   a. User support
   b. Telecommunications support
   c. Software support
   d. Configuration management

Explanation   The correct answer is b; telecommunications support and operations categories are included in the Telecommunications Security domain. The other answers are included.

Reference   National Institute of Standards and Technology (1995), FIPS 31-1974, chapter 14, page 157.[34]

16. Systems in Class (C2): Controlled Access Protection enforce a more finely grained discretionary access control than in (C1) systems in order to facilitate all but one of the following. Which one?

    a. Making users individually accountable for their action through log-in procedures
    b. Allowing for encryption of user password data
    c. Allowing for auditing of security-related events
    d. Allowing for resource isolation

Explanation The correct answer is b. (C2) Controlled Access Protection does not provide for encryption mechanisms. The other answers are facilitated in Class (C2) systems.

References National Research Council (1991), Appendix A, page 244;[36] U.S. Department of Defense (1985b), or Orange Book.[40]

17. The underlying principles that support the security policy within organizations include all but one of the following. Which one is *not* included?

    a. Authorization
    b. Least privilege
    c. Non-repudiation
    d. Separation of duty

Explanation The correct answer is c. Non-repudiation is not an underlying principle of security policy, but merely a component of an overall computer security implementation. The fourth underlying principle is *redundancy*. The other answers are included principles.

Reference Summers (1997), page 8.[37]

18. When considering operations security, the basic principles of management control in choosing the means to secure information and operations include all but one of the following. Which one is *not* included?

    a. Individual accountability
    b. Auditing
    c. Encryption
    d. Separation of duty

Explanation The correct answer is c. Encryption is not a basic principle of management control, but merely a component of an overall computer security implementation. The other answers are included principles.

Reference National Research Council (1991), chapter 2, page 57.[36]

19. The principle of separation of duty mandates that functions be divided between people so that no one person can commit fraud. Examples of these types of separation of duty include all but one of the following. Which one is *not* included?

a. Executive management and board of directors
b. Computer operations and programming staff
c. Personnel who accept cash and those who post master accounting records
d. Computer operations and functional user

Explanation   The correct answer is a. There are no separation of duties issues between executive management and the board of directors. In fact, it is very common for executive management to be on the board. The other answers are included.

Reference   Vallabhaneni (2000), page 311.[42]

20. With regard to operations security, the basic principles of preventing breaches of security include all but one of the following. Which one is *not* included?

a. Business continuity planning
b. Management controls as guidance
c. User authentication
d. Non-repudiation

Explanation   The correct answer is a because business continuity planning does not prevent breaches of security. Answer b, management controls as guidance, helps steer operations personnel in the proper direction, prevent or detect mischief and harmful mistakes, and give early warning of vulnerabilities. Answer c, user authentication, supports the principle of individual accountability, which answers the question of who is responsible. When people know that their actions can be tracked and traced back to them, this acts as a deterrent to improper behavior. Answer d, non-repudiation, a more stringent form of authentication, provides further incentive for users not to commit breaches of security because it ensures that the user cannot claim later that a statement attributed to him or her was forged or that he or she never made it.

Reference   National Research Council (1991), chapter 2, pages 56–57.[36]

21. Organizations can describe their needs for information security and trust in systems in terms of confidentiality, integrity, and availability, although these requirements may be emphasized differently, depending on the mission of the organization. With this in mind, which one of the following statements is false?

a. A funds transfer system may require strong integrity controls.
b. Requirements for applications connected to external systems will differ from those for applications without such interconnection.
c. Although the U.S. Department of Defense has articulated requirements for controls to ensure confidentiality, there is no articulation for systems based on other requirements and management controls, such separation of duty, auditability, and recovery.
d. For a national defense system, the chief concern may be ensuring the confidentiality of non-classified information.

Explanation   The correct answer is d because the chief concern is ensuring confidentiality of classified information. The other answers are true.

Reference   National Research council (1991), chapter 2, pages 49–51.[36]

22.   Typical markings for media could include all but which of the following, and would have a Label of Company Confidential?

a. Privacy Act Information.
b. Company Proprietary.
c. Joe's Backup Tape.
d. Press Release.

Explanation   The correct answer is d, press release. This type of information is made available to the public through authorized company channels. Answers a, b, and c are different types of information records typically found in the sensitive information category.

Reference   National Institute of Standards and Technology (1995), chapter 14 (Marking).[34]

23.   Information security policy defines generic security roles and spells out the responsibilities of each role so that employees know what management expects from them. Of the following, which role does *not* match the responsibility?

a. Information resource owner = Responsible for the security of resources he or she owns
b. System user = Responsible for providing access control to the system he or she uses
c. Service provider = Responsible for disaster recovery plan for services provided
d. Application owner = Responsible for providing access control based on user ID

Explanation   The correct answer is b because system users should be responsible for using systems only in authorized ways. The information resource owner should determine access control to the systems, and the application owner may be the one responsible for actually providing access controls based on user ID.

Reference   Summers (1997), chapter 12.[37]

24.   The most fully developed policies for confidentiality reflect the concerns of:

a. The stock exchange.
b. The U.S. national security community.
c. The banking industry.
d. The pharmaceutical industry.

Explanation   The correct answer is b because this community has been willing to pay to get policies defined and implemented, and because the state of the information it seeks to protect is deemed very high. The other three answers are false.

Reference   National Research council (1991), chapter 2, pages 52–53.[36]

25.   Some experts feel that the rise in global competition suggests that we are entering an Age of Information Warfare. Information warfare consists of deliberate attacks on the following aspects of data, with the exception of:

a. Availability and utility.
b. Confidentiality and possession.
c. Integrity and authenticity.
d. Corporate calender.

Explanation   The correct answer is d. Answers a, b, and c are characteristics of information warfare.

Reference   Kabay (1999), chapter 1 (Information Warfare).[33]

Chapter 8

Business Continuity Planning and Disaster Recovery Planning Domain

The Business Continuity Planning and Disaster Recovery Planning domain addresses actions to preserve the business in the face of disruptions to normal business operations, including both natural and man-made events. Information systems and processing continuity are subject to many natural and man-made threats. Organizations must continually plan for potential business disruption and test the recovery plans for their automated systems. Moreover, these organizations must continue to reengineer the continuity planning process, given the challenges of evolving technologies, including distributed computing and the World Wide Web.

Measures taken to ensure business continuity and disaster recovery have always been a challenge in the IT environment. The current information processing environment is much more complex to manage than that in the past. As systems and networks become more distributed, the control and manageability of these systems travels further away from a central source. In the world of Web applications, much of the control lies outside the organization that owns the resources. Thus, management may well be aware that continuity planning (CP) is important, but does not effectively execute on its plans.

In this domain, the successful candidate will understand the structured approach to contingency planning, including measures to demonstrate its value. Business continuity planning, of course, is necessary to ensure that the systems critical to keeping the organization viable are processed at an alternate site in time to avoid an intolerable business impact. The concepts of a business impact analysis (BIA) will be examined as key tools to assist in the identification of critical applications, systems, and supporting resources.

Key Discussion Terms

- Backup procedures
- Business continuity plan
- Business impact analysis
- Cold site
- Contingency plan
- Continuity of operations
- Crisis management
- Criticality
- Disaster
- Business continuity
  (business process/function focused)
- Disaster declaration
- Disaster recovery plan
- Emergency response phase
- Recovery phase
- Hot site
- Off site
- Site restoration phase
- Warm site
- Disaster recovery
  (technology focused)

Practice Study Questions

1. There are many reasons why a Business Continuity Planning/Disaster Recovery Planning (BCP/DRP) infrastructure and processes should be in place in the enterprise. Of the following, which is *not* an appropriate reason?

   a. Satisfy fiduciary responsibilities of the board or directors or senior management
   b. Writing an overview hard-copy plan to have on the shelf so the auditors have something to read
   c. Good business practice — standard of due care
   d. Legal or regulatory mandates

   Explanation Answer b is the correct answer. The other answers specify valid reasons for BCP/DRP infrastructure and processes, and are therefore incorrect answers.

   Reference Devlin and Emerson (1999), pages I-1–4.[13]

2. Continuity of business operations or business processes is addressed in which one of the following types of recovery plan?

   a. Disaster recovery plans
   b. Emergency response/crisis management plans
   c. Business continuity plans
   d. Restoration plans

   Explanation Answer c is the correct answer and is taken from the discussion in the cited references. The other answers are incorrect because they represent other components of the recovery planning infrastructure.

   Reference Tipton and Krause (2000), Vol. 2, pages 502 and 563.[17]

3. Recovery of IT technologies or network communications capabilities is addressed in what type of recovery plan?

   a. Disaster recovery plan
   b. Emergency response/crisis management plan
   c. Business continuity plan
   d. Restoration plan

   Explanation Answer a is the correct answer and is taken from the discussion on Business Impact Assessments on page 502 of the *Information Security Management Handbook* (Tipton and Krause, 2000).[17] The other answers are incorrect because they represent other components of the recovery planning infrastructure.

   References Vallabhaneni (2000), page 337;[18] Hare (1999), page 27;[14] Tipton and Krause, chapter 26, starting on page 563.[17]

4. The business impact analysis (BIA) phase of the BCP/DRP development methodology is necessary for all except one of the following reasons. Which one?

a. Identify and prioritize time-critical business processes.
b. Identify which data files in off-site storage will be needed in case of a disaster.
c. Determine business process recovery time objectives.
d. Raise management and employee awareness of potential loss impacts and threat mitigation.

Explanation   Answer b is the correct answer. The other answers represent reasons why a BIA should be performed.

Reference   Tipton and Krause (2000), Vol. 2, page 502.[17]

5. The primary audience for the business impact analysis (BIA) is:

a. All levels of management concerned with continuity of time-critical business processes
b. The auditors
c. IT management
d. All employees

Explanation   Answer a is the correct answer and is taken from the cited reference. Answer d is partially correct but is too broad in definition; management and selected employees will be in the audience, but not all employees. Answer b is incorrect because the BIA should have nothing to do with satisfying audit criticisms. Answer c is incorrect because it only focuses on one narrow group of management.

Reference   Tipton and Krause (2000), Vol. 2, page 502.[17]

6. The individual(s) with overall responsibly for authorizing expenditures and initiating next-step activities and recommendations that come out of the business impact analysis (BIA) is (are):

a. The BCP/DRP manager.
b. Senior management.
c. IT manager/Director.
d. Shareholders.

Explanation   Answer b is the *most* correct answer and is taken from the cited reference. The other individuals mentioned in answers a, c, and d have little or no role to play in "authorizing" overall enterprise expenditures and initiating next steps.

Reference   Tipton and Krause (2000), Vol. 2, page 504.[17]

7. The business impact analysis (BIA) should quantify and qualify loss potential in terms of all except one of the following:

   a. Financial (monetary) loss
   b. Operational (customer service related) loss
   c. Image/loss of confidence impacts
   d. Outside vendor loss

Explanation Answer d is the correct answer. The other answers are valid because they all represent the type of information the BIA should present.

Reference Hare (1999), page 27.[14]

8. The business impact analysis (BIA) should be used to consider appropriate recovery strategies in the next phase of the BCP/DRP development methodology. The BIA should be used to answer all but one of the following questions. Which one?

   a. Number of time-critical business processes to be recovered
   b. Approximate numbers and types of supporting resources needed to recover time-critical business processes
   c. The location of the emergency operations site(s)
   d. Recovery time objectives of time-critical business processes and their supporting resources

Explanation Answer c is the *most* correct answer. The other answers are valid in relation to the type of information the BIA should be relied upon to deliver during the recovery alternative strategy phase of the development methodology.

Reference Tipton and Krause (2000), Vol. 2, page 519.[17]

9. If the recovery time objective for enterprises' IT computer operations is longer that five days, each of the following may be an acceptable alternative; however, the one alternative that traditionally typifies the greatest cost in terms of declaration fees, subscription fees, usage fees, etc. is a:

   a. Cold site.
   b. Warm site.
   c. Hot site.
   d. Drop-ship arrangement with an appropriate IT equipment manufacturer.

Explanation Answer c is the *best* answer, given the amount of information in the question. While it could be argued that any of these answers is correct, it is generally acknowledged that given the extended recovery time frame of five days, the hot-site solution would generally be considered to be most costly in terms of declaration fees, subscription fees, usage fees, etc.

References   Vallabhaneni (2000), page 341;[18] Hutt, Bosworth, and Hoyt (1995), page 719.[15]

10. Of the following recovery alternatives and a short time for recovery (36 hours or less), which is considered to be the most unreliable or failure prone as compared to the others?

   a. Hot site
   b. Reciprocal/mutual agreements
   c. Drop-ship arrangement with an appropriate IT equipment manufacturer
   d. Mobile recovery units

Explanation   Answer b is the *best* answer, given the amount of information in the question. The other answers represent alternatives that have been successfully used in the past given the recovery time frame. Reciprocal agreements are not considered effective primarily due to "configuration management" issues. They must be closely managed at all times; and if they are not, they tend to be very failure prone.

Reference   Vallabhaneni (2000), page 341;[18] Hutt, Bosworth, and Hoyt (1995), page 7-19.[15]

11. When selecting a recovery site for either DRP or BCP purposes, the facility should *not* be located:

   a. As close as possible to the primary site.
   b. In another state/country.
   c. Close enough to become operational quickly, but not too close to get hit with the same disaster.
   d. In another enterprise-occupied facility a comfortable distance from the primary site.

Explanation   Answer a is the *best* answer, given the amount of information in the question. The other answers represent appropriate locations, given the individual circumstances of the recovery scenario under consideration.

Reference   Vallabhaneni (2000), page 514.[18]

12. Emergency or crisis management planning focuses primarily on reacting to all but one of the following event types. Which one?

   a. Fire, electrical, or falling water-related emergencies
   b. Natural disasters (hurricane, earthquake)

c. Bomb threats
d. Computer restart/recovery

Explanation Answer d is the *best* answer, given the amount of information in the question. Answers a, b, and c represent what emergency response/crisis management plans should address.

Reference Vallabhaneni (2000), page 515.[18]

13. For DRP purposes, when determining IT/network operations recovery strategies, which one of the following should *not* be considered?

a. Communications network connectivity and bandwidth recovery requirements
b. Recovery requirements for systems and applications that support time-critical business processes to be recovered
c. IT and network communications recovery team members roles and responsibilities
d. Physical security of the primary site

Explanation Answer d is the *best* answer because physical security considerations are not of primary concern during the development of IT/network operations recovery. Answers a, b, and c are all considerations when determining appropriate recovery strategies.

Reference Vallabhaneni (2000), page 343.[15]

14. The traditional five phases of the BCP/DRP development methodology are:

a. Project scope and planning, business impact analysis, recovery alternative strategy development, recovery plan development, recovery plan testing and maintenance strategy development.
b. Project scope and planning, risk management review, recovery plan development, plan testing, and maintenance strategy development.
c. Project scope and planning, recovery strategy development, recovery plan development, recovery plan testing, and maintenance strategy development.
d. Project scope and planning, business impact analysis, recovery plan development, and risk management review.

Explanation Answer a is the correct answer. Answers b, c, and d are all methodology steps that are either out of order, are not primary methodology phase activities, or are sub-phase activities.

Reference Tipton and Krause, *1996–97 Yearbook Edition,* page S-75.[16]

15. Following a disruption or disaster, all of the following are responsibilities of the recovery team management organization within the BCPs/DRPs except:

a. Manage damage assessment activities for their area of concern.
b. Brief shareholders on the event.
c. Coordinate activation and operation of the backup facilities locations.
d. Coordinate restoration activities relative to the primary site.

Explanation   Answer b is the *most* correct answer. The other answers represent activities that BCP/DRP recovery team management should undertake.

Reference   Devlin and emerson (1999), page I-6-1.[13]

16. During the recovery alternative strategy development phase of the BCP/DRP development methodology, all activities except one should be performed. Which activity should *not* be performed?

a. Utilize BIA business process priorities to map to both IT and business operations support resources.
b. Conduct benchmarking/peer review assessments of competitors.
c. Prepare cost estimates for acquisition of recovery resources required.
d. Obtain senior management concurrence on acquiring appropriate recovery resources.

Explanation   Answer b is the *most* correct answer. Conducting benchmarking/peer review assessments of competitors is usually a meaningful exercise; however, this should be performed as part of the current state assessment/BIA phase of the project rather than during development of recovery strategies. The other answers are what is typically considered a part of this phase.

References   Devlin and emerson (1999), page I-7-5;[3] Tipton and Krause (2000), Vol. 2, page 503.[17]

17. During the recovery plan development phase of the BCP/DRP development methodology, which of the following answers contains the most correct activities that should take place within this phase?

a. (1) Document recovery planning team roles and responsibilities and assign tasks to specific team members, (2) identify and establish appropriate emergency operation center (EOC) locations, (3) define specific activities and tasks for the recovery of time-critical components for the operations under consideration, (4) document inventory requirements (hardware, software, networks, space, data, etc.).
b. (1) Document restoration procedures, (2) identify press and media contacts (3) develop press kits, (4) visit off-site backup location.

c. (1) Document emergency response plans, (2) develop emergency response testing procedures, (3) conduct tests, (4) document results and report to senior management.

d. (1) Document vendor contact and recovery strategies, (2) identify vendor contacts, (3) define specific activities and tasks for the recovery of vendor communications, (4) test vendor contact and recovery plans.

Explanation Answer a is the *most* correct answer, meaning that during this phase of the methodology these are the most likely activities that should take place, at least on a high level. The other answers incorrectly describe activities for this phase of the methodology.

Reference Devlin and Emerson (1999), chapter II-2, page II-2-1;[13] Hutt, Bosworth and Hoyt (1995), page 7-29.[15]

18. The benefit of regularly testing DRPs include all but one of the following. Whcih one?

a. To train internal IT and off-site vendor personnel in configuring off-site backup systems and networks
b. To assess whether the written DRP plans are accurate and up-to-date
c. To determine recovery time objective to time-critical applications
d. To ascertain that backup site systems, applications, databases and networks are sized properly to fit the circumstances

Explanation Answer c is the *most* correct answer. Determining time criticality of applications should have been performed during the BIA phase of the methodology. The other answers are benefits of testing DRPs.

References Devlin and Emerson (1999), chapter I-8, page I-8-1;[13] Hutt, Bosworth and Hoyt (1995), page 7-31.[15]

19. Specific responsibility for DRP traditionally rests with which individual(s)?

a. The BCP/DRP manager
b. The board of directors or executive management
c. The IT director/manager
d. The internal auditor

Explanation Answer c is the *most* correct answer. The others do have some degree of responsibility in the long run; however, specific responsibility for testing the DRP is that of the IT director/manager.

Reference Hutt, Bosworth, and Hoyt (1995), page 7-4.[15]

20. A vital records program is an essential prerequisite to a well-rounded BCP/DRP process implementation. All but one of the following should be considered for an effective vital records program. Which one?

   a. Assignment of responsibility for identifying and backing up critical information
   b. Maintenance of current inventories of information needed to recreate data
   c. Storing critical data/information at an off-site backup location an appropriate distance from the primary site
   d. Ensuring that all employees store critical vital records necessary for the execution of their job function at an off-site location such as their residence or in the trunk of their car

Explanation   Answer d is the obvious correct answer. Under no circumstances should critical information be stored at a residence or in a private automobile as a matter of policy or practice of the enterprise. The remaining answers are all part of a vital records program.

Reference   Hutt, Bosworth, and Hoyt (1995), page 7-8.[15]

21. Another important element of a well-rounded BCP/DRP process implementation is the development, testing, and maintenance of emergency response procedures. What is the primary purpose for developing emergency response procedures?

   a. Development of building evacuation plans
   b. Documenting bomb threat procedures
   c. Documenting earthquake evacuation plans and procedures
   d. Ensuring human life safety and security

Explanation   Answer d is the obvious correct answer because life safety issues are paramount to the concept of emergency response planning. The remaining answers are all part of an emergency response procedure document.

References   Hutt, Bosworth, and Hoyt (1995), page 7-9;[15] Devlin and Emerson (1999) page II-14-1.[13]

22. Off-site storage is another important component of the overall BCP/DRP process. Methods for achieving appropriate off-site data backup include all but one of the following. Which one?

   a. Backing up software and data to tape files and moving them to a secure off-site location
   b. Electronic vaulting of data to an off-site location
   c. Mirroring data and systems files in hardware that is remote to the primary system

    d. Backing up software and data to files and storing them in a fireproof vault in the primary location

Explanation Answer d is the correct answer. There are no precise guidelines on how far away the data/media must be stored relative to the primary location, but storing in any location within the primary site is considered bad practice. The remaining answers are all consistent with an appropriate off-site backup process.

Reference Vallabhaneni (2000), page 345.[18]

23. Understanding the breadth and scope of enterprise insurance coverage relative to potential recovery of losses sustained as the result of a disaster is an important component of the BCP/DRP equation. Which one of the following types of insurance coverage is relevant to BCP/DRP planning?

    a. Business interruption, media reconstruction, extra-expense
    b. Business interruption, casualty, medical, extra-expense
    c. Business interruption, media reconstruction, leasehold
    d. Fraud, media reconstruction, extra-expense, medical

Explanation Answer a is the correct answer. The others types of insurance coverage are not necessary to be understood relative to the DRP/BCP process.

Reference Hutt, Bosworth, and Hoyt (1995), page 8-2.[15]

24. An enterprisewide approach to BCP/DRP should include the development of several types of plans that, all together, comprise a strong BCP/DRP function. The different types of plans are:

    a. Business continuity plans for business operations; disaster recovery plans for IT and communications; and media kits and communications plans.
    b. Business continuity plans for business operations; disaster recovery plans for IT and communications; and off-site data storage plans.
    c. Management plans for reacting to an emergency prior to recovery.
    d. Business continuity plans for business operations; disaster recovery plans for IT and communications; and emergency response/crisis management plans.

Explanation Answer d is the correct answer. The others present types of plans that are really sub-components of the emergency response/crisis management plan.

Reference Tipton and Krause (2000), Vol. 2, page 511.[17]

25. A documented DRP should most correctly contain which of the following sections?

    a. IT recovery team structure; detailed activities and tasks for recovery of time-critical IT system and network operations; EOC location; reporting structure; inventory information (hardware, software, data, space, communications, transportation, people, etc.)

    b. BCP scope, assumption, approach; BCP recovery team structure; off-site backup location; EOC location; reporting structure; inventory information (hardware, software, data, space, communications, transportation, people, etc.)

    c. IT DRP scope, assumption, approach; BCP recovery team structure; detailed activities and tasks for recovery of time-critical operations; EOC location; reporting structure; emergency response procedures

    d. IT DRP scope, assumption, approach; IT recovery team structure; detailed activities and tasks for recovery of time-critical systems and network operations; EOC location; reporting structure; inventory information (hardware, software, data, space, communications, transportation, people, etc.)

Explanation Answer d is the correct answer. The others present types of plans that are really sub-components of the BCP/DRP formalized plans.

Reference Hutt, Bosworth, and Hoyt (1995), page 7-29.[15]

Chapter 9

Law, Investigations, and Ethics Domain

The Law, Investigations, and Ethics domain addresses computer crime laws and regulations. It reviews investigative measures and techniques used to determine if a crime has been committed and methods to gather evidence. It also reviews the ethical constraints that provide a code of conduct for the security professional.

In this domain we discuss methods for determining if a computer crime has been committed and the laws that would be applicable to the crime. We examine laws prohibiting specific types of computer crime and methods to gather and preserve evidence of a computer crime. We review investigative methods and techniques. Finally, we study ways in which RFC 1087 and the (ISC)² Code of Ethics can be applied to resolve ethical dilemmas.

Key Discussion Terms

- Chain of evidence
- Computer abuse
- Computer crime
- Computer fraud
- Copyright
- Discovery
- Due care
- Due diligence
- Entrapment
- Evidence
- Ethics

- Hearsay
- Intellectual property
- Liability
- Patent
- Privacy
- Proprietary data
- Prudent Man Rule
- Tampering
- Theft
- Trademark
- Trade secret

Practice Study Questions

1. Under the U.S. Best Evidence Rule, the court will accept a duplicate of evidence during a trial rather than the original, under which one of the following circumstances?

   a. Original is difficult to read.
   b. Original was destroyed in the normal course of business.
   c. Customer or information owner will not allow the original to be used.
   d. Original is written in a language other than what the court uses.

   Explanation   Answer b is the correct answer and is taken verbatim from the cited reference. The other answers are incorrect. In addition to this circumstance, duplicates will be allowed if the original was lost or destroyed by fire, flood, or other acts of God; and if the original is in the possession of a third party who is beyond the court's subpoena power.

   Reference   Tipton and Krause (2000), page 608.[30]

2. In the United States, any evidence collected in violation of the Fourth Amendment is not admissible and is considered to be:

   a. "Fruit of the Poisonous Tree."
   b. "Serpent's Fruit."
   c. "Achilles' Heal."
   d. "Forbidden Fruit."

   Explanation   Answer a is the correct answer, and is taken verbatim from the cited reference. The other answers are incorrect because they are not terms that are formally used in U.S. courts.

   Reference   Tipton and Krause (2000), page 609.[30]

3. Under the U.S. Federal Rules of Evidence, all business records, including computer records, are considered:

   a. Inadmissible.
   b. Relevant.
   c. Best evidence.
   d. Hearsay.

   Explanation   Answer d is the correct answer and is taken verbatim from the cited reference. Business records are considered hearsay because they are second-hand evidence; they are not gathered from personal knowledge of a witness, but from another source. The other answers are incorrect because they do not correctly describe the nature of business records as they apply to a court of law.

   Reference   Tipton and Krause (2000), page 609.[30]

4. All legally incorporated U.S. enterprises are required to have which one of the following to turn in to government authorities when determining the status of an enterprise?

   a. Message authentication codes
   b. Uniform codes of conduct
   c. Official books of record
   d. Traffic analysis requirements

   Explanation Answer c is the correct answer and is taken verbatim from the cited reference. The other answers are incorrect because they are not required by law to determine enterprise status.

   Reference Tipton and Krause (2000), page 665.[30]

5. The United Kingdom's Data Protection Act of 1984 applies to the:

   a. Commercial sector.
   b. Private sector.
   c. Government sector.
   d. International sector.

   Explanation Answer a is the correct answer and is taken verbatim from the cited reference. The other answers are incorrect because they are not specified within the law.

   Reference Tipton and Krause (2000), page 666.[30]

6. Privacy laws generally have at least three characteristics, one of these being that they:

   a. Require uniformity across state lines.
   b. Provide notice to the subject of the existence of a database containing the subject's personal data (usually by requiring registration of the database).
   c. Restrict disclosure of information not in accordance with the laws of the jurisdictions involved.
   d. Provide technical requirements governing access to personal data.

   Explanation Answer b is the correct answer and is taken verbatim from the cited reference. The other characteristics include:

   ■ Provide a process for the subject to inspect and to correct the personal data.
   ■ Provide a requirement for maintaining an audit trail of accessors to the private data.

   Answers a, c, and d are incorrect.

   Reference Tipton and Krause (2000), page 667.[30]

7. A trademark is:

   a. The legal protection against copying and the specific rights allowing copying given to original works, which may be in printed or photographically or electronically stored words, music, visual arts, and performing arts.
   b. Provides exclusive legal rights to inventors for the use and commercial exploitation of their inventions.
   c. A unique address by which an Internet resource can be identified and found by Web browser software.
   d. A design showing the origin or ownership of merchandise and reserved to the owner's exclusive use.

Explanation   Answer d is the correct answer and is taken verbatim from the cited reference. The other answers are incorrect because they do not define the term. Answer a defines a copyright; answer b defines a patent; and answer c defines a domain name.

Reference   Tipton and Krause (2000), page 667.[30]

8. Any nation wishing to enforce its laws with regard to data transmitted within or across its borders must have the ability to monitor/intercept the data and:

   a. The ability to prosecute within the country.
   b. The ability to interpret and understand the data.
   c. The ability to export encryption.
   d. The ability to conduct a formal investigation.

Explanation   Answer b is the correct answer and is taken verbatim from the cited reference. The other answers are incorrect because they do not meet the requirement.

Reference   Tipton and Krause (2000), page 670.[30]

9. Message authentication works by:

   a. Employing the use of continuous stream messages.
   b. Sharing passphrases or passwords.
   c. Applying a cryptographic algorithm to a message in such a way as to produce a resulting message authentication code (MAC).
   d. Applying asymmetric key systems.

Explanation   Answer c is the correct answer and is taken verbatim from the cited reference. The other answers are incorrect because they do not rely upon secret codes or ciphers, as required by message authentication.

Reference   Tipton and Krause (2000), page 672.[30]

10. The purpose of a digital signature is to:

   a. Authenticate the sender's identity and prevent repudiation.
   b. Ensure the integrity of the message contents.
   c. Provide the sender's Internet information.
   d. Authorize the receiver to return the message.

Explanation   Answer a is the correct answer and is taken verbatim from the cited reference. The other answers are incorrect because the nature and design of digital signatures cannot ensure the integrity of the contents, provide the sender's Internet information, or provide authorization to the receiver for sending a return message.

Reference   Tipton and Krause (2000), page 674.[30]

11. The U.S. Foreign Corrupt Practices Act prohibits which activity, even if it is legal and traditional in a country in which you are doing business?

   a. Monitoring network traffic
   b. Sharing user IDs and passwords
   c. Accepting gifts from International companies
   d. Giving gifts by U.S. corporations

Explanation   Answer d is the correct answer, and is taken verbatim from the cited reference. The other answers are incorrect because they do not appear within the act.

Reference   Tipton and Krause (2000), page 675.[30]

12. The top-level domain (TLD) name indicates the:

   a. Protocol being used at the Web site.
   b. Country of jurisdiction.
   c. Type of entity that owns the domain.
   d. The specific organization or individual to whom the domain belongs.

Explanation   Answer c is the correct answer and is taken verbatim from the cited reference. For example:

- .com — commercial organizations
- .edu — educational organizations
- .gov — government organizations
- .mil — military organizations
- .net — sites that form part of the Internet infrastructure, sites of Internet service providers, and other large network sites
- .org — nonprofit organizations

The other answers are incorrect.

Reference   Imparl (2000), page II 4-1.[28]

13. When something occurs that will go into the messages log, it appears first in the:

a. Browser cache file.
b. DOS slack file.
c. Message buffer in memory.
d. Vmcore file.

Explanation Answer c is the correct answer and is taken verbatim from the cited reference. Log information often does appear in the other choices, but never before the message buffer in memory.

Reference Stephenson (2000), page 155.[29]

14. There are three basic ways to recover passwords, none of which are guaranteed to work. They are:

a. Password cracking, physical password recovery, and inference.
b. Examining logs, examining slack space, and examining unallocated space.
c. Social engineering, sniffing, and witness interviews.
d. Password cracking, witness interviews, and sticky notes.

Explanation Answer a is the correct answer and is taken verbatim from the cited reference. Logs, slack space, and unallocated space typically do not contain cleartext passwords (at least they should not). And, while witnesses may be able to give you passwords, or you may be able to find them on sticky notes, these methods are not reliable; and if the organization's information security program is effective, they should not be options.

Reference Stephenson (2000), page 159.[29]

15. The four general areas of the disk where evidence might hide, in addition to the active data area, include:

a. Slack space, unallocated space, swap files, and cache files.
b. Backup files, free space, archive space, and dedicated space.
c. Memory, share drives, cache files, and boot files.
d. Diskettes, CDs, microfiche, and backup tape.

Explanation Answer a is the correct answer and is taken verbatim from the cited reference. The other answers, while possible sources of evidence, are not groups of choices that represent possibilities all of which are necessarily located on the computer disk, thus making answer a the *best* answer.

Reference Stephenson (2000), page 247.[29]

16. An NTI tool that performs two calculations on a file and reports the results in the form of a unique file fingerprint is:

a. SafeBack.
b. CRCMD5.
c. MD5.
d. PGP.

Explanation Answer b is the correct answer and is taken verbatim from the cited reference. The other answers are incorrect; answers a, c, and d all describe tools but do not fit the provided description.

Reference Stephenson (2000), page 250.[29]

17. Any applet that attempts to use your system in an inappropriate manner is considered a(an):

a. Java applet.
b. ICMP applet.
c. Hostile applet.
d. Mobile code applet.

Explanation Answer c is the correct answer and is taken verbatim from the cited reference. The other answers do not fit the description and thus are incorrect.

Reference Stephenson (2000), page 275.[29]

18. An attack that involves an attacker creating a misleading context in order to trick the victim into making an inappropriate security-relevant decision is known as a:

a. Spoofing attack.
b. Surveillance attack.
c. Denial-of-service attack.
d. Social engineering attack.

Explanation Answer a is the correct answer and is taken verbatim from the cited reference. Answer b is incorrect because a surveillance attack occurs as a result of an attacker passively watching traffic and recording information provided by the victim on Web forms. Answer c is incorrect because a denial-of-service attack occurs as a result of the attacker flooding the network bandwidth to the point of making it inaccessible. Answer d is not correct because a social engineering attack occurs from an attacker speaking directly with a victim to obtain information needed for inappropriate access.

Reference Stephenson (2000), page 285.[29]

19. To meet U.S. Federal Rules of Evidence 803(6), the witness must have custody of the records in question on a regular basis, rely on those records in the regular course of business, and:

a. Properly mark the evidence.
b. Show who had control or possession of the evidence.
c. Know that they were prepared in the regular course of business.
d. Be extremely careful not to damage the evidence.

Explanation Answer c is the correct answer and is taken verbatim from the cited reference. The other answers, while good measures and practices, are not specifically mentioned within this regulation.

Reference Tipton and Krause (2000), page 610.[30]

20. If evidence is not properly protected, the person or agency responsible for the collection and storage of the evidence may be:

a. Held in contempt of court.
b. Responsible for replacement value.
c. Eliminated from testifying.
d. Held liable for damages.

Explanation Answer d is the correct answer and is taken verbatim from the cited reference. The entity typically cannot be held in contempt for poor handling of evidence, be responsible for the material replacement value, or be eliminated from testimony.

Reference Tipton and Krause (2000), page 612.[30]

21. There are two forms of surveillance used in computer crime investigations. They are:

a. Physical surveillance and telephone wiretapping.
b. Physical surveillance and computer surveillance.
c. Physical surveillance and logs examination.
d. Hidden microphones and physical surveillance.

Explanation Answer b is the correct answer and is taken verbatim from the cited reference. The other answers may be applicable; but in the combinations they are presented, they are not the best choice and thus they are incorrect.

Reference Tipton and Krause (2000), page 629.[30]

22. In 1997, the U.S. Supreme Court declared unconstitutional the Communications Decency Act of 1996 ban on which of the following:

a. Pornographic images
b. Indecent Internet speech

c. Gambling
d. Live video sites

Explanation   Answer b is the correct answer and is taken verbatim from the cited reference. The other answers, while controversial, are incorrect because they are not specifically cited in the act.

Reference   Tipton and Krause (2000), page 655.[30]

23. According to RFC 1855, Netiquette Guidelines, one-to-one communications are defined as those in which a person is communicating with another person as if:

   a. Writing a letter.
   b. In a social situation.
   c. Others are listening.
   d. Face-to-face.

Explanation   Answer d is the correct answer and is taken verbatim from the cited reference. The other answers, while possibly applicable, are incorrect because they are not specifically cited in RFC 1855.

Reference   Tipton and Krause (2000), page 657.[30]

24. A common argument made by systems hackers is that they are simply making use of idle machines. They argue that because some systems are not used at a level near their capacity, the hacker is entitled to use them. This argument is flawed because:

   a. Few systems are ever used near their capacity.
   b. These systems are usually not in service to provide a general-purpose user environment.
   c. Spikes in system usage put the hacked system at risk, even if the hacker is not purposefully damaging the system.
   d. Someone else is still paying for the system services.

Explanation   Answer b is the correct answer and is taken verbatim from the cited reference. The other answers, while possibly applicable, are incorrect because they are *not* the best answer.

Reference   Ermann, Williams, and Shauf (1997), page 131.[27]

25. When an author or programmer of a piece of software retains no legal rights and has not attached a copyright notice, it is then referred to as:

   a. Shareware
   b. Freeware
   c. Public domain
   d. Entrapment

Explanation　Answer c is the correct answer. Answers a and b could be forms of public domain, or may still be owed by the author. Answer d is a process for the purpose of detecting attempted penetrations.

Reference　Icove, Seger, and VanStorch, page 423.[56]

Chapter 10

Physical Security Domain

The Physical Security domain focuses on the critical foundation layer of an effective information security program; the physical security layer. Both chapters in this domain define the methodology and thought processes that should be deployed to assess risk and implement mitigating controls. Those processes include:

1. Understanding the facility and the systems environment
2. Classifying facilities into categories
3. Weighing considerations of owned versus leased facilities
4. Defining the protection priorities
5. Deciding what needs to be protected
6. Identifying critical assets
7. Analyzing the threats
8. Analyzing natural threats
9. Analyzing man-made threats
10. Analyzing environmental threats
11. Considering the human factors
12. The psychology of physical security
13. Awareness and training
14. Social engineering
15. Teaming with other risk management functions

As one author relates, "With the common acceptance that nothing is 100 percent secure, information security uses the depth of its layers to achieve the highest form of security. A weakness in any one of these layers will cause security to break. Physical protection is the first step in the layered approach of information security. If it is nonexistent, or exercised in malpractice, information security will fail."

Key Discussion Terms

- Biometric
- CER
- Defense in depth
- Degauss
- Dumpster diving
- Electronic emanation
- EMI
- EPO
- False positive/Negative
- IDS
- Mantrap

- Montreal Protocol
- MTBF/MTTR
- Passive ultrasonic
- Photometric IDS
- PIDAS
- Piggy-back
- Remanence
- RFI
- Shoulder-surfing
- Tamper alarm
- Taut wire

Practice Study Questions

1. Incoming material from the delivery area should be:

  a. Immediately delivered to the addressee.
  b. Inspected for potential hazards.
  c. X-rayed.
  d. Held in the delivery area until called for.

Explanation Answer b is correct; incoming material should be inspected before it is moved from the delivery area to the point of use if the point of use is in a secure area (although many companies insist on inspection no matter where the point of use is). Answer a is therefore incorrect. Answer c would be "overkill" in most environments (where a visual inspection is sufficient), and answer d is unnecessary when an effective pre-delivery inspection is carried out.

Reference ISO/IEC 17799:2000, Section 7.1.5, Isolated Delivery and Loading Areas.[44]

2. *Supporting facilities* for IT infrastructure include:

  a. Soda and snack vending machines.
  b. Electrical supply and cabling.
  c. Radio and television in the break rooms.
  d. Cleaning staff.

Explanation Supporting facilities include electrical supply and cabling, so answer b is correct. While answers a and c might seem to qualify as supporting facilities, they are not absolutely necessary for the conduct of business. Cleaning staff (answer d) are support personnel — and necessary support personnel — but not support facilities.

Reference ISO/IEC 17799:2000, Section 7.2, Equipment Security.[44]

3. Items requiring special protection should be:

  a. Labeled as such.
  b. Isolated to reduce the amount of protection required.
  c. Kept in locked facilities.
  d. Eliminated.

Explanation The correct answer is b. Those items that need special protection — even in a secure area — should be moved to an isolated position so that protection needs are reduced because of their isolation. Answer a would draw attention to those items and be counter to protecting them. Answer c might suffice but may not always be practical (not every special protection item can be locked away). Answer d is also impractical.

Reference   ISO/IEC 17799:2000, Section 7.2.1, Equipment Security.[44]

4. Eating and drinking in proximity to information processing facilities should be:

   a. Punishable by dismissal.
   b. Done only in a recovery situation.
   c. Subject to carefully considered policy statements.
   d. Allowed only at certain periods.

Explanation   The correct answer is answer c. An organization should consider its policy toward eating and drinking in proximity to sensitive facilities. Answer a seems much too harsh even if eating and drinking in such areas is not allowed by policy, while answer b would again be subject to policy (policy should not be waived in recovery situations). Answer d would also depend on the organization's policy but would seem to be pointlessly restrictive (eating and drinking would probably be allowed or not — and not restricted by time.)

Reference   ISO/IEC 17799:2000, Section 7.2.1, Equipment Security.[44]

5. The use of special protection methods, such as keyboard membranes, should be considered:

   a. In case the sprinklers are activated.
   b. In industrial environments.
   c. When eating and drinking is allowed in sensitive facilities.
   d. To preserve the resale value of the equipment.

Explanation   The correct answer is answer b. Special protection methods are necessary in dust- or dirt-intensive environments where such particles are liable to enter and damage sensitive equipment. Answer a is incorrect because fire suppression equipment in computer facilities should be of the inert gas variety. Answer c is incorrect because, where eating and drinking is allowed, it should be allowed only away from direct contact with equipment. Answer d is incorrect because resale value is not a consideration when adding special protection.

Reference   ISO/IEC 17799:2000, Section 7.2.1, Equipment Security.[44]

6. Equipment supporting critical business functions should be equipped with:

   a. An uninterruptible power supply.
   b. An internal fire suppression system.

c. Dial-in access.

d. A list of emergency contact personnel.

Explanation The correct answer is answer a — to allow an orderly shutdown in the event of power failure. Fire suppression systems (answer b) are installed to protect rooms, not particular pieces of equipment. Answer c does nothing to promote the physical security of the equipment, and answer d (a list of emergency contact personnel) is the answer to a business continuity planning question.

Reference ISO/IEC 17799:2000, Section 7.2.2, Power Supplies.[44]

7. In equipment rooms, emergency power switches should be located near:

a. The help desk.

b. Emergency exits.

c. The operator console.

d. A window.

Explanation Emergency power switches should be located near the emergency exits in equipment rooms to facilitate rapid power-down in case of emergency. Thus, answer b is correct. Neither the help desk nor the operator console are likely to be near the emergency exit, so answers a and c are incorrect. Answer d is just plain silly.

Reference ISO/IEC 17799:2000, Section 7.2.2, Power Supplies.[44]

8. For sensitive or critical equipment, controls should include all except:

a. The use of alternate routings or transmission media.

b. Sweeps for unauthorized devices attached to the cables.

c. Locked rooms or boxes at cable inspection and termination points.

d. Encryption.

Explanation The correct answer is answer d. Answers a, b, and c should be considered with fiber-optic cabling and armored conduit.

Reference ISO/IEC 17799:2000, Section 7.2.3, Cabling Security.[44]

9. Repairs to and service of processing equipment should be carried out by:

a. The manufacturer.

b. In-house staff only.

c. Authorized maintenance personnel.

d. Building maintenance.

Explanation Because equipment aftercare can be contracted to vendors other than the original equipment vendor, answer c is the correct answer. For the same reason, answer a is incorrect as is answer b. Building maintenance staff will rarely be qualified to perform repair and maintenance on information processing equipment, so answer d is also incorrect.

Reference ISO/IEC 17799:2000, Section 7.2.4, Equipment Maintenance.[44]

10. Security for equipment and information used outside a company's premises (e.g., for home working) should be:

   a. Determined by the person using the equipment or information.
   b. Commensurate with the security of the premises where it is being used.
   c. The responsibility of the information security department.
   d. Equivalent to the security on the company's regular premises.

Explanation The correct answer is d. Security should be no less rigorous when equipment is used off-site or information is accessed from or taken home. Security is determined by policy and standards and so answer a is incorrect. The owner of the equipment and information is responsible for the security of those assets and thus answer c is incorrect. Answer b is incorrect because the premises where equipment is being used off-site would rarely start out having security equivalent to that on the company's premises.

Reference ISO/IEC 17799:2000, Section 7.2.5, Security of Equipment Off-Premises.[44]

11. Portable computers should be:

   a. Disguised whenever possible while traveling.
   b. Kept on the company's premises.
   c. Used only for noncritical functions.
   d. Checked luggage on all flights.

Explanation According to FBI figures for 1999, portable computers were the most frequently stolen items in U.S. airports during that year. Consequently, it makes sense to disguise them whenever possible. Thus, answer a is correct. Answer b would defeat the purpose of having a portable computer, as would answer c. Answer d would most probably result in a broken computer and quite possibly result in a lost computer.

Reference ISO/IEC 17799:2000, Section 7.2.5, Security of Equipment Off-Premises — A.[44]

12. Home working controls should be determined by:

    a. The cost of the equipment or information taken home.
    b. The information security department.
    c. A risk assessment.
    d. The company's Chief Information Officer.

Explanation Although answer a is part of the correct answer, it is incorrect. The correct answer is c — a risk assessment (which will take into account a value placed in the equipment and information). The information security department should not be responsible for deciding which controls are necessary (they should be advising the owners of assets on that subject), so answer b is incorrect, which means that answer d — unless that person is designated as the owner of the assets — is also incorrect.

Reference ISO/IEC 17799:2000, Section 7.2.5, Security of Equipment Off-Premises.[44]

13. When no longer needed, storage media should be:

    a. Set aside in case it is needed in the future.
    b. Given to charity.
    c. Thrown out.
    d. Physically destroyed or securely overwritten.

Explanation The key here is that all storage media, once retired from use, must be physically destroyed or securely overwritten to prevent the possibility of recovery of data from the media itself. Therefore, answer d is correct. Answers b and c do not achieve the objective and are incorrect. Answer a would invite the chance that someone would try to recover data from the media, "just to see if it could be done."

Reference ISO/IEC 17799:2000, Section 7.2.6, Secure Disposal or Re-use of Equipment.[44]

14. Protection for processing equipment or media against strong electro-magnetic fields is usually found in:

    a. ISO/IEC 17799 standards.
    b. Common Criteria.
    c. Manufacturers' instructions.
    d. Operating procedures.

Explanation Answer c is correct. The manufacturers of media and equipment are qualified to instruct on required protection against destructive electromagnetic fields. ISO/IEC 17799 is a standard for information security programs; thus, answer a is not correct. Similarly,

Common Criteria is a framework for evaluating security, which makes answer b incorrect. Answer d — operating procedures — would refer to the means of operating the equipment under normal circumstances.

Reference ISO/IEC 17799:2000, Section 7.2.5, Security of Equipment Off-Premises.[44]

15. The security perimeter of a building or site containing information-processing facilities should be:

    a. Guarded by physical security guards.
    b. Well-lit.
    c. Physically sound.
    d. A minimum of 20 feet from the public right-of-way.

    Explanation The correct answer is c. The perimeter must have no gaps or areas where break-ins can easily occur. Answer a is incorrect because it is not necessary to have perimeters patrolled by humans. While answer b is desirable from a health and safety point of view, it is not a requirement under the ISO/IEC 17799 standard. Answer d is incorrect because there is no prescribed distance between security perimeters and the public right-of-way.

    Reference ISO/IEC 17799:2000, Section 7.1.1 Physical Security Perimeter.[44]

16. Environmental conditions inside a processing facility should be:

    a. Kept at a constant 72°F.
    b. Monitored.
    c. Dust-free.
    d. Kept in a state of low humidity.

    Explanation Answer b is the correct answer — monitored for conditions that could adversely affect the operation of information processing facilities. Answer a is incorrect because the mean temperature in a processing facility will depend on a number of factors. Answer c is incorrect because it is "overkill;" and answer d is incorrect because, while most processing facilities are low-humidity, once again the exact level of humidity required depends on a number of local factors.

    Reference ISO/IEC 17799:2000, Section 7.2.1, Equipment Siting and Protection.[44]

17. One consideration about nearby premises (when creating a secure processing facility) is:

    a. The building blocking light from the processing facility.
    b. The impact of a disaster occurring in neighboring premises.

c. The type of people who work next door.

d. Shared parking.

Explanation   The correct answer is b. A fire, an explosion in the street, or water leakage in common stairwells or floors should all be considered when siting a processing facility. Answer a is incorrect simply because ambient light is not a consideration. Answer c is incorrect because a neighboring company's staff is not the concern of the company siting the processing center. Answer d is incorrect because parking at the facility is not a direct physical security concern — although it can be a personnel security concern.

Reference   ISO/IEC 17799:2000, Section 7.2.1, Equipment Siting and Protection.[44]

18.   Delivery or holding areas should be designed so that:

a. Delivery staff can unload without gaining access to other parts of the building.

b. Delivery staff can take the deliveries directly to the addressee.

c. Delivery staff have access to facilities such as break rooms and toilets.

d. Delivery staff can be monitored by video camera at all times.

Explanation   Answer a is the correct answer. Delivery staff must be allowed to do its job without posing a security threat to other parts of the building. Therefore, answer b is incorrect. Answer c is incorrect because, while it may be desirable for delivery staff to have such access, it is not a consideration of physical security for a processing facility. Answer d is not correct because that is a matter of policy for the site owner.

Reference   ISO/IEC 17799:2000, Section 7.1.5, Isolated Delivery and Loading Areas.[44]

19.   Authentication controls for entry to secure areas include:

a. A sign-in book.

b. A requirement to show a form of identification.

c. A swipe card plus PIN.

d. A security guard.

Explanation   Answer c is the only correct answer. A swipe card, plus PIN, plus an audit trail that is regularly examined are the only effective controls listed in this question. A sign-in book (answer a) is not a control because it does not require any kind of validation. Nor does showing a form of identification — by itself (answer b). Answer d is incorrect because the mere presence of a security guard accomplishes nothing.

Reference   ISO/IEC 17799:2000, Section 7.1.2, Physical Entry Controls.[44]

20. Suitable intrusion detection systems — installed to professional standards — should be in place to cover:

    a. Employee locker areas.
    b. All external doors and accessible windows.
    c. Management offices.
    d. Rooms containing sensitive or expensive processing equipment.

Explanation The purpose of intrusion detection systems is primarily to cause an alarm when someone attempts to breach the external perimeter. Therefore, answer b is correct. Internal areas, such as employee locker areas and management offices, are not generally protected by such systems so answers a and c are incorrect. Similarly, rooms containing sensitive or expensive equipment would be protected by means other than intrusion detection systems and thus answer d is incorrect.

Reference ISO/IEC 17799:2000, Section 7.1.3, Securing Offices, Rooms and Facilities.[44]

21. When it is necessary to remove equipment from the premises, the equipment should be:

    a. Clearly labeled as belonging to the company.
    b. Logged out and logged back in again.
    c. Given only to trusted employees.
    d. Kept in locked carrying cases when not in use.

Explanation Answer b is correct. An audit trail of who has equipment and its location can be created through logging in and out. Answer a is incorrect because it may attract the attention of thieves to the equipment. Answer c is incorrect because the concept of a "trusted employee" is fraught with legal problems. Answer d is incorrect because it may be impractical.

Reference ISO/IEC 17799:2000, Section 7.3.2, Removal of Property.[44]

22. Where appropriate, paper and computer media should be stored in:

    a. Locked cabinets or other forms of security furniture.
    b. A central storage facility.
    c. Fireproof cabinets.
    d. The employee's desk drawer.

Explanation Answer a is correct; paper (preprinted forms and such) and computer media such as diskettes should be kept in locked furniture to avoid theft. Answer b is not correct because it adds a level of effort to the normal course of business (retrieving the media each day and returning it each evening). Answer c may be desirable but is not a good standard due to cost (however, backup copies of computer media should be kept off-site in such a protected facility); and answer d is incorrect because most desk drawers are not locked or, where they are, are easily forced.

Reference ISO/IEC 17799:2000, Section 7.3.1, Clear Desk and Clear Screen Policy.[44]

23. Sensitive or critical business information should be:

a. Clearly labeled as such.
b. Locked away when not in use.
c. Taken off-site each night.
d. Subjected to inventory and stored in a central location.

Explanation Answer b is correct; lock sensitive or critical business information, preferably in a fireproof cabinet when it is not actually in use. Answer a is incorrect; sensitive or critical information should not be clearly labeled as such because labeling it will attract the attention of potential thieves. Answer c is not practical because the movement of data would increase the risk of loss or damage. Answer d is not a physical security concern.

Reference ISO/IEC 17799:2000, Section 7.3.1, Clear Desk and Clear Screen Policy.[44]

24. When personal computer and computer terminals are unattended but still "in session," they should be:

a. Available for use by other staff.
b. Switched off.
c. Logged off.
d. Locked up with a device such as a cable lock.

Explanation Answer c is the best answer. When personal computers, etc., are unattended, they should be logged off and should require the entry of a password to resume the session. This should be done by the operator; but in the event the operator fails to do so, "timeout" software should do it. Answer a is incorrect in this situation because other staff should not know the password to unlock the terminal. Answer b is incorrect because, with appropriate procedures and software ("timeout"), it is unnecessary. Answer d is incorrect only because it is "overkill" as far as protecting the session is concerned.

Reference ISO/IEC 17799:2000, Section 7.3.1, Clear Desk and Clear Screen Policy.[44]

25. Sensitive or classified information, when printed, should be:

    a. Bound and labeled.
    b. Immediately taken from the printer.
    c. Shredded.
    d. Put in the recipient's delivery box.

Explanation The correct answer is answer b; sensitive or classified information should be delivered immediately to the intended recipient, which means taking it from the printer immediately to shield it from "prying eyes." Likewise, answer d is incorrect because leaving such information in a delivery box opens it to unauthorized access. Answer a is not correct because there is no security need to bind any particular kind of print, and answer c is not correct because shredding information before the recipient has seen it rather defeats the purpose of printing it.

Reference ISO/IEC 17799:2000, Section 7.3.1, Clear Desk and Clear Screen Policy.[44]

APPENDICES

Appendix A

Bibliography

Access Control Systems and Methodology

1. International Standards Organization. Information Technology — Code of Practice for Information Security Management, ISO/IEC 17799:2000(E). Geneva, Switzerland: ISO, 2000.
2. Ford, Warwick and Michael S. Baum, *Secure Electronic Commerce*. New Jersey: Prentice-Hall, 1997.
3. King, Christopher M., Curtis E. Dalton, and T. Ertem Osmanoglu. *Security Architecture: Design, Deployment and Operations*. California: Osborn/McGraw-Hill, 2001.
4. Summers, Rita C. *Secure Computing: Threats and Safeguards*. New York: McGraw-Hill, 1997.
5. Tipton, Harold F. and Micki Krause, Editors. *Information Security Management Handbook, 4th edition*. New York: Auerbach Publications, 2000.
6. Tudor, Jan Killmeyer, *Information Security Architecture*. New York: Auerbach Publications, 2001.

Applications and System Development Security

7. Fites, Philip, and Martin P.J. Kratz. *Information Systems Security: A Practitioner's Reference*. London: International Thomson Computer Press, 1996.
8. Hutt, Arthur E., Seymour Bosworth, and Douglas B. Hoyt. *Computer Security Handbook, third edition*. New York: John Wiley and Sons, 1995.
9. National Institute of Standards and Technology. *An Introduction to Computer Security: The NIST Handbook, Special Publication 800-12*. Washington, D.C.: U.S. Government Printing Office, 1995.
10. Pfleeger, Charles P. *Security in Computing, second edition*. Upper Saddle River, NJ: Prentice-Hall, 1996.
11. Summers, Rita C. *Secure Computing: Threats and Safeguards*. New York: McGraw-Hill, 1997.
12. Vallabhaneni, Rao S. *CISSP Examination Textbooks*. Schaumburg, IL: SRV Professional Publications, 2000.

Business Continuity Planning and Disaster Recovery Planning

13. Devlin, Ed, Leo Wrobel, Mark B. Desman, and Cole Emerson. *Business Resumption Planning, 1999 edition.* New York: Auerbach Publications, 1999.
14. Hare, Chris. *CISSP Certified CBK Study Guide: Business Continuity Planning Domain.* Posted at http://www.cccure.org, March 1999.
15. Hutt, Arthur E., Seymour Bosworth, and Douglas B. Hoyt. *Computer Security Handbook, third edition.* New York: John Wiley and Sons, 1995.
16. Tipton, Harold F. and Micki Krause, Editors. *Information Security Management Handbook, 1996–97 Yearbook Edition,* Auerbach Publications.
17. Tipton, Harold F. and Micki Krause, Editors. *Information Security Management Handbook, 4th edition.* New York: Auerbach Publications, 2000.
18. Vallabhaneni, Rao S. *CISSP Examination Textbooks.* Schaumburg, IL: SRV Professional Publications, 2000.

Cryptography

19. Atkinson, R. "Security Architecture for the Internet Protocol," RFC 1825, Naval Research Laboratory, August 1995.
20. Fites, Philip, and Martin P.J. Kratz. *Information Systems Security: A Practitioner's Reference.* London: International Thomson Computer Press, 1996.
21. Guttman, E., L. Leong, and G. Malkin. "Users' Security Handbook," RFC 2504, Sun Microsystems, February 1999.
22. Housley, R., W. Ford, W. Polk, and D. Solo. "Internet X.509 Public Key Infrastructure Certificate and CRL Profile," RFC 2459, SPYRUS, January 1999.
23. Krawczyk, H., M. Bellare, and R. Canetti. "HMAC: Keyed-Hashing for Message Authentication," RFC 2104, IBM, February 1997.
24. Piper, D. "The Internet IP Security Domain of Interpretation for ISAKMP," RFC 2407, Network Alchemy, November 1998.
25. Postel, Jon and Joyce Reynolds. "File Transfer Protocol," RFC 959, ISI, October 1985.
26. Schneier, Bruce. *Applied Cryptography.* New York: John Wiley and Sons, 1996.

Law, Investigations, and Ethics

27. Ermann, M. David, Mary B. Williams, and Michele S. Shauf. *Computers, Ethics and Society, second edition.* New York: Oxford University Press, 1997.
28. Imparl, Steven D., JD. *Internet Law — The Complete Guide.* Specialty Technical Publishers, 2000.
29. Stephenson, Peter. *Investigating Computer-Related Crime.* New York: CRC Press LLC, 2000.
30. Tipton, Harold F. and Micki Krause, Editors. *Information Security Management Handbook, 4th edition.* New York: Auerbach Publications, 2000.
31. Economic Espionage Act of 1996; U.S. Congressional Record of 1996; http://cybercrime.gov/EEAleghist.htm.

Operations Security

32. Depuis, Clement. *CISSP Study Booklet on Operations Security.* Posted at http://www.cccure.org. April 5, 1999.

33. Kabay, Michel E. *The NCSA Guide Enterprise Security*, McGraw-Hill Computer Communications Series, 1999.
34. National Institute of Standards and Technology. *An Introduction to Computer Security: The NIST Handbook, Special Publication 800-12*. Washington, D.C.: U.S. Government Printing Office, 1995.
35. National Institute of Standards and Technology. *NIST Generally Accepted Principles and Practices for Securing Information Technology Systems*. Washington, D.C.: U.S. Government Printing Office, September 1996.
36. National Research Council. *Computers at Risk: Safe Computing in the Information Age*. Washington, D.C.: National Academy Press, 1991.
37. Summers, Rita C. *Secure Computing: Threats and Safeguards*. New York: McGraw-Hill, 1997.
38. Tipton, Harold F. and Micki Krause, Editors. *Information Security Management Handbook, 1996–97 Yearbook Edition*, Auerbach Publications.
39. U.S. Department of Defense. *Technical Rationale Behind CSC-STD-003-85*. Washington, D.C.: U.S. Government Printing Office, 1985a. (The Yellow Book.)
40. U.S. Department of Defense. *Trusted Computer System Evaluation Criteria*. Washington, D.C.: U.S. Government Printing Office, 1985b. (The Orange Book.)
41. U.S. Department of Defense. *Trusted Network Interpretation of the Trusted Computer System Evaluation Criteria*. Washington, D.C.: U.S. Government Printing Office, 1987. (The Red Book.)
42. Vallabhaneni, Rao S. *CISSP Examination Textbooks*. Schaumburg, IL: SRV Professional Publications, 2000.

Physical Security

43. Carroll, John M. *Computer Security, third edition*. Woburn, MA: Butterworth-Heinemann, 1996.
44. International Standards Organization. Information Technology — Code of Practice for Information Security Management, ISO/IEC 17799:2000. Geneva, Switzerland: ISO, 2000.

Security Architecture and Models

45. Common Criteria for Information Technology Security Evaluation, Version 2.1. August 1999.
46. Fites, Philip and Martin P.J. Kratz. *Information Systems Security: A Practitioner's Reference*. London: International Thomson Computer Press, 1996.
47. King, Christopher M., Curtis E. Dalton, and T. Ertem Osmanoglu. *Security Architecture: Design, Deployment and Operations*. California: Osborn/McGraw-Hill, 2001.
48. Pfleeger, Charles P. *Security in Computing, second edition*. Upper Saddle River, NJ: Prentice-Hall, 1996.
49. Summers, Rita C. *Secure Computing: Threats and Safeguards*. New York: McGraw-Hill, 1997.
50. Tudor, Jan Killmeyer. *Information Security Architecture*. New York: Auerbach Publications, 2001.
51. Vallabhaneni, Rao S. *CISSP Examination Textbooks, Vol. 1*. Schaumburg, IL: SRV Professional Publications, 2000.

Security Management Practices

52. Bryson, Lisa C. "Protect Your Boss and Your Job: Due Care in Information Security," *Computer Security Alert, Number 146.* San Francisco, May 1995.

53. D'Agenais, Jean and John Carruthers. *Creating Effective Manuals.* Cincinnati, OH: South-Western Publishing Co., 1985.

54. Fites, Philip and Martin P.J. Kratz. *Information Systems Security: A Practitioner's Reference.* London: International Thomson Computer Press, 1996.

55. Glass, Robert L. *Building Quality Software.* Englewood Cliffs, NJ: Prentice-Hall, 1992.

56. Icove, David, Karl Seger, and William VonStorch. *Computer Crime: A Crime-fighter's Handbook.* California: O'Reilly and Associates, 1995.

57. International Information Security Foundation. *Generally Accepted Systems Security Principles (GASSP),* Version 2.0. Gaithersburg, MD, July 1999; Version 1.0, June 1997.

58. International Standards Organization. Information Technology — Code of Practice for Information Security Management, ISO/IEC 17799:2000(E). Geneva, Switzerland: ISO, 2000.

59. Jackson, K.M. and J. Hruska. *Computer Security Reference Book.* Boca Raton, FL: CRC Press, 1992.

60. National Institute of Standards and Technology. *An Introduction to Computer Security: The NIST Handbook, Special Publication 800-12.* Washington, D.C.: U.S. Government Printing Office, 1995.

61. National Security Agency. "Online Course: Overview and Risk Management Terminology." Posted at www.ncisse.org/Courseware/NSAcourse/lesson1/lesson. PPT. 1997.

62. Parker, Donn. "Risk Reduction Out, Enablement and Due Care In," *Computer Security Institute Journal,* Volume XVI, Number 4, Winter 2000.

63. Peltier, Tom. "How to Build a Comprehensive Security Awareness Program," *Computer Security Institute Journal,* Volume XVI, Number 2, Spring 2000.

64. Peltier, Thomas R. *Information Security Policies, Standards, Procedures and Guidelines.* Boca Raton, FL: CRC Press, 2001a.

65. Peltier, Thomas R., *Information Security Risk Analysis.* New York: Auerbach Publications, 2001b.

66. Russell, Deborah and G.T. Gangemi, Sr. *Computer Security Basics.* California: O'Reilly and Associates, 1991.

67. Tipton, Harold F. and Micki Krause, Editors. *Information Security Management Handbook,* New York: Auerbach Publications, 1999.

Telecommunications and Network Security

68. Anonymous. *Maximum Security: A Hacker's Guide to Protecting Your Internet Site and Network,* second edition. Indianapolis: Sams Publishing, 1998.

69. Cassidy, Kyle and Joseph Dries. *The Concise Guide to Enterprise Networking and Security.* http://quepublishing.com, 2000.

70. Fites, Philip and Martin P.J. Kratz. *Information Systems Security: A Practitioner's Reference.* London: International Thomson Computer Press, 1996.

71. Russell, Deborah and G.T. Gangemi Sr. *Computer Security Basics.* California: O'Reilly and Associates, 1991.

72. Scambray, Joel, Stuart McClure, and George Kurtz. *Hacking Exposed: Network Security Secrets and Solutions, second edition.* New York: Osborne/McGraw-Hill, 2001.
73. Tipton, Harold F. and Micki Krause, Editors. *Information Security Management Handbook, 4th edition.* New York: Auerbach Publications, 2000.

Appendix B

Sample CISSP Exam

1. Automatic control devices for access to sensitive areas should:

    a. Have backup power supplies.
    b. Provide a log of every attempted access.
    c. Be supplemented by a human guard.
    d. Create an alarm at a failed access attempt.

2. The basic component of a General Program Policy consists of four basic elements. Among these elements are Purpose or Topic, Scope, and Responsibilities. Which of the following is the fourth component?

    a. Thesis
    b. Provisions
    c. Compliance
    d. Supplemental information

3. A sensitivity label is a piece of information that represents the security level of an object and that describes the sensitivity (e.g., classification) of the date object. Sensitivity levels are used as a basis for:

    a. Identifying the owner of the object.
    b. Determining the retention period for the object.
    c. Determining mandatory access control decisions of the object.
    d. Providing a schedule for rotation of the object to an off-site location.

4. The primary audience for the Business Impact Assessment is:

    a. All levels of management concerned with continuity of time-critical business processes.
    b. The auditors.
    c. IT management.
    d. All employees.

5. The principle of concentric controlled perimeters is meant to:

   a. Provide different types of control at different points.
   b. Repeat and reinforce access control.
   c. Slow an intruder's progress toward the protected area.
   d. Create a show of strength to deter intruders.

6. Maintenance hooks are a security risk because:

   a. They allow entry into the code without the usual checks.
   b. They are trap doors.
   c. They permit remote access to code.
   d. They are undocumented.

7. Which is true about DES?

   a. It is based on public key cryptography.
   b. It uses stream ciphers.
   c. It was developed by the U.S. Department of Defense.
   d. It uses private key cryptography.

8. In a secure area, the organization's information processing facilities and third-party processing facilities must be:

   a. Connected to the same uninterruptible power system (UPS).
   b. Managed by the same operations staff.
   c. Composed of the same hardware and software configurations.
   d. Kept physically separate.

9. During the recovery plan development of the BCP/DRP development methodology, all activities except this one should be performed:

   a. Document recovery planning team roles and responsibilities and assign tasks to specific team members.
   b. Identify and establish appropriate emergency operation center (EOC) locations.
   c. Define specific activities and tasks for the recovery of time-critical components for the operations under consideration.
   d. Perform a risk management review or assessment/analysis.

10. Audit trails maintain a record of activity and, in conjunction with appropriate tools and procedures, can provide a means to accomplish which of the following?

   a. Individual accountability and separation of duties
   b. Prudent Man Concept
   c. Physical security
   d. Reconstruction of events

11. There are three primary kinds of spoofing; they are e-mail spoofing, Web-site spoofing, and:

   a. System masquerades.
   b. Gopher spoofing.
   c. IP spoofing.
   d. Social engineering.

12. All of the following are effective in combating malicious software with the exception of:

   a. Using only commercial software obtained from reliable vendors.
   b. Testing all new software on isolated computers.
   c. Creation and retention of backup copies of executable files.
   d. Monthly use of virus detection software.

13. Overall enterprisewide responsibility for BCP/DRP ultimately rests with which individual(s)?

   a. The BCP/DRP manager
   b. The board of directors and/or executive management
   c. The IT director/manager
   d. The internal auditor

14. The purpose of Business Continuity Plans is to:

   a. Counteract interruptions to preserve business activities and to protect time-critical business processes.
   b. Mitigate disasters before they occur.
   c. Comply with audit requirements.
   d. Meet management by objective requirements.

15. Making computer users aware of their security responsibilities and presenting them with the correct practices helps change their behavior. This process of raising end-user consciousness is part of:

   a. An in-house education program.
   b. A new product training course.
   c. An employee awareness program.
   d. Skill development.

16. The security perimeter should have:

   a. Signs indicating what it is.
   b. No external windows.
   c. A way to control physical access.
   d. Fire suppression equipment.

17. Crackers are defined as:

   a. Software programs designed to compromise password and other files.
   b. People who violate systems for monetary or personal gain.
   c. Automated scripts used to perform penetration tests on external environments.
   d. Tools used to exploit online sessions by sniffing packets and obtaining unencrypted information.

18. A Trojan horse differs from a virus in the following two very important aspects:

   a. First, it is not found on UNIX boxes; second, it could stand alone as an independent executable file.
   b. First, it does not replicate or infect other files; second, it has a limit to how many times it can occur on a system.
   c. First, it does not replicate or infect other files; second, it cannot be found by anti-virus software using virus signature files.
   d. First, it does not replicate or infect other files; second, it could stand alone as an independent executable file.

19. Cleanliness of media is important and, as such, demands special handling and storage. All except one of the following media handling techniques should be considered:

   a. Do not leave media that are to be shipped on the loading dock.
   b. The media transport time should be as short as practical, preferably no longer than five days.
   c. Leave the tape cartridges in their protective packaging until ready to use them.
   d. Use sharp instruments to unpack tape cartridges to avoid jagged cuts in packing materials.

20. Emergency or Crisis Management Planning focuses primarily on what goal?

   a. Ensuring that all employees have a radio
   b. Preparing to recapture lost data
   c. Preparing to withstand a nuclear attack
   d. Ensuring human security and life safety

21. Which of the following is *not* a function of the System Resource Manager as pertaining to systems architecture?

   a. It allocates CPU.
   b. It allocates main storage.
   c. It allocates input/output devices to user programs.
   d. It allocates user group memberships.

22. The U.S. Freedom of Information Act (FOIA) regulates:

    a. Dissemination of and access to data.

    b. How government agencies collect, use, maintain, or disseminate information pertaining to individuals.

    c. Private industry in collecting, using, maintaining, and disseminating information pertaining to individuals.

    d. What constitutes records for the purposes of the Internal Revenue laws.

23. Disaster Recovery Plans must focus primarily on:

    a. Recovery of all business functionality.

    b. Recovery of telecommunications circuits.

    c. Recovery of time-critical business processes.

    d. Recovery of IT technologies and communications network resources that support time-critical business processes.

24. Directories and internal telephone books identifying locations of sensitive information processing facilities should:

    a. Be kept in locked cabinets.

    b. Be under the control of designated staff.

    c. Be clearly marked.

    d. Not be readily accessible to the public.

25. Which of the following storage mediums is regarded as the most secure against unauthorized erasure?

    a. Floppy disks

    b. Virtual memory

    c. Optical disks

    d. On-board hard disks

26. ARP is an acronym for:

    a. Address Resolution Protocol.

    b. Advanced Research Project.

    c. Anti-virus Resolution Protocol.

    d. Address Research Project.

27. The Clark–Wilson model relies on four requirements:

    a. Integrity, confidentiality, availability, and recoverability

    b. Recoverability, auditability, reproducabilty, and reporting capacity

    c. Integrity, serviceability, auditability, and stability

    d. External consistency, separation of duty, internal consistency, and error recovery

28. An agreement used to give notice that information is confidential or secret to employees and other third parties is termed either a confidentiality agreement or:

    a. An employment agreement.
    b. A condition of employment.
    c. A non-disclosure agreement.
    d. Top-secret clearance.

29. What kind of document is a high-level statement of enterprise beliefs, goals, and objectives and the general means for their attainment for a specified subject area?

    a. Policy
    b. Procedure
    c. Standard
    d. Guideline

30. The lower layers of the OSI model (layers 1, 2, and 3) deal with:

    a. Defining the characteristics of the systems at the two ends of the communication.
    b. The end-user interface.
    c. The application.
    d. Defining the network facilities necessary to transfer a message.

31. One method often used to reduce the risk to a local area network that has external connections is by using:

    a. Passwords.
    b. Dial-back.
    c. Firewall.
    d. Token Ring.

32. Which of the following is a media-control task?

    a. Off-site storage of backup media
    b. Erasing each volume at the end of its retention period
    c. Cleaning and checking media on a regular basis
    d. Both b and c

33. A polymorphic virus is a type of malicious code that:

    a. Can change its appearance.
    b. Can make multiple copies of itself.
    c. Imitates the behavior of another form of virus.
    d. Resembles many other types of viruses.

34. Loss potential exists as a result of the threat–vulnerability pair. Reducing either the threat or the vulnerability reduces what?

    a. Risk
    b. Impact
    c. Concern
    d. Issue

35. The Orange Book is the common name for:

    a. The Trusted Network Interpretation of the Trusted Computer System Evaluation Criteria, or TNI (U.S. DoD, 1987).
    b. Trusted Computer System Evaluation Criteria (U.S. DoD, 1985d.)
    c. The Technical Rationale Behind CSC-STD-003-85 (U.S. DoD, 1985b).
    d. All of the above.

36. The business records exception to the hearsay rule, Fed. R. Evid. 803(6), in general refers to any memorandum, report, record, or data compilation (1) made at or near the time of the event, and (2):

    a. By a customer who was conducting business with the organization.
    b. By, or from information transmitted by, an employee during normal business hours.
    c. Transmitted using a digital signature.
    d. By, or from information transmitted by, a person with knowledge if the record was kept in the course of a regularly conducted business activity, and it was the regular practice of that business activity to make the record.

37. When selecting a recovery site for either DRP or BCP purposes, the facility should be located:

    a. As close as possible to the primary site.
    b. In another state/country.
    c. Close enough to become operational quickly, but not too close to get hit with the same disaster.
    d. In the basement.

38. Intrusion management is a four-step process. The steps are:

    a. Avoidance, testing, detection, and investigation.
    b. Identification, authentication, investigation, and prosecution.
    c. Avoidance, detection, investigation, and prosecution.
    d. Detection, communication, investigation, and recovery.

39. The ISO/IEC 17799 International Standard on Information Security characterizes information security as the preservation of CIA: Confidentiality, Integrity, and which of the following?

a. Authenticity
b. Accountability
c. Availability
d. Assurance

40. In relationship to cryptography, *work factor* is a term that can be defined as:

a. The amount of time it takes an encryption algorithm to encrypt the data.
b. The amount of time it takes an encryption algorithm to decrypt the data.
c. The amount of effort it takes to defeat an encryption scheme.
d. The amount of processing power necessary to create a public/private key-pair.

41. The use of VLANs (virtual local area networks), IP subnets, NAT (network address translation), and routing provide security through which of the following?

a. The separation of network resources to prevent systems from directly interacting with each other
b. The hiding of network resources from the boundary protection devices that protect them from attack
c. Improving the flow of traffic throughout the network to make detection and response to an attack more efficient and effective
d. These methods cannot be used to improve the security of a network

42. The following describes what information security tenet? Baseline versions of a product are saved and protected in such a way that they will exist even if something happens to the original version.

a. Change control
b. Version control
c. Software deployment
d. Configuration management

43. Delivery areas should be controlled and:

a. Adequately heated and ventilated to prevent deterioration of materials.
b. Be separate from the main building.
c. Be separate from information processing facilities.
d. Monitored with video-monitoring equipment.

44. A magnetic medium requires environmental controls to protect it from the most common risks, which include all but one of the following. Which risk is *not* included?

    a. Temperature
    b. Liquids
    c. Magnetism
    d. Air

45. Physical security barriers should be:

    a. Made of non-flammable material.
    b. From real floor to real ceiling.
    c. Insulated for sound.
    d. Monitored by video camera.

46. A secret, undocumented entry point into a program module is referred to as a:

    a. Control bypass.
    b. Trap door.
    c. Pseudo-flaw.
    d. Black hole.

47. The protection mechanisms within a computing system that collectively enforce security policy are known as the TCB. What does this acronym represent?

    a. Terminal Connection Board
    b. Trusted Computing Base
    c. Trusted Connection Boundary
    d. Trusted Cipher Base

48. Computer support and operation refers to:

    a. System planning.
    b. System design.
    c. System administration.
    d. None of the above.

49. The IPSec standard includes a specification for which of the following security components?

    a. Authentication headers
    b. Support for non-IP protocols
    c. High availability
    d. Message playback

50. In configuration management, the goal from an operational security standpoint is to:

   a. Know what changes occur.
   b. Prevent security from being changed.
   c. Know when security can be reduced.
   d. Know when security can be eliminated.

51. In an IPSec packet, what is the goal of an authentication header?

   a. To provide integrity and authentication
   b. To provide confidentiality and availability
   c. To provide advanced routing features
   d. To provide the decrypting device with information on what the encrypting protocol is used for

52. Which of the following best describes the security provided by process isolation in distinct address space?

   a. It ensures that processes running concurrently will not interfere with each other by accident or design.
   b. It ensures that every process executed has a unique address in memory.
   c. It ensures that a computer user can access only one process at a time.
   d. It ensures that an executing process cannot communicate with any other process.

53. Zones of control (sometimes referred to as enclaves) do *not* require different levels of security than the corporate network at the:

   a. Intranet.
   b. Extranet.
   c. Internet.
   d. Remote access.

54. Which of the following is *not* a passive telecommunications attack (by definition, is restricted to observation or other methods that do not alter the data within a system)?

   a. Eavesdropping
   b. Traffic analysis
   c. Disclosure by observation of a screen
   d. Computer virus

55. Separation of duties functions on the principle that employees are less tempted to do wrong if:

   a. They must cooperate with another employee to do so.
   b. They must submit transactions in the proper sequence.

    c. They must perform specific functions at specific times.

    d. Management performs strict oversight of their work.

56. Non-repudiation is:

    a. Something to which access is controlled.

    b. Equivalent to administratively directed access controls.

    c. An expression of policy in a form that a system can enforce, or that analysis can use for reasoning about the policy and its enforcement.

    d. An authentication that with high assurance can be asserted to be genuine.

57. Which item is *not* a VPN component?

    a. Tunneling

    b. Encryption

    c. Availability

    d. Authentication

58. Which of the following is *not* an example of an intrusion detection system?

    a. An outsourced monitoring service

    b. Anti-virus software

    c. Automated review of logs searching for anomalous behavior

    d. An incident response team on immediate standby

59. The first case successfully prosecuted under the Computer Fraud and Abuse Act of 1986 was:

    a. The Robert T. Morris worm.

    b. Kevin Mitnick computer hacking.

    c. The Melissa virus.

    d. Clifford Stoll's cyber-spy case.

60. VPNs (virtual private networks) do *not* provide the following:

    a. Secure Internet-based remote access via a peer-to-peer VPN

    b. Secure, dedicated private network connections

    c. Secure extranet access

    d. Secure end-to-end data flow via a gateway-to-gateway VPN

61. There are two primary types of message flooding; they are:

    a. Disabling services and freezing up X-Windows.

    b. Malicious use of Telnet and packet flooding.

    c. Broadcast storms and attacking with LYNX clients.

    d. E-mail and log flooding.

62. Which layer of the OSI model is responsible for security?

a. Application
b. Transport
c. Session
d. Physical

63. The industry best practice for password selection by clients is:

a. Six characters in length, changed every 60 days, frozen after five invalid access attempts.
b. Eight characters in length, changed every 90 days, frozen after three invalid access attempts.
c. Six characters in length, changed every 90 days, frozen after three invalid access attempts.
d. Eight characters in length, changed every 60 days, frozen after five invalid access attempts.

64. Penetration testing stresses a system to identify security flaws in the following manner:

a. Through interviews and access to applications, access risks are identified.
b. Using commercial and public tools, an attack is simulated on a network.
c. Using commercial and public tools, reports are run to determine policy compliance.
d. Using password-cracking tools, an attack is simulated on an application.

65. Buildings that are or are in a secure area should:

a. Be clearly marked to deter entry.
b. Give minimum indication of their purpose.
c. Be no more than two floors high.
d. Allow access only to personnel and not to vehicles.

66. The efficient use of resources when attempting to mitigate a business risk is often described as a positive:

a. Operating expense ratio.
b. Return on investment.
c. Risk assessment.
d. Security analysis.

67. How many layers are in the TCP/IP protocol stack?

a. One
b. Seven

    c. Five
    d. Four

68. The computer controlling automatic access control devices must be:

    a. Remote from the secured area.
    b. Protected as well as the other computers in the secure area.
    c. Isolated from the remainder of the network.
    d. Running a hardened operating system.

69. Which is *not* a component of public key infrastructure?

    a. Certificate authority
    b. Symmetric encryption
    c. Digital certificate
    d. Certificate revocation

70. In the seven-layer OSI model, what does each layer depend on from the layers below it?

    a. Protocols
    b. Services
    c. Entities
    d. Data

71. Accountability is defined as:

    a. Meeting schedules and budgets in a fiscally secure manner.
    b. Gathering and retaining records pertaining to financial matters.
    c. Performing actions within a job role that are governed by security policy.
    d. Ensuring that access to information is consistent and correct.

72. Which of the following do not need to be a part of the TCB?

    a. Operating system kernels
    b. Protected subsystems
    c. Trusted applications
    d. Untrusted applications

73. The method for separating a process from other processes that relies on using different hardware facilities is known as:

    a. Logical separation.
    b. Isolation.
    c. Temporal separation.
    d. Physical separation.

74. Which of the following is *not* an active telecommunications attack (by definition, attack on the data in the network is altered)?

a. Playback
b. Denial of service
c. Sniffing
d. Spoofing

75. Digital signatures used in combination with e-mail do *not* provide:

a. Integrity.
b. Confidentiality.
c. Authentication.
d. Non-repudiation.

76. When using e-mail, which of the following is the *best* way to secure a message?

a. Send the message only to the person you want to see it.
b. Write the message assuming that someone is listening in.
c. Encrypt the message before sending it.
d. Sign the message using a digital signature.

77. Fallback equipment and backup media should be sited at a safe distance to avoid:

a. Theft.
b. Damage from an incident that affects the main site.
c. Mistaken use as "production version" equipment and media.
d. Corruption from constant handling.

78. Responsible senior management should formalize decisions and next-step actions following their concurrence with business impact analysis results to:

a. Satisfy shareholder concerns.
b. Satisfy audit requirements.
c. Communicate precise recovery time objectives for prioritized business processes and supporting resources within the enterprise.
d. Provide vendors with guidelines for providing recovery services to the enterprise.

79. When considering operations security, controls should be placed on system software commensurate with the risk, including:

a. Authorization for system changes. A combination of logical and physical access controls can be used to protect software and backup copies.
b. Use of powerful system utilities that can potentially compromise the integrity of operating systems and logical access controls.

    c. Policies for loading and executing new software on a system.

    d. All of the above.

80. Which best describes the definition of protocol?

    a. Multiple communications networks

    b. A set of rules for how information is exchanged over a communications network

    c. Layering of networks

    d. Layering of suites

81. One of the primary reasons that computer systems have bugs is:

    a. Malicious code.

    b. Faulty system design.

    c. Programming errors.

    d. Program specifications.

82. The *principle of least privilege* supports which domain implementation method?

    a. Providing protected entry points into a network

    b. Providing privilege checking within a system or application access

    c. Providing hardware that allows access to certain functions

    d. Providing many small domains

83. What application does PGP help protect?

    a. E-mail

    b. Web browsing

    c. File transfers (FTP)

    d. Telnet

84. A time bomb is a type of what form of malicious software?

    a. Virus

    b. Trojan horse

    c. Logic bomb

    d. Worm

85. Robert T. Morris designed the Internet Worm to do all of the following except:

    a. Determine where it could spread.

    b. Spread its infection.

    c. Exhaust Internet resources.

    d. Remain undiscovered and undiscoverable.

86. Personnel should be aware of the activities within a secured area:

    a. If the activities constitute a hazard to the employees' health.
    b. Where the nearest accessible fire exit is through the secured area.
    c. Only on a need-to-know basis.
    d. When those activities create input to the personnel's jobs.

87. According to Eugene Spafford, computer break-ins are ethical only:

    a. To catch a person committing fraud.
    b. To prove the security of a computer network system.
    c. In extreme situations, such as a life-critical emergency.
    d. Whenever corporate management has been forewarned of the break-in attempts.

88. Cryptography addresses which of the following security issues?

    a. Confidentiality and availability
    b. Integrity and availability
    c. Fault tolerance and integrity
    d. Confidentiality and integrity

89. Visitors to restricted areas should be:

    a. Only technical staff.
    b. Made to wear badges.
    c. Kept to designated areas.
    d. Allowed in only at particular times.

90. The objective of secure areas is:

    a. To lower insurance costs.
    b. To keep traffic to a minimum.
    c. To prevent unauthorized access to business premises.
    d. To prevent the unauthorized removal of equipment.

91. *Access control* supports the principles of:

    a. Ownership, need-to-know, and data classification.
    b. Authorization, least privilege, and separation of duty.
    c. Connectivity, password controls, and session controls.
    d. Privacy, monitoring, and compliance.

92. A program that moves through an address space by making a copy of itself in a new location is known as a:

    a. Virus.
    b. Worm.

    c. Trojan horse.

    d. Logic bomb.

93. The primary reasons that each aspect of computer support and operations should be documented include all but one of the following. Which one is *not* included?

    a. To ensure continuity and consistency

    b. To eliminate security lapses and oversights

    c. To provide new personnel with sufficiently detailed instructions

    d. To satisfy audit requirements

94. The files required to perform a batch update are:

    a. Master file and transaction file.

    b. Batch file and record file.

    c. Update file and production file.

    d. Sequential file and master file.

95. SHA1 and MD5 are two examples of?

    a. Key exchange mechanisms.

    b. Hashing algorithms.

    c. Certificate authorities.

    d. Symmetric encryption algorithms.

96. A possible danger to a system, whether it be a person, thing, or event, that might exploit a vulnerability of the system is termed a:

    a. Problem.

    b. Danger.

    c. Concern.

    d. Threat.

97. According to Orange Book criteria, which of the following is required for C1 security?

    a. Labels

    b. Trusted recovery

    c. System architecture (software engineering)

    d. Object reuse

98. Which term relates to a cryptographic key exchange?

    a. Diffie–Hellman

    b. Cipher block chaining

    c. Elliptical curve cryptography

    d. Steam cipher encryption

99. The characteristic of information being disclosed only to authorized persons, entities, and processes at authorized times and in the authorized manner is known as:

    a. Integrity.
    b. Availability.
    c. Accountability.
    d. Confidentiality.

100. If the recovery-time objective for an enterprise's IT computer operations is 24 hours or less, the most appropriate recovery alternative would be a:

    a. Cold site.
    b. Warm site.
    c. Hot site.
    d. Drop ship arrangement with an appropriate IT equipment manufacturer.

101. Which of the following is *not* a defined mode of access in the Bell–LaPadula model?

    a. Read-only
    b. Write-only
    c. Read-and-write
    d. Execute

102. Digital certificates are based on what international standard?

    a. X.25
    b. X.400
    c. 802.3
    d. X.509

103. There are generally two types of denial-of-service attacks that are the most prevalent. They are:

    a. Planting and Trojan horses.
    b. TCP hijacking and IP address spoofing.
    c. TCP SYN attack and ICMP Ping flood.
    d. Buffer overflow and sniffing.

104. The concept of *least privilege*, as it pertains to operations security, means that:

    a. An operator needs access to documentation about operating system internals.
    b. An operator must have full access to the media library.
    c. An operator must be able to adjust resource quotas.
    d. Both a and c are correct.

105. An enterprisewide approach to BCP/DRP should include the development of several types of plans that together comprise a strong BCP/DRP function. The different types of plans are:

    a. Business continuity plans for business operations; disaster recovery plans for IT and communications; and off-site data storage plans.

    b. Business continuity plans for business operations; disaster recovery plans for IT and communications; and emergency response/crisis management plans for reacting to an emergency prior to recovery

    c. Business continuity plans for business operations; disaster recovery plans for IT and communications; and building evacuation plans.

    d. Business continuity plans for business operations; disaster recovery plans for IT and communications; and media kits and communications plans.

106. The acronym ITSEC represents:

    a. Information Technology Security Evaluation Criteria.
    b. Information Transfer Systems Evaluation Criteria.
    c. Internationally Tested Security Evaluation Certificate.
    d. Information Technology Systems Evaluation Certificate.

107. On a DOS disk, the space taken up by the "real" file when you erase it is called:

    a. Slack space.
    b. Unallocated space.
    c. Swap files.
    d. Cache files.

108. The objective of separation of duties is to protect each of the following from compromise, except for:

    a. Applications.
    b. Policies.
    c. Controls.
    d. Vendors.

109. The best technique to identify and authenticate a person to a system is to:

    a. Establish biometric access through a secured server or Web site.
    b. Make sure the person knows something to identify and authenticate him/herself, and has something to do the same.
    c. Maintain correct and accurate ACLs (access control lists) to allow access to applications.
    d. Allow access only through user ID and password.

110. A change control board is intended to evaluate all proposed changes on the basis of:

    a. Cost-effectiveness and impact.
    b. Desirability and correctness.
    c. Privacy and security.
    d. Timeliness and comprehensiveness.

111. "...to prove the content of a writing, recording, or photograph, the original writing, recording, or photograph is required, except as otherwise provided in these rules or by Act of Congress" is taken from the:

    a. Chain of Custody Rule
    b. Hearsay Rule
    c. Best Evidence Rule
    d. Distinctive Evidence Rule

112. Which one of the following is a major component of the Common Criteria Standard?

    a. User Profile
    b. Protection Profile
    c. Desktop Profile
    d. Network Profile

113. Which of the following are generally not characteristic of biometric systems?

    a. Accuracy, speed, and throughput rate
    b. Uniqueness of the biometric organ and action
    c. Subject and system contact requirements
    d. Increased overhead of administration and support time

114. Following a disruption, the purpose of the recovery team management organization outlined within the BCPs/DRPs is to:

    a. Develop recovery procedures to address the specific situation.
    b. Arrange for the press to visit the damaged location.
    c. Protect human life and to facilitate timely recovery of time-critical operational components in order to protect enterprise assets.
    d. Go to the backup site and recover operations.

115. *Spoofing*, or *masquerading*, is a means of tampering with communications by:

    a. Changing data fields in financial transactions.
    b. Convincing a user to submit information to an alias system.
    c. Pretending to be someone in order to access specific information.
    d. Allowing packets to be sent from one host to another trusted host.

116. Reciprocal/mutual agreements for off-site backup are normally considered a poor recovery alternative because:

    a. Auditors do not like this practice.
    b. Slow response to requests to recover operations.
    c. Network incompatibilities.
    d. Difficulties in keeping agreements, plans, and configurations managed and up-to-date.

117. Discretionary access control (DAC) refers to what common configuration requirement of TCSEC levels C2 through D?

    a. Objects in a computer system must meet minimum security requirements.
    b. Owners of objects in a computer system can determine the ability of users to access the objects.
    c. Object access control lists can be modified, depending on the criticality of the object.
    d. Objects in a computer system must be secured using the strictest method possible.

118. The U.S. Economic Espionage Act of 1996 defines someone as undertaking economic espionage if they knowingly perform any of five activities. One of these activities includes:

    a. Intentionally, without authorization, accessing any non-public computer of a department or agency of the United States, accessing such a computer of that department or agency that is exclusively for the use of the U.S. Government.
    b. Not obtaining consent for the collection, use, or disclosure of personal information.
    c. Causing loss aggregating at least $5000 in value during any one-year period to one or more individuals.
    d. Receiving, buying, or possessing a trade secret, knowing the same to have been stolen or appropriated, obtained, or converted without authorization.

119. The *custodian* of information has the primary responsibility for:

    a. Logically ensuring that information is properly safeguarded from unauthorized access, modification, or disclosure.
    b. Implementing safeguards such as ACLs to protect information.
    c. Accessing information in a manner controlled by ACL safeguards and supported by policy.
    d. Physically ensuring that information is safeguarded and maintained in a secure manner.

120. The process of investigating a target environment and the relationships of dangers to the target is known in information security circles as:

 a. Value analysis.
 b. Risk analysis.
 c. Risk assessment.
 d. Safeguard checking.

121. The concept of non-repudiation means that:

 a. The sender can verify that the receiver has read the message.
 b. The receiver can prove that the sender sent the message.
 c. The sender can verify the receiver's private key.
 d. The receiver can verify that the certificate authority has not been compromised.

122. The concepts of due care and due diligence are key to operations security undertakings. Examples of due diligence include all but one of the following. Which one is *not* included?

 a. Good housekeeping
 b. Requesting that employees acknowledge and sign off on computer security requirements
 c. Issuing appropriate formalized security policies and procedures
 d. Allowing unrestricted access to both public and private spaces

123. The NSA (National Security Agency) has published the TCSEC, often referred to as the Orange Book. What does the acronym TCSEC stand for?

 a. Total Computer Security Enhancement Conventions
 b. Trusted Compliant Security Evaluation Classification
 c. Total Confidential System Examination Considerations
 d. Trusted Computer System Evaluation Criteria

124. The absence or weakness of a risk-reducing safeguard is known as:

 a. An uncertainty.
 b. A detection.
 c. An exposure.
 d. A vulnerability.

125. A shared resource matrix is a technique commonly used to locate:

 a. Malicious code.
 b. Security flaws.
 c. Trap doors.
 d. Covert channels.

126. What is the definition of cryptography?

    a. The art or science of secret writing
    b. The practice of defeating attempts to hide information
    c. The study of secret writing and defeating the science of secret writing
    d. The secure exchange of information over a local area network

127. To protect audit trails, the audit database must be protected. Which of the following techniques can help counter attacks on the audit database?

    a. Write-once optical disks
    b. Cryptographic protection
    c. Remote storage of audit trails
    d. All of the above

128. What is one drawback to using authentication headers?

    a. Single-factor authentication
    b. Increased packet size
    c. Authentication headers are proprietary
    d. Only 56-bit encryption algorithms support authentication headers

129. What does the acronym DES represent?

    a. Dual Encryption Standard
    b. Data Encryption Standard
    c. Data Encryption Scheme
    d. Dual Encryption Scheme

130. Hazardous or combustible materials should be:

    a. Taken to a local landfill.
    b. Inventoried.
    c. Stored a safe distance from secure areas.
    d. Handled and disposed of only by a licensed vendor.

131. U.S. criminal law identifies a crime as being a wrong against:

    a. A private citizen.
    b. Society.
    c. The U.S. Government.
    d. Taxpayers.

132. Under ITSEC evaluation, what assurance class represents inadequate assurance that the target of evaluation has met its requirements?

    a. E0
    b. E1

c. E2

d. E3

133. What kinds of cases are much easier to convict because the burden of proof required for a conviction is much less?

a. Misdemeanor

b. Civil

c. Criminal

d. Domestic

134. The traditional five phases of the BCP/DRP development methodology are:

a. Project scope and planning, business impact analysis, recovery alternative strategy development, recovery plan development, and recovery plan testing and maintenance strategy development.

b. Project scope and planning, risk management review, recovery plan development, plan testing and maintenance strategy development.

c. Project scope and planning, recovery strategy development, recovery plan development, recovery plan testing, and maintenance strategy development.

d. Project scope and planning, business impact analysis, recovery plan development, and risk management review.

135. A non-interference access control model is best suited for:

a. Systems that require strict access flow and do not easily accommodate flexibility in information flow.

b. Systems that are stand-alone and do not communicate with others in a networking capacity.

c. Systems that do not require classification schemes and have all public information.

d. Systems that rely on state machine architectures and capabilities.

136. U.S. criminal law falls under two main jurisdictions; they are:

a. Federal and local.

b. County and local.

c. Federal and state.

d. National and international.

137. Real evidence is:

a. Things such as tools used in the crime.

b. Made up of tangible objects that prove or disprove guilt.

c. Evidence used to aid the jury in the form of a model, experiment, chart, or an illustration offered as proof.

d. Oral testimony, whereby the knowledge is obtained from any of the witness' five senses.

138. Which of the following applies to the notion of a specific security policy maintaining a *secure state* as defined by Bell–LaPadula?

    a. The policy must define the hierarchy of integrity levels.
    b. The policy must prevent unauthorized users from making modifications.
    c. The policy must define logging of subject activity.
    d. The policy must define the permitted modes of access between subjects and objects.

139. According to RFC 1087, any activity is characterized as unethical and unacceptable that purposely:

    a. Destroys the integrity of computer-based information.
    b. Results in fraud.
    c. Threatens e-mail message delivery.
    d. Participates in gambling.

140. The process in which an independent security evaluation team checks on compliance with software development standards on an unannounced basis is known as:

    a. Independent evaluation.
    b. Security audit.
    c. Validation.
    d. Certification.

141. Which of the following is *not* one of the three integrity goals addressed by the Clark–Wilson model?

    a. Prevent unauthorized users from making modifications.
    b. Prevent unauthorized users from viewing classified objects.
    c. Prevent authorized users from making improper modifications.
    d. Maintain internal and external consistency.

142. The basic phases of a system life cycle are:

    a. Design, programming, installation, operation, and retirement.
    b. Planning, development, testing, operation, and disposal.
    c. Initiation, development/acquisition, implementation, operation, and disposal.
    d. Planning, programming, testing, installation, operation, and retirement.

143. In distributed systems, the basic security problem is knowing:

    a. Who to trust.
    b. When to reconnect.

c. How to name resources.
d. The order of transactions.

144. Which of the following is a generally accepted implementation of a role-based authentication model:

a. People are assigned access to an application through certain communications paths.
b. People are assigned access to an application by group identifiers, not individual accounts.
c. People are assigned access to an application through groups by job function or location.
d. People are assigned access to an application directly by their own account.

145. Which of the following should clients consider *best practice* for password selection?

a. Use randomly generated passwords during a log-in sequence.
b. Do not re-use passwords when expiration is indicated.
c. Select six-character passwords with special characters included.
d. Use the same eight-character password on all systems to which access is allowed.

146. Photographic, video, or audio recording equipment should be allowed in secure areas:

a. Only in specific, highly exceptional circumstances.
b. Only when accompanied by physical security personnel.
c. Only for the purpose of company publicity.
d. Only when the normal staff complement is not present.

147. Vacant secure areas should be:

a. Locked and periodically checked.
b. Cleared of all equipment.
c. Made ready to be used as non-secure areas.
d. Kept open.

148. Physical evidence is:

a. Things such as tools used in the crime.
b. Evidence presented to the court in the form of business records, manuals, printouts, etc.
c. Evidence used to aid the jury in the form of a model, experiment, chart, or an illustration offered as proof.
d. Oral testimony, whereby the knowledge is obtained from any of the witness' five senses.

149. The portion of risk that remains due to management decisions, unconsidered factors, or incorrect conclusions is termed:

    a. Loss.
    b. Residual risk.
    c. Insurance.
    d. A threat factor.

150. Within an access control model, the *subject* is:

    a. The entity that performs an action.
    b. The entity that is acted upon.
    c. The user account.
    d. The program.

151. A secure area might be:

    a. In the basement of the building.
    b. A locked office or offices inside a security perimeter.
    c. Made up of several different buildings in several locations.
    d. Close to neighboring premises.

152. Record retention programs are important so that both paper and computer records are maintained to satisfy all but one of the following management requirements.

    a. Legal requirements
    b. Audit requirements
    c. Tax guidelines
    d. ACLU requirements

153. What is the definition of cryptanalysis?

    a. The art or science of secret writing
    b. The practice of defeating attempts to hide information
    c. The study of secret writing and defeating the science of secret writing
    d. The exchange of information securely over a local area network

154. What is the greatest challenge to the security of private key cryptographic systems?

    a. Keeping the key secure
    b. Authenticating the user
    c. Export restrictions
    d. The security of the certificate authority

155. The two basic principles that underlie most well-constructed software are:

   a. Data hiding and abstraction.
   b. Segmentation and accountability.
   c. Layering and modularity.
   d. Isolation and separation of duties.

156. What is one advantage to using 3-DES over DES?

   a. 3-DES supports digital signatures and DES does not.
   b. IPSec standards allow the use of 3-DES only.
   c. 3-DES is standards based, and DES is proprietary.
   d. 3-DES is based on a longer encryption key than DES.

157. Configuration management is another important component of operations security and is defined as:

   a. Controlling modification to system hardware, firmware, software, and documentation against improper modification.
   b. Security safeguards designed to detect and prevent unauthorized access.
   c. Ensuring availability of critical systems components.
   d. Maintenance of essential DP services after a major outage.

158. Direct evidence is:

   a. Things such as tools used in the crime.
   b. Evidence presented to the court in the form of business records, manuals, printouts, etc.
   c. Evidence used to aid the jury in the form of a model, experiment, chart, or an illustration offered as proof.
   d. Oral testimony, whereby the knowledge is obtained from any of the witness' five senses.

159. Any action, device, procedure, technique, or other process that reduces the vulnerability of a system or asset to an acceptable level is best identified as a:

   a. Safeguard.
   b. Precaution.
   c. Safety measure.
   d. Countermeasure.

160. Which of the following is *not* one of the Ten Commandments of Computer Ethics published by the Computer Ethics Institute?

   a. Thou shalt not use a computer to harm other people.
   b. Thou shalt not use a computer to steal.

    c. Thou shalt not use a computer to perform a denial-of-service attack.

    d. Thou shalt not use use other people's computer resources without authorization or proper compensation.

161. In the system development life cycle, when should security requirements be developed?

    a. During the initiation phase

    b. At the same time that other requirements for the system are developed

    c. During system testing

    d. As part of the sensitivity assessment

162. What is the proper definition of a lattice-based access control environment?

    a. A lattice security structure is mathematically based and represents the meaning of security levels within a flow model.

    b. A lattice security structure defines access control lists needed for TCSEC compliance.

    c. A lattice security model does not change once requirements have been defined.

    d. Lattice models support military definitions of clearance and need-to-know processes.

163. The formal authorization by a management official for a system to operate and an explicit acceptance of risk is known as:

    a. Certification.

    b. Acceptance.

    c. Quality control statement.

    d. Accreditation.

164. Which of the following is *not* used for sending information securely over the Internet:

    a. SSL

    b. S-HTTP

    c. HTML

    d. SET

165. The characteristic of a resource or an asset that implies its value or importance, and may include its vulnerability, is known as:

    a. Public data.

    b. Sensitivity.

    c. Internal use.

    d. A threat.

166. Which of the following is *not* a communication threat?

    a. Masquerade
    b. Playback
    c. Repudiation
    d. Proxy

167. What makes up a security association?

    a. The security parameter index and the source address
    b. The security parameter index and the MD5 hash
    c. The MD5 hash and the source address
    d. The security parameter index and the destination address

168. The primary purpose of the Business Impact Analysis is to:

    a. Create management awareness and support.
    b. Satisfy audit requirements.
    c. Identify and prioritize time-critical business processes and recovery-time objectives.
    d. Provide a route map for resources that support business functions.

169. In public key cryptography, which key does the sender use to encrypt the data?

    a. Sender's public key
    b. Sender's private key
    c. Recipient's public key
    d. Recipient's private key

170. The security of a system should also be documented and would typically include all but one of the following. Which is *not* included?

    a. IT facilities telephone books
    b. Security plans
    c. Risk analysis
    d. Security policies and procedures

171. What is the most commonly employed network protocol for remote access systems?

    a. DECNet
    b. SNA
    c. IPX/NetBIOS
    d. TCP/IP

172. The formal testing of the security safeguards implemented in a computer system to determine whether they meet applicable requirements and specifications is known as:

    a. Certification.
    b. Accreditation.
    c. Security testing.
    d. Acceptance.

173. A security perimeter is:

    a. Always manned by a security guard.
    b. Something that builds a barrier.
    c. A wall with a locked door.
    d. A necessary part of a data center.

174. Which of the following represents a Star Property in the Bell–LaPadula model?

    a. Subject cannot read upward to an object of higher secrecy classification.
    b. Subject cannot write upward to an object of higher secrecy classification.
    c. Subject cannot write downward to an object of lower secrecy classification.
    d. Subject cannot read or write upward or downward to an object outside their own secrecy classification.

175. Third-party access to secure areas should be:

    a. Restricted and granted only when required.
    b. Denied.
    c. Granted on the same basis as other employees.
    d. Granted only with a physical escort.

176. Which is the most secure type of modem?

    a. Dial-back modems
    b. Password modems
    c. Encryption modems
    d. Silent modems

177. U.S. criminal conduct is broken down into two classifications, depending upon severity. They are:

    a. First offence and repeat offence.
    b. Juvenile and adult.
    c. Tort and felony.
    d. Felony and misdemeanor.

178. A sniffer attack has which of the following characteristics?

   a. It uses hardware called a sniffer to intercept packets being transferred in a telecommunications session.
   b. It uses pen test capabilities to access a system and then gather passwords for continued access.
   c. It uses a technique called tunneling to get under a certain safeguard within a system.
   d. It uses transportation procedures to convert information within an application.

179. The closest definition of the *principle of least privilege* is:

   a. People should perform job roles based on clearly written job descriptions.
   b. People should know how to execute all functions in an application or department.
   c. People should be authorized only to the resources they need to do their jobs.
   d. People performing increasingly more responsible job functions should have increased system access rights.

180. Salami attacks are effective because:

   a. The amount of funds diverted is so small that it is not easily noticed.
   b. The number of affected transactions is so limited that they are not noticeable.
   c. They involve electronic funds transfers.
   d. They are committed by individuals with detailed knowledge of the system.

181. General non-mandatory recommendations designed to achieve the policy objectives by providing a framework within which to implement procedures are known as:

   a. Guidelines.
   b. Policies.
   c. Laws.
   d. Procedures.

182. Which of the following telecommunications media is *most* resistant to tapping?

   a. Microwave
   b. Twisted pair
   c. Fiber optic
   d. Coaxial cable

183. Something of value or what security professionals are trying to protect. This can include data, information, personnel, facilities, applications, hardware, software, or transmission devices. This item of value is known in information security as:

   a. An asset.
   b. A program.
   c. A code.
   d. Top secret.

184. In a policy on employee responsibilities for handling organization information, this individual — the creator of the information or the primary user of the information — is classified as the:

   a. Custodian.
   b. Steward.
   c. User.
   d. Owner.

185. Access rights to secure areas should be:

   a. Given only to the people who work there.
   b. Given by the manager of the area.
   c. Reviewed regularly and updated regularly.
   d. Given to emergency services personnel.

186. Business Continuity Plans must focus primarily on:

   a. Recovery of all business functionality.
   b. Recovery of telecommunications circuits.
   c. Recovery of time-critical business processes and supporting resources.
   d. Recovery of IT department off-site data files.

187. Bulk supplies, such as stationery, should:

   a. Be stored in a cool, dark, dry space.
   b. Be delivered only to designated bulk-handling facilities.
   c. Be stored somewhere other than a secure facility.
   d. Be examined regularly for wastage.

188. Visitors to a restricted area should be:

   a. Supervised.
   b. Granted access for only a specific date and time.
   c. Issued instructions on security procedures.
   d. All of the above.

189. Layer 4 of the OSI (Open System Integration) stack is known as:

   a. The data-link layer.
   b. The transport layer.
   c. The network layer.
   d. The presentation layer.

190. What is the most widely used standard for digital certificates?

   a. X.17799
   b. X.509
   c. POP3
   d. X.25

191. Which of the following *best* describes the principle of hardware segmentation as it relates to systems architecture?

   a. Machines are stored in different physical locations.
   b. Disks are split into multiple logical drive letters.
   c. Virtual memory is divided into segments.
   d. Computers are given unique IP addresses.

192. A Vital Records program is an essential prerequisite to a well-rounded BCP/DRP process implementation. All but one of the following should be considered for an effective Vital Records program. Which one should *not* be considered?

   a. Assignment of responsibility for identifying and backing up critical information
   b. Maintenance of current inventories of information needed to recreate data
   c. Storing critical data/information at an off-site backup location an appropriate distance from the primary site
   d. Ensuring that all employees store critical vital records necessary for the execution of their job function at an off-site location such as their residence or in the trunk of their car

193. The employee, department or third-party entity entrusted with ensuring that information assets or resources are appropriately maintained, secured, processed, archived, and available as directed by the owner is:

   a. The custodian.
   b. The user.
   c. Management.
   d. The ISSO.

194. Mandatory activities, actions, rules, or regulations designed to provide policies with the support structure and specific direction are:

    a. Guidelines.
    b. Processes.
    c. Practices.
    d. Standards.

195. Which of the following is covered by U.S. Title 18 of the U.S. Code, Section 1030, also known as the Computer Fraud and Abuse Act?

    a. Obtaining free telephone service by fraud
    b. Disrupting computer services
    c. Monitoring employee communications
    d. Trafficking in passwords

196. Information hiding is a design principle whereby:

    a. The program module operates as if surrounded by a shield.
    b. A program module is isolated from the negative effects of other modules.
    c. How a program module does its task is concealed.
    d. The data processed by a program module is concealed.

197. Authentication protocols can combine certain elements that can be effective against "man-in-the-middle" attacks. What is the definition of such an attack?

    a. Active sniffers are used to inspect packets being transmitted from one system to another.
    b. Active spoofing is used to masquerade an intruder's whereabouts on a system.
    c. Active session hijacking moves the destination of one session to another location.
    d. Active attackers intercede in protocol exchange that modifies data moving in both directions.

198. The security of the physical security perimeter is:

    a. Consistent with the value of the assets being protected.
    b. The outer doors to the building.
    c. Constantly monitored.
    d. The responsibility of information security.

199. There are several types of detection methods for finding viruses. The most common is the:

    a. Heuristic scanner.
    b. Pattern scanner.
    c. Integrity checker.
    d. Behavior blocker.

200. To update anti-virus software the quickest, which location is best to update first?

    a. Mail server (Notes, Exchange)
    b. Network server
    c. PC
    d. Internet gateway virus server

201. What is the definition of cryptology?

    a. The art or science of secret writing
    b. The practice of defeating attempts to hide information
    c. The study of secret writing and defeating the science of secret writing
    d. The exchange of information securely over a local area network

202. Mandatory access control is related to which of the following?

    a. Permanent and irreversible access rules defined within an operating system
    b. Controls defined by the security administrator, or within his or her policy, that are classified as mandatory
    c. Control capability defined within an operating system that the security administrator or his or her policy may opt to utilize
    d. Controls enforced by the reference monitor

203. Every program or system component must operate with the minimum set of privileges it needs to accomplish its task. This is the definition of:

    a. Least privilege.
    b. Open design.
    c. Separation of privilege.
    d. Economy of mechanism.

204. Understanding the breadth and scope of enterprise insurance coverage relative to potential recovery of losses sustained as the result of a disaster is an important component of the BCP/DRP equation. All but one of the following types of insurance coverage are relevant to BCP/DRP planning. Which one is *not* relevant?

    a. Business interruption
    b. Media reconstruction

    c. Medical

    d. Extra-expense

205. "Processes have no more privilege than is required to perform authorized functions" is a definition of which system architecture principle?

    a. Enforcement of greatest access

    b. Execution of lowest rights

    c. Implementation of highest privilege

    d. Enforcement of least privilege

206. One major difference between the ITSEC and TCSEC is that the ITSEC:

    a. Does not address networking.

    b. Includes availability and integrity as security goals.

    c. Provides for bundled ratings for functionality and assurance.

    d. Addresses only commercial requirements.

207. Behavior that is unexpected is referred to as an anomaly. An example of an anomaly detection system would be:

    a. Using statistical profiles to measure behavior.

    b. Using misuse signatures to measure activity.

    c. Using checksums to measure quantity.

    d. Using probes to measure traffic.

208. Which of the following ITSEC functionality and assurance class ratings corresponds most closely to a C2 rating under TCSEC criteria?

    a. F-B3, E6

    b. F-B3, E5

    c. F-C2, E2

    d. F-C1, E1

209. The information flow model is also known as:

    a. The non-interference model.

    b. The lattice-based access control model.

    c. The risk-acceptance model.

    d. The discrete model.

210. The process applied when transactions fail to complete after making some updates to an online file is known as a:

    a. Checkpoint.

    b. Recovery.

    c. Restart.

    d. Back-out.

211. Before evidence can be presented in a U.S. case, it must be competent, relevant, and material to the issue, and it must be:

a. Presented in compliance with the rules of evidence.
b. Returned to the owner following case closure.
c. Reliable.
d. Relevant.

212. Which of the following represents a *Simple Security Property* in the Bell–LaPadula model?

a. Subject cannot read upward to an object of higher secrecy classification.
b. Subject cannot read downward to an object of lower secrecy classification.
c. Subject cannot write upward to an object of higher secrecy classification.
d. Subject cannot write downward to an object of lower secrecy classification.

213. The goal of the System Security Engineering Capability Maturity Model (SSE CMM) is to lead to the development of software that performs computing tasks as well as:

a. Follows a structured system development life cycle.
b. Employs modularity and encapsulation.
c. Meets ISO 9000 standards.
d. Enforces security requirements.

214. There are four types of computer-generated evidence. They are visual output on the monitor, film recorder (includes magnetic representation on disk, tape, or cartridge, and optical representation on CD), printed evidence on a plotter, and:

a. Voice mail messages.
b. Scanned images.
c. Generated business files.
d. Printed evidence on a printer.

215. Which algorithms does PGP support?

a. DES and El Gamal
b. IDEA and DES
c. DES and PPTP
d. PPTP and IDEA

216. The benefit of regularly testing business continuity plans and disaster recovery plans include all but one of the following. Which one is *not* included?

    a. To ascertain the level of discomfort recovery team members will sustain without complaint

    b. To assess whether the written plans are accurate and up-to-date

    c. To train recovery planning personnel in their roles and responsibilities

    d. To satisfy audit criticisms or to ensure compliance with applicable laws or regulations

217. To best protect the network from viruses, where should anti-virus software be placed?

    a. On the firewall

    b. On the PC

    c. On the router

    d. On the server

218. The following statement describes what information security tenet? For management to be able to rely on information that is as intended and is not contaminated or corrupted by malicious acts, uncorrected error conditions, or other failures.

    a. Accountability

    b. Authenticity

    c. Access control

    d. Integrity

219. Protecting the integrity of programs and documentation is the main security motivation for using:

    a. Configuration management.

    b. Separation of duties.

    c. Modular programming.

    d. System development controls.

220. In public key cryptography, which key does the recipient use to decrypt the data?

    a. Sender's public key

    b. Sender's private key

    c. Recipient's public key

    d. Recipient's private key

221. All vehicles entering or leaving a restricted area should be:

    a. Stopped.
    b. Clearly marked as to their reason for being there.
    c. Accompanied by a security person.
    d. Subject to search.

222. Another component of operations security is the logging of media for inventory purposes. The information contained in media logs includes all but one of the following. Which one is *not* included?

    a. Control or tracking numbers
    b. Times and dates of transfers
    c. Names and signatures of the individuals involved
    d. Number of bytes of information contained on the media

223. The Business Impact Analysis is also used as the primary input into the next phase of the BCP/DRP development methodology, which is:

    a. Identifying recovery team members.
    b. Developing testing and maintenance objectives.
    c. Document recovery planning.
    d. Determining appropriate recovery strategies and resource needs.

224. For BCP purposes, when determining business operations recovery strategies, all but one of the following should be considered. Which one should *not* be considered?

    a. Distance to the backup facility
    b. Time-critical business processes to be recovered
    c. Recovery team members roles and responsibilities
    d. Insurance coverage for replacement of the primary site equipment

225. Computer operators should be able to:

    a. Authorize users to access the system.
    b. Set the time and date on the system.
    c. Maintain and manage the audit log files.
    d. Run tools to format, compress, and analyze data.

226. A classic form of risk analysis was presented to the information security profession when it was included in the FIPS PUB 65 in 1979. This process requires the use of the formula of *Loss = Impact × Frequency of Occurrence*. The results will give the user:

    a. A threat analysis.
    b. A quantitative risk analysis.
    c. The annual loss exposure.
    d. The frequency of threat.

227. *Secondary storage*, as it relates to systems architecture, is:

    a. Memory directly accessible to the CPU.
    b. Extending the apparent size of RAM by using part of the hard disk.
    c. A storage location in memory with direct access to peripherals.
    d. A nonvolatile medium to store data even after power-off.

228. The technique in which an operating system strictly limits what system resources a program can access is known as:

    a. Segmentation.
    b. Segregation.
    c. Confinement.
    d. Isolation.

229. The process of identifying, controlling, and minimizing or eliminating security risks that may affect information systems, for an acceptable cost, is known as:

    a. A vulnerability assessment.
    b. Risk management.
    c. An information security policy.
    d. A safeguard review.

230. Off-site storage is another important component of the overall BCP/DRP process. Controls relative to storing data off-site include all but one of the following. Which control is *not* incldued?

    a. The off-site storage location is physically and environmentally secure.
    b. Record-keeping of the movement of data/media to and from the off-site storage location provides an adequate audit trail.
    c. Data storage location(s) must be within three miles of the primary site.
    d. Only authorized personnel are allowed access to the off-site storage facility or have the ability to request transfer of data/media.

231. Which of the following is *not* an attribute of an open system?

    a. It provides a standard interface.
    b. It provides a non-standard interface.
    c. It permits interoperability with other systems.
    d. It permits use of non-proprietary languages.

232. Operations security is:

    a. Used to identify and define the physical security of computer facilities and media.
    b. Used to define and control access to software.

c. Used to identify the controls over hardware, media, and the operations with access privileges to any of these resources.
d. Used to define and control access to computer systems.

233. Which one of the following mechanisms do manual key exchanges use?

a. PKI
b. Kerberos
c. Shared secrets
d. Diffie–Hellman

234. The Business Impact Analysis quantifies and qualifies loss potential in terms of:

a. People, processes, and technology.
b. Financial (monetary) loss and operational (customer service related) loss impact potentials.
c. Communications network downtime.
d. Overtime hour estimates.

235. One reason why intellectual property is a special ethical issue when applied to software is because:

a. Computer software is expensive to create.
b. Computer software typically has many features.
c. Computer software is easy to reproduce and distribute.
d. Computer software takes a long time to program.

236. The mandatory, step-by-step processes that must be done to complete a task or assignment are known as:

a. Policies.
b. Standards.
c. Guidelines.
d. Procedures.

237. Configuration management normally addresses:

a. Hardware and software.
b. Networking.
c. Tape library management.
d. Both a and b

238. During the recovery alternative strategy development phase of the BCP/DRP development methodology, all activities except one should be performed. Which activity should *not* be performed?

a. Utilize BIA business process priorities to map to both IT and business operations support resources.
b. Prepare cost estimates for acquisition of the recovery resources required.

    c. Obtain senior management concurrence on acquiring appropriate recovery resources.

    d. Document recovery plans.

239. A virus scanner works on all the following principles, except for:

    a. Viruses must be in memory to execute.

    b. Viruses can be completely invisible.

    c. Viruses execute in a particular way.

    d. Viruses use certain methods to spread.

240. A *single-state* computer:

    a. Simultaneously processes the data of two or more security levels.

    b. Executes only non-privileged instructions.

    c. Processes data of a single security level at one time.

    d. Contains the data of only one security level or classification.

241. Which of the following is a requirement for a system operating in system-high security mode?

    a. Each user has a valid personnel clearance for the least sensitive information processed on the system.

    b. Each user has a valid personnel clearance for the most restricted information processed by the system.

    c. Each user has a valid need-to-know for *all* the information contained within the system.

    d. Each user has a valid need-to-know for *some* of the information contained within the system.

242. What does the acronym ESP represent?

    a. Encrypted secure packet

    b. Encrypted secure payload

    c. Encapsulated secure packet

    d. Encapsulated secure payload

243. In what field of an IPSec packet might one find the MD5 message digest?

    a. In the data field

    b. In the encapsulated secure payload

    c. In the authentication header

    d. In the destination field

244. One of the key processes used in a personnel security program is a method that allows organizations to assess threats presented to them by individuals. This process is normally conducted prior to hiring and is termed:

a. Background investigation.
b. Resumé skimming.
c. Reference checking.
d. Credential verification.

245. Another important element of a well-rounded BCP/DRP process imple-mentation is the development, testing, and maintenance of emergency response procedures. All but one of the following should be considered for inclusion in an effective emergency response procedure. Which one should *not* be included?

a. Building evacuation plans
b. Bomb threat procedures
c. Earthquake evacuation plans and procedures
d. Detailed business impact analysis information on time-critical IT applications

246. Which of the following is *incorrect* when access to an application or process is changed?

a. Revocation of rights to an application or process should be automatic when a role changes within an ACL.
b. Revocation of rights to an application or process should be automatic when an employee leaves the company.
c. Revocation of rights to an application or process should be automatic when a security breach is observed.
d. Revocation of rights to an application or process should be auto-matic, based on job rotation.

247. The written recovery plan (either BCP or DRP) should *most* correctly contain all of the following sections:

a. Recovery team structure; detailed activities and tasks for recovery of time-critical operations; EOC location; reporting structure; inven-tory information (hardware, software, data, space, communications, transportation, people, etc.)
b. Plan scope, assumption, approach; recovery team structure; detailed activities and tasks for recovery of time-critical operations; EOC location; reporting structure; inventory information (hardware, soft-ware, data, space, communications, transportation, people, etc.)
c. Plan scope, assumption, approach; recovery team structure; detailed activities and tasks for recovery of time-critical operations; EOC location; reporting structure; emergency response procedures
d. Plan scope, assumption, approach; recovery team structure; off-site backup location; EOC location; reporting structure; inventory infor-mation (hardware, software, data, space, communications, transpor-tation, people, etc.)

248. Unsupervised working in secure areas should be avoided:

    a. Because it allows for employee wastage of company time.
    b. To prevent opportunities for malicious activities.
    c. Because it is against OSHA regulations.
    d. Because mistakes can be missed and can cause production outages.

249. Mandatory access control (MAC) techniques are usually used for highly secured, noncommercial computing systems. What are the characteristics of a MAC-compliant system?

    a. Internal and external controls (physical and software) must be employed to be certified as a MAC-compliant system.
    b. MAC-implemented systems enforce policy about which computers connect to one another and what data can pass on a connection.
    c. Access control lists (ACLs) and user authentication constitute a MAC environment.
    d. Mandatory access is only permitted if allowed by mandatory rules and discretionary rights.

250. The statement "Subject cannot modify objects of higher integrity" represents which property of the Biba Access Control Model?

    a. Simple Integrity Property
    b. Simple Security Property
    c. Star Property
    d. Integrity Star Property

Appendix C

Sample CISSP Exam with Answers

1. Automatic control devices for access to sensitive areas should:

   a. Have backup power supplies.
   b. Provide a log of every attempted access.
   c. Be supplemented by a human guard.
   d. Create an alarm at a failed access attempt.

   Explanation   Although most automatic control devices do offer the option for backup power supplies, some data center owners prefer the doors to "fail open" in the event of a power failure (as do some local fire regulations); thus, answer a is incorrect. Answer b is correct — because the secondary point of having automatic access control (after actually controlling access) is to be able to see what access attempts were made and which were successful. Answer c is incorrect simply, because a human guard is not necessary at every access and exit point in a security perimeter; and answer d is not correct because many organizations prefer to monitor access attempts rather than alert potential intruders.

   Domain   Physical Security

   Reference   Carroll (1996).[43]

2. The basic component of a General Program Policy consists of four basic elements. Among these elements are Purpose or Topic, Scope, and Responsibilities. Which of the following is the fourth component?

   a. Thesis
   b. Provisions

c. Compliance
d. Supplemental information

Explanation Answer c is the correct answer and can be found in the cited reference. Answer a is an element found in a Topic-specific policy; answer b is sometimes used by policy writers to explain why policy was written; and answer d is usually found in an application-specific policy.

Domain Security Management Practices

Reference National Institute of Standards and Technology (1995), pages 38–39.[60]

3. A sensitivity label is a piece of information that represents the security level of an object and that describes the sensitivity (e.g., classification) of the data object. Sensitivity levels are used as a basis for:

a. Identifying the owner of the object.
b. Determining the retention period for the object.
c. Determining mandatory access control decisions of the object.
d. Providing a schedule for rotation of the object to an off-site location.

Explanation Answer c is the correct answer and is taken from the cited reference. The other answers are incorrect because they are each too narrow or just plain incorrect.

Domain Operations Security

Reference Vallabhaneni (2000), page 320.[42]

4. The primary audience for the Business Impact Assessment is:

a. All levels of management concerned with continuity of time-critical business processes.
b. The auditors.
c. IT management.
d. All employees.

Explanation Answer a is the correct answer and is taken from the cited reference. Answer d is partially correct but is too broad in definition; management and selected employees will be in the audience but not all employees. Answer b is incorrect because the BIA should have nothing to do with satisfying audit criticisms. Answer c is incorrect because it only focuses on one narrow group of management.

Domain Business Continuity Planning and Disaster Recovery Planning

Reference Tipton and Krause (2000), Vol. 2, page 502.[17]

5. The principle of concentric controlled perimeters is meant to:

    a. Provide different types of control at different points.
    b. Repeat and reinforce access control.
    c. Slow an intruder's progress toward the protected area.
    d. Create a show of strength to deter intruders.

Explanation Correct answer a means that concentric perimeters allow for, for example, the control of vehicles at the outer perimeter, material and personnel control at the building perimeter, equipment and personnel control at the data center perimeter, etc. Answer b is incorrect because repeating access control is costly and wasteful. Answer c is incorrect because any point of access control is intended to prevent intrusion — not simply "slow progress." Answer d is incorrect because creating a show of strength is not the purpose of any access control; the purpose of access control is to prevent unauthorized access.

Domain Physical Security

Reference Carroll (1996).[43]

6. Maintenance hooks are a security risk because:

    a. They allow entry into the code without the usual checks.
    b. They are trap doors.
    c. They permit remote access to code.
    d. They are undocumented.

Explanation Answer a is the correct answer. It is the best answer provided. The most significant risk that maintenance hooks present is that they permit circumvention of normal checks designed into the system. Answer c may also be correct but it cannot be considered to be as significant as answer a. Answers b and d are incorrect because the difference between a maintenance hook and a trap door is that the maintenance hook is documented and the trap door is not.

Domain Applications and System Development Security

Reference Fites and Kratz (1996), page 445.[7]

7. Which is true about DES?

    a. It is based on public key cryptography.
    b. It uses stream ciphers.
    c. It was developed by the U.S. Department of Defense.
    d. It uses private key cryptography.

Explanation Answer d is the correct answer. Answer a is incorrect because it is the complete opposite of answer d. Answer b is incorrect because DES is a block cipher. Answer c is incorrect because DES was developed by IBM.

Domain   Cryptography

Reference   Fites and Kratz (1996), page 26.[20]

---

8. In a secure area, the organization's information processing facilities and third-party processing facilities must be:

    a. Connected to the same uninterruptible power system (UPS).
    b. Managed by the same operations staff.
    c. Composed of the same hardware and software configurations.
    d. Kept physically separate.

    Explanation   The correct answer here is answer d; third-party processing facilities must be kept physically separate from the organization's facilities to simplify access controls and to avoid the risk of activity being carried out on the "wrong" platforms. Answer a is incorrect because a UPS can well be shared by more than one computing environment — if the UPS is appropriately rated. Answer c is incorrect because there is no security concern inherent in the configuration of two environments.

    Domain   Physical Security

    Reference   ISO/IEC 17799:2000, Section 7.1.3, Securing Offices, Rooms and Facilities — F.[44]

---

9. During the recovery plan development of the BCP/DRP development methodology, all activities except this one should be performed:

    a. Document recovery planning team roles and responsibilities and assign tasks to specific team members.
    b. Identify and establish appropriate emergency operation center (EOC) locations.
    c. Define specific activities and tasks for the recovery of time-critical components for the operations under consideration.
    d. Perform a risk management review or assessment/analysis.

    Explanation   Answer d is the *most* correct answer, meaning that during this phase of the methodology, risk assessment should not be performed; it should have been done long before this. The other answers include activities that should take place during this phase.

    Domain   Business Continuity Planning and Disaster Recovery Planning

    Reference   Devlin and Emerson (1999), chapter II-2, page II-2-1;[13] Hutt, Bosworth, and Hoyt (1995), page 7-29.[15]

10. Audit trails maintain a record of activity and, in conjunction with appropriate tools and procedures, can provide a means to accomplish which of the following?

    a. Individual accountability and separation of duties
    b. Prudent Man Concept
    c. Physical security
    d. Reconstruction of events

    Explanation Answer d is the correct answer and is taken from the cited reference. Answer a is incorrect because audit trails do not establish separation of duties, although they do provide for individual accountability if set up properly. The Prudent Man Concept incorporates concepts of due care and due diligence, and an audit trail alone does not accomplish this.

    Domain Operations Security

    Reference National Institute of Standards and Technology (1996), Section 3.13.[35]

11. There are three primary kinds of spoofing; they are e-mail spoofing, Web-site spoofing, and:

    a. System masquerades.
    b. Gopher spoofing.
    c. IP spoofing.
    d. Social engineering.

    Explanation Answer c is the correct answer and is taken verbatim from the cited reference. The other answers are incorrect. A system masquerade (answer a) is not a form of spoofing; it replaces a legitimate computer with the masquerading computer. Gopher spoofing (answer b) is not a primary kind of spoofing, but rather a subset of IP spoofing. Social engineering (answer d) is not a type of spoofing at all, but rather a type of user masquerade.

    Domain Law, Investigations, and Ethics

    Reference Stephenson (2000), page 53.[29]

12. All of the following are effective in combating malicious software with the exception of:

    a. Using only commercial software obtained from reliable vendors.
    b. Testing all new software on isolated computers.
    c. Creation and retention of backup copies of executable files.
    d. Monthly use of virus detection software.

Explanation Answer d is the correct answer. To be effective, virus detection software must be used more frequently than once a month. Answers a, b, and c are effective controls for countering malicious code.

Domain Applications and System Development Security

Reference Pfleeger (1996) page 190.[10]

13. Overall enterprisewide responsibility for BCP/DRP ultimately rests with which individual(s)?

a. The BCP/DRP manager
b. The board of directors and/or executive management
c. The IT director/manager
d. The internal auditor

Explanation Answer b is the *most* correct answer. The others do have some degree of responsibility in the long run; however, overall final responsibilities rest, as always, with the board of directors and management.

Domain Business Continuity Planning and Disaster Recovery Planning

Reference Hutt, Bosworth, and Hoyt (1995), page 7-4.[15]

14. The purpose of Business Continuity Plans is to:

a. Counteract interruptions to preserve business activities and to protect time-critical business processes.
b. Mitigate disasters before they occur.
c. Comply with audit requirements.
d. Meet management by objective requirements.

Explanation Answer a is the correct answer and is taken verbatim the cited reference. The other answers are incorrect because they are each too narrow. Answer b is incorrect because BCPs should be designed to help organizations recover following an event, not to mitigate or avoid the event from happening. Answer c is incorrect because it is too narrow, although many plans are written for precisely this reason. Answer d is incorrect because it is simply incorrect.

Domain Business Continuity Planning and Disaster Recovery Planning

Reference Hare (1999), page 27.[14]

15. Making computer users aware of their security responsibilities and presenting them with the correct practices helps change their behavior. This process of raising end-user consciousness is part of:

a. An in-house education program.
b. A new product training course.

c. An employee awareness program.

d. Skill development.

Explanation Answer c is the correct answer and is found in the cited reference. Answers a, b, and d are related to the overall process of improving end-user use of security systems, but mainly focus on learning to use specific tools, where awareness is a process in behavior modification.

Domain Security Management Practices

Reference National Institute of Standards and Technology (1995), page 143.[60]

16. The security perimeter should have:

a. Signs indicating what it is.

b. No external windows.

c. A way to control physical access.

d. Fire suppression equipment.

Explanation Answer c is correct according to the cited reference. Answer a is incorrect because the owner of the site may not want to publicize the existence of the protected area. Answer b is incorrect because external windows can be as well-protected as any other part of the perimeter and so need not be banned. Answer d is incorrect because fire suppression is a function that would most appropriately take place inside and outside the security perimeter.

Domain Physical Security

Reference ISO/IEC 17799:2000, page 33.[44]

17. Crackers are defined as:

a. Software programs designed to compromise password and other files.

b. People who violate systems for monetary or personal gain.

c. Automated scripts used to perform penetration tests on external environments.

d. Tools used to exploit online sessions by sniffing packets and obtaining unencrypted information.

Explanation Answer b is correct. Crackers and hackers (although the terms are used interchangeably within the industry at times) are people, not software tools. This leaves the other answers incorrect.

Domain Access Control Systems and Methodology

Reference King, Dalton, and Osmanoglu (2001), page 452.[3]

18. A Trojan horse differs from a virus in the following two very important aspects:

   a. First, it is not found on UNIX boxes; second, it could stand alone as an independent executable file.
   b. First, it does not replicate or infect other files; second, it has a limit to how many times it can occur on a system.
   c. First, it does not replicate or infect other files; second, it cannot be found by anti-virus software using virus signature files.
   d. First, it does not replicate or infect other files; second, it could stand alone as an independent executable file.

Explanation   Answer d is the correct answer and is taken verbatim from the cited reference. The other answers are incorrect. A Trojan horse can be found on UNIX boxes; it can occur many times on a system; and it cannot typically be found using virus signature files.

Domain   Law, Investigations, and Ethics

Reference   Stephenson (2000), page 36.[29]

19. Cleanliness of media is important and, as such, demands special handling and storage. All except one of the following media handling techniques should be considered:

   a. Do not leave media that are to be shipped on the loading dock.
   b. The media transport time should be as short as practical, preferably no longer than five days.
   c. Leave the tape cartridges in their protective packaging until ready to use them.
   d. Use sharp instruments to unpack tape cartridges to avoid jagged cuts in packing materials.

Explanation   Answer d is the correct answer. One would want to avoid using sharp instruments altogether. The other answers are techniques that should be considered.

Domain   Operations Security

Reference   Vallabhaneni (2000), page 321.[42]

20. Emergency or Crisis Management Planning focuses primarily on what goal?

   a. Ensuring that all employees have a radio
   b. Preparing to recapture lost data
   c. Preparing to withstand a nuclear attack
   d. Ensuring human security and life safety

Explanation Answer d is the *best* answer, given the amount of information in the question. Answers a, b, and c are simply not appropriate.

Domain Business Continuity Planning and Disaster Recovery Planning

Reference Vallabhaneni (2000), page 515.[18]

21. Which of the following is *not* a function of the System Resource Manager as pertaining to systems architecture?

    a. It allocates CPU.
    b. It allocates main storage.
    c. It allocates input/output devices to user programs.
    d. It allocates user group memberships.

Explanation Answer d is correct because this is a human administrator function and not one performed by the operating system. Answers a, b, and c are valid functions and are therefore incorrect.

Domain Security Architecture and Models

Reference Fites and Kratz (1996), page 157.[46]

22. The U.S. Freedom of Information Act (FOIA) regulates:

    a. Dissemination of and access to data.
    b. How government agencies collect, use, maintain, or disseminate information pertaining to individuals.
    c. Private industry in collecting, using, maintaining, and disseminating information pertaining to individuals.
    d. What constitutes records for the purposes of the Internal Revenue laws.

Explanation Answer a is the correct answer and is taken verbatim from the cited reference. The other answers are incorrect because they each describe other laws. Answer b is incorrect because it describes the Privacy Act of 1974. Answer c is incorrect because it describes the Fair Credit Reporting Act. Answer d is incorrect because it describes IRS Revenue Ruling 71-20.

Domain Law, Investigations, and Ethics

Reference Ermann, Williams, and Shauf (1997), page 241.[27]

23. Disaster Recovery Plans must focus primarily on:

    a. Recovery of all business functionality.
    b. Recovery of telecommunications circuits.

c. Recovery of time-critical business processes.

d. Recovery of IT technologies and communications network resources that support time-critical business processes.

Explanation   Answer d is the correct answer and is taken the cited reference. Answer a is incorrect because it defines technology-focused DRPs as recovering too wide a scope of business functions. Answer b is incorrect because it focuses narrowly upon an IT (DRP) recovery plan component. Answer c is incorrect because it focuses on the goal of the BRP, not the DRP.

Domain   Business Continuity Planning and Disaster Recovery Planning

Reference   Vallabhaneni (2000), page 337;[18] Hare (1999), page 27;[14] Tipton and Krause (2000), starting on page 563.[17]

24. Directories and internal telephone books identifying locations of sensitive information processing facilities should:

a. Be kept in locked cabinets.
b. Be under the control of designated staff.
c. Be clearly marked.
d. Not be readily accessible to the public.

Explanation   Answer d is the correct answer. Documents such as these should be kept away from the public but still be available for authorized use. Therefore, answers a and b are both incorrect (because they would impede such access). Answer c is incorrect because it defeats the intent of keeping them out of ready access to the public.

Domain   Physical Security

Reference   ISO/IEC 17799:2000, Section 7.1.3, Security Offices, Rooms and Facilities — G.[44]

25. Which of the following storage mediums is regarded as the most secure against unauthorized erasure?

a. Floppy disks
b. Virtual memory
c. Optical disks
d. On-board hard disks

Explanation   Answer c is correct because optical disks cannot be erased. Answer a is incorrect because floppy disks are erasable at any time. Answer b is incorrect because virtual memory is volatile. Answer d is incorrect because hard disk erase protection is achieved through system control, not by the medium itself.

Domain Security Architecture and Models

Reference Fites and Kratz (1996), page 369.[46]

26. ARP is an acronym for:

    a. Address Resolution Protocol.
    b. Advanced Research Project.
    c. Anti-virus Resolution Protocol.
    d. Address Research Project.

Explanation Answer a is the correct answer. ARP provides a dynamic mapping of a 32 bit-bit IP address to a 48-bit physical hardware address.

Domain Telecommunications and Network Security

Reference Scambray, McClure, and Kurtz (2001), page 448.[72]

27. The Clark–Wilson model relies on four requirements:

    a. Integrity, confidentiality, availability, and recoverability
    b. Recoverability, auditability, reproducabilty, and reporting capacity
    c. Integrity, serviceability, auditability, and stability
    d. External consistency, separation of duty, internal consistency, and error recovery

Explanation Answer d is correct. The other answers are simply misleading terms.

Domain Access Control Systems and Methodology

Reference Summers (1997), pages 144–147.[4]

28. An agreement used to give notice that information is confidential or secret to employees and other third parties is termed either a confidentiality agreement or:

    a. An employment agreement.
    b. A condition of employment.
    c. A non-disclosure agreement.
    d. Top-secret clearance.

Explanation Answer c is the correct answer and can be found in the cited reference. Answer a is generally used with senior-level executives and employees with access to competitive advantage information. Answer b is incorrect because one might find a non-disclosure agreement as a requirement for employment. Answer d is a clearance level usually restricted to Department of Defense-type information access.

Domain Security Management Practices

Reference ISO/IEC 17799:2000, Section 6.1.3, page 11.[58]

29. What kind of document is a high-level statement of enterprise beliefs, goals, and objectives and the general means for their attainment for a specified subject area?

   a. Policy
   b. Procedure
   c. Standard
   d. Guideline

Explanation   Answer a is the correct answer, and can be found in the cited reference. Answer b implies that mandatory, step-by-step processes be required to complete a specific task. Answer c implies mandatory actions, devices, or methods be used to support a policy; and answer d implies recommended actions, devices, or methods that can be adopted but are not mandatory.

Domain   Security Management Practices

Reference   Peltier (2001a), Section 3.1.[64]

30. The lower layers of the OSI Model (layers 1, 2, and 3) deal with:

   a. Defining the characteristics of the systems at the two ends of the communication.
   b. The end-user interface.
   c. The application.
   d. Defining the network facilities necessary to transfer a message.

Explanation   Answer d is the correct answer. The lower layers are the physical, data-link, and network layers. They define the interfaces necessary for transfer. Answer a is incorrect because it defines how the user accesses the network. Answer b is incorrect because the middle layers (presentation, session, and transport) are responsible for networking management, establishing a communications session between the two sides and preparing information for the application.

Domain   Telecommunications and Network Security

Reference   Russell and Gangemi (1991), page 216.[71]

31. One method often used to reduce the risk to a local area network that has external connections is by using:

   a. Passwords.
   b. Dial-back.
   c. Firewall.
   d. Token Ring.

Explanation Answer c is the correct answer. A firewall will best protect the LAN if properly set up and maintained.

Domain Telecommunications and Network Security

Reference Russell and Gangemi (1991), page 203.[71]

32. Which of the following is a media-control task?

    a. Off-site storage of backup media
    b. Erasing each volume at the end of its retention period
    c. Cleaning and checking media on a regular basis
    d. Both b and c

Explanation Answer d is the correct answer and is taken from the cited reference. Every organization has a media control responsibility, and each volume in the media library must be labeled in both human-readable and machine-readable forms. A correct inventory of all media is also important to track entry of a volume into the library, removal of a volume, and each return. Other media-control tasks include those listed in b and c (above). Answer a is a function of business continuity planning, although media management is involved.

Domain Operations Security

Reference Summers (1997), chapter 12.[37]

33. A polymorphic virus is a type of malicious code that:

    a. Can change its appearance.
    b. Can make multiple copies of itself.
    c. Imitates the behavior of another form of virus.
    d. Resembles many other types of viruses.

Explanation Answer a is the correct answer. A polymorphic virus is a form of malicious code that can change its appearance, making it more difficult to scan for. Answer b is incorrect because it describes the behavior of a worm. Answers c and d are distracters.

Domain Applications and System Development Security

Reference Pfleeger (1996), page 188.[10]

34. Loss potential exists as a result of the threat–vulnerability pair. Reducing either the threat or the vulnerability reduces what?

    a. Risk
    b. Impact
    c. Concern
    d. Issue

Explanation Answer a is correct and can be found in the cited reference. Answer b is the element in risk analysis that tries to identify what level of damage might occur if a threat were to be successful. Answers c and d are sub-elements of the overall risk definition.

Domain Security Management Practices

Reference Fites and Kratz (1996), page 51.[54]

35. The Orange Book is the common name for:

a. Trusted Network Interpretation of the Trusted Computer System Evaluation Criteria, or TNI (U.S. DoD, 1987).
b. Trusted Computer System Evaluation Criteria (U.S. DoD, 1985b.)
c. The Technical Rationale Behind CSC-STD-003-85 (U.S. DoD, 1985a).
d. All of the above.

Explanation Answer b is the correct answer because this is the common name for the Department of Defense document containing the basic definition of the TCSEC, and the name is derived from the color of its cover. Answer a is the Red Book. Answer c is the Yellow Book, which contains guidance for applying the TCSEC to specific environments.

Domain Operations Security

Reference U.S. Department of Defense (1985b), the Orange Book;[40] (1987), the Red Book;[41] (1985a), the Yellow Book.[39]

36. The business records exception to the Hearsay Rule, Fed. R. Evid. 803(6), in general refers to any memorandum, report, record, or data compilation (1) made at or near the time of the event, and (2):

a. By a customer who was conducting business with the organization.
b. By, or from information transmitted by, an employee during normal business hours.
c. Transmitted using a digital signature.
d. By, or from information transmitted by, a person with knowledge if the record was kept in the course of a regularly conducted business activity, and it was the regular practice of that business activity to make the record.

Explanation Answer d is the correct answer and is taken verbatim from the cited reference. The other answers are incorrect.

Domain Law, Investigations, and Ethics

Reference Stephenson (2000), page 135.[29]

37. When selecting a recovery site for either DRP or BCP purposes, the facility should be located:

    a. As close as possible to the primary site.
    b. In another state/country.
    c. Close enough to become operational quickly, but not too close to get hit with the same disaster.
    d. In the basement.

Explanation   Answer c is the best answer, given the amount of information in the question. Answers a and d are simply not appropriate. Answer b could be partially correct, given a particular circumstance, but answer c is *more* correct for this question.

Domain   Business Continuity Planning and Disaster Recovery Planning

Reference   Vallabhaneni (2000), page 514.[18]

38. Intrusion management is a four-step process. The steps are:

    a. Avoidance, testing, detection, and investigation.
    b. Identification, authentication, investigation, and prosecution.
    c. Avoidance, detection, investigation, and prosecution.
    d. Detection, communication, investigation, and recovery.

Explanation   Answer a is the correct answer and is taken verbatim from the cited reference. The other answers are incorrect because identification and authentication (answer b) are functional areas of vulnerability, but not part of the four-step process; prosecution (answer c) can be a result of investigation, but not part of the four-step process itself; and communication (answer d) should be part of the detection and investigation processes, and recovery is a subset of the detection and investigation processes as well.

Domain   Law, Investigations, and Ethics

Reference   Stephenson (2000), page 64.[29]

39. The ISO/IEC 17799 International Standard on Information Security characterizes information security as the preservation of CIA: Confidentiality, Integrity, and which of the following?

    a. Authenticity
    b. Accountability
    c. Availability
    d. Assurance

Explanation   Answer c is the correct answer and is taken from the cited reference. The other answers are incorrect because they are generally viewed as elements of Integrity.

Domain Security Management Practices

Reference National Institute of Standards and Technology (1995), Section 1.4, Important Terminology, page 7.[60]

40. In relationship to cryptography, *work factor* is a term that can be defined as:

  a. The amount of time it takes an encryption algorithm to encrypt the data.
  b. The amount of time it takes an encryption algorithm to decrypt the data.
  c. The amount of effort it takes to defeat an encryption scheme.
  d. The amount of processing power necessary to create a public/private-key pair.

Explanation Answer c is correct. Work factor has to do with the amount of effort and not just the length of time it takes a CPU to process something. Answers a, b, and d are all incorrect because they deal with encryption taking place and not the process of defeating encryption.

Domain Cryptography

Reference Schneier (1996), page 7.[26]

41. The use of VLANs (virtual local area networks), IP subnets, NAT (network address translation), and routing provide security through which of the following?

  a. The separation of network resources to prevent systems from directly interacting with each other
  b. The hiding of network resources from the boundary protection devices that protect them from attack
  c. Improving the flow of traffic throughout the network to make detection and response to an attack more efficient and effective
  d. These methods cannot be used to improve the security of a network

Explanation Answer a is the correct answer. Separation of resources will provide security when using the weakest link theory. If one resource is compromised, the attacker is not able to jump to other resources. Answer b is incorrect; if the network resources hide from the boundary protection devices, they will not know what to protect. Answer c is incorrect; improving the flow of traffic does not make it more secure. Answer d is incorrect because answer a is correct.

Domain Telecommunications and Network Security

Reference Tipton and Krause (2000), Vol. 2, page 192.

42. The following describes what information security tenet? Baseline versions of a product are saved and protected in such a way that they will exist even if something happens to the original version.

    a. Change control
    b. Version control
    c. Software deployment
    d. Configuration management

Explanation   Answer d is the correct answer and can be found in the reference cited. Answer a is a process in which system changes are authorized. Answer b is the process used to ensure that all areas have the proper software level or release. Answer c is the process for the orderly distribution of products to the user community.

Domain   Security Management Practices

Reference   Glass (1992), page 203.[55]

43. Delivery areas should be controlled and:

    a. Adequately heated and ventilated to prevent deterioration of materials.
    b. Be separate from the main building.
    c. Be separate from information processing facilities.
    d. Monitored with video-monitoring equipment.

Explanation   Answer c is correct — to help avoid unauthorized access to the information processing facility Typically, delivery areas have less-effective access controls than information processing facilities and thus should be as far as possible from those facilities. Answer a refers to material handling and workplace comfort. Answer b defeats the purpose of having a delivery area (if a second delivery must be made from there to the main building), and answer d is a matter of policy for the facilities management group.

Domain   Physical Security

Reference   ISO/IEC 17799:2000, Section 7.1.5, Isolated Delivery and Loading Areas.[44]

44. A magnetic medium requires environmental controls to protect it from the most common risks, which include all but one of the following. Which risk is *not* included?

    a. Temperature
    b. Liquids
    c. Magnetism
    d. Air

Explanation   Answer d is the best answer. Air alone does not present a significant environmental risk to magnetic media. Temperature and liquid spillage can result in damage to the media itself, and magnetism can result in the loss of data contained on the media.

Domain   Operations Security

Reference   National Institute of Standards and Technolgoy (1995), chapter 14, page 162 (Environmental Protection).[34]

45.   Physical security barriers should be:

   a. Made of non-flammable material.
   b. From real floor to real ceiling.
   c. Insulated for sound.
   d. Monitored by video camera.

Explanation   Answer b is correct. Physical security barriers should extend beyond raised floors and false ceilings to prevent access through those spaces (ISO/IEC 17799 7.1.1 D). Answer a is incorrect because physical security barriers should not be relied upon to also be fire barriers. Answer c is incorrect because there is no need to prevent sound leakage from a protected area, and answer d is incorrect because video monitoring of the entire perimeter of a protected area may be more costly than the value of the asset being protected warrants.

Domain   Physical Security

Reference   ISO/IEC 17799:2000, page 34.[44]

46.   A secret, undocumented entry point into a program module is referred to as a:

   a. Control bypass.
   b. Trap door.
   c. Pseudo-flaw.
   d. Black hole.

Explanation   Answer b is the correct answer. "Trap door" is the term normally used to refer to a secret, undocumented access point into a module. Answer a describes what a trap door is, but uses non-standard terminology. Answer c is incorrect because a pseudo-flaw, although secret from a potential intruder, is not undocumented. Answer d is a distracter.

Domain   Applications and System Development Security

Reference   Pfleeger (1996), page 195.[10]

47. The protection mechanisms within a computing system that collectively enforce security policy are known as the TCB. What does this acronym represent?

    a. Terminal Connection Board
    b. Trusted Computing Base
    c. Trusted Connection Boundary
    d. Trusted Cipher Base

Explanation   Answer b is the correct answer. Answers a, c, and d are simply fictitious terms and therefore incorrect.

Domain   Security Architecture and Models

Reference   Fites and Kratz (1996), page 163.[46]

48. Computer support and operation refers to:

    a. System planning.
    b. System design.
    c. System administration.
    d. None of the above.

Explanation   Answer c is the correct answer and is taken from the cited reference. Answers a and b are related to applications development.

Domain   Operations Security

Reference   National Institute of Standards and Technology (1995), chapter 14.[34]

49. The IPSec standard includes a specification for which of the following security components?

    a. Authentication headers
    b. Support for non-IP protocols
    c. High availability
    d. Message playback

Explanation   Answer a is the correct answer. Answer b is incorrect because IPSec does not support non-IP protocols. Answer c is incorrect because encryption mechanisms do not often have high availability options due to security complications. Answer d is incorrect because encryption standards help to eliminate message playback.

Domain   Cryptography

Reference   Atkinson (1995).[19]

50. In configuration management, the goal from an operational security standpoint is to:

    a. Know what changes occur.
    b. Prevent security from being changed.
    c. Know when security can be reduced.
    d. Know when security can be eliminated.

Explanation Answer a is correct; the other answers are not the goal of security in configuration management. Security may or may not need to be changed at some point, but the most important concept is to be in a position to *know* what changes have occurred.

Domain Operations Security

Reference National Institute of Standards and Technology (1995), chapter 14, page 160 (Configuration Management).[34]

51. In an IPSec packet, what is the goal of an authentication header?

    a. To provide integrity and authentication
    b. To provide confidentiality and availability
    c. To provide advanced routing features
    d. To provide the decrypting device with information on what the encrypting protocol is used for

Explanation Answer a is the correct answer. Answer b is incorrect because encryption does not concern itself with availability. Answer c is incorrect because the IPSec standard does not include advance routing features. Answer d is incorrect because the security association contains that information.

Domain Cryptography

Reference Atkinson (1995).[19]

52. Which of the following best describes the security provided by process isolation in distinct address space?

    a. It ensures that processes running concurrently will not interfere with each other by accident or design.
    b. It ensures that every process executed has a unique address in memory.
    c. It ensures that a computer user can access only one process at a time.
    d. It ensures that an executing process cannot communicate with any other process.

Explanation Answer a is correct because process isolation ensures that processes cannot affect instructions by writing to each other's memory. Answer b is a reasonable definition of process isolation but does not explain its benefit. Answers c and d are false statements.

Domain   Security Architecture and Models

Reference   Fites and Kratz (1996), page 151.[46]

53. Zones of control (sometimes referred to as enclaves) do *not* require different levels of security than the corporate network at the:

a. Intranet.
b. Extranet.
c. Internet.
d. Remote access.

Explanation   Answer a is the the correct answer. Typically, companies do not add additional security to access their intranets. Answers b, c, and d are incorrect; all require additional security than that required by the corporate network.

Domain   Telecommunications and Network Security

Reference   Tipton and Krause (2000), Vol. 2, page 152.[73]

54. Which of the following is *not* a passive telecommunications attack (by definition, is restricted to observation or other methods that do not alter the data within a system)?

a. Eavesdropping
b. Traffic analysis
c. Disclosure by observation of a screen
d. Computer virus

Explanation   Answer d is the correct answer. The objective of a computer virus is to replicate and cause harm. Answer a is incorrect; eavesdropping is the unauthorized interception of information-bearing emanations through the use of methods other than wiretapping. Answer b is incorrect; traffic analysis is the inference of information from observation of traffic flows (presence, absence, amount, direction, and frequency). Answer c is incorrect; monitors emit a frequency that can be eavesdropped.

Domain   Telecommunications and Network Security

Reference   Fites and Kratz (1996), page 193.[70]

55. Separation of duties functions on the principle that employees are less tempted to do wrong if:

a. They must cooperate with another employee to do so.
b. They must submit transactions in the proper sequence.
c. They must perform specific functions at specific times.
d. Management performs strict oversight of their work.

Explanation Answer a is the correct answer. The aim of separation of duties is to force cooperation between individuals in order to violate security controls. Answers b, c, and d are incorrect because they address performance requirements and do not relate to the division of job functions to prevent illicit behavior.

Domain Applications and System Development Security

Reference Pfleeger (1996), page 224.[10]

56. Non-repudiation is:

    a. Something to which access is controlled.
    b. Equivalent to administratively directed access controls.
    c. An expression of policy in a form that a system can enforce, or that analysis can use for reasoning about the policy and its enforcement.
    d. An authentication that with high assurance can be asserted to be genuine.

Explanation Answer d is the correct answer and is taken from the cited reference. Answer a refers to an object; answer b refers to nondiscretionary access controls; and answer c refers to a model.

Domain Operations Security

Reference National Research Council (1991), page 295.[36]

57. Which item is *not* a VPN component?

    a. Tunneling
    b. Encryption
    c. Availability
    d. Authentication

Explanation Answer c is the correct answer. VPNs do not guarantee availability. Answers a, b, and d are all components of a VPN.

Domain Telecommunications and Network Security

Reference Tipton and Krause (2000), Vol. 2, page 161.[73]

58. Which one of the following is *not* an example of an intrusion detection system?

    a. An outsourced monitoring service
    b. Anti-virus software
    c. Automated review of logs searching for anomalous behavior
    d. An incident response team on immediate standby

Explanation Answer d is the correct answer. An incident response team goes into action when an incident occurs; it does not detect the incident.

Domain Telecommunications and Network Security

Reference Tipton and Krause (2000), Vol. 2, page 583.[73]

59. The first case successfully prosecuted under the Computer Fraud and Abuse Act of 1986 was:

    a. The Robert T. Morris worm.
    b. Kevin Mitnick computer hacking.
    c. The Melissa virus.
    d. Clifford Stoll's cyber-spy case.

Explanation Answer a is the correct answer, as taken verbatim from the cited reference. The other answers are incorrect because they were not the first case successfully prosecuted under the Computer Fraud and Abuse Act of 1986.

Domain Law, Investigations, and Ethics

Reference Ermann, Williams, and Shauf (1997), page 58.[27]

60. VPNs (virtual private networks) do *not* provide the following:

    a. Secure Internet-based remote access via a peer-to-peer VPN
    b. Secure, dedicated private network connections
    c. Secure extranet access
    d. Secure end-to-end data flow via a gateway-to-gateway VPN

Explanation Answer d is the correct answer. VPNs cannot secure the dataflow past the gateway; this leaves the connection between the gateway and the host insecure. Answer a is incorrect; peer-to-peer VPNs provide security from host to host. Answer b is incorrect; a VPN can provide secure, dedicated, private network connections. Answer c is incorrect; a VPN can provide secure extranet access.

Domain Telecommunications and Network Security

Reference Tipton and Krause (2000), Vol. 2, page 172.[73]

61. There are two primary types of message flooding; they are:

    a. Disabling services and freezing up X-Windows.
    b. Malicious use of Telnet and packet flooding.
    c. Broadcast storms and attacking with LYNX clients.
    d. E-mail and log flooding.

Explanation   Answer d is the correct answer and is taken verbatim from the cited reference. Answers a, b, and c all describe attacks, but not message flooding attacks.

Domain   Law, Investigations, and Ethics

Reference   Stephenson (2000), page 46.[29]

62. Which layer of the OSI model is responsible for security?

   a. Application
   b. Transport
   c. Session
   d. Physical

Explanation   Answer c is the correct answer. The session layer typically deals with starting up new tasks, if necessary, and with security (for example, authentication of nodes). Answer a (the application layer) is incorrect because it defines how the user accesses the network. Answer b (the transport layer) is incorrect because this layer is responsible for general network management functions and resource optimization. Answer d is incorrect because the physical layer establishes the physical, mechanical, and electrical connections and transmits the actual bits.

Domain   Telecommunications and Network Security

Reference   Russell and Gangemi (1991), page 216.[71]

63. The industry best practice for password selection by clients is:

   a. Six characters in length, changed every 60 days, frozen after five invalid access attempts.
   b. Eight characters in length, changed every 90 days, frozen after three invalid access attempts.
   c. Six characters in length, changed every 90 days, frozen after three invalid access attempts.
   d. Eight characters in length, changed every 60 days, frozen after five invalid access attempts.

Explanation   Answer c is correct. The other answers, although perhaps applicable in certain instances, are not considered best practice at this time.

Domain   Access Control Systems and Methodology

Reference   Tipton and Krause (2000), pages 53–54.[5]

64. Penetration testing stresses a system to identify security flaws in the following manner:

    a. Through interviews and access to applications, access risks are identified.
    b. Using commercial and public tools, an attack is simulated on a network.
    c. Using commercial and public tools, reports are run to determine policy compliance.
    d. Using password-cracking tools, an attack is simulated on an application.

Explanation Answer b is correct. A classic *pen test* is dedicated to examining open ports on a network for exploit potential. The other answers are applicable within a full vulnerability assessment, of which a pen test is a component.

Domain Access Control Systems and Methodology

Reference King, Dalton, and Osmanoglu (2001), pages 458–461.[3]

65. Buildings that are or are in a secure area should:

    a. Be clearly marked to deter entry.
    b. Give minimum indication of their purpose.
    c. Be no more than two floors high.
    d. Allow access only to personnel and not to vehicles.

Explanation The correct answer is b; buildings that form or that are secure areas should not give an indication of their purpose because doing so might incite attempts at unauthorized access. Answer a is incorrect for the same reason. Answer c is incorrect because the security of a building depends more on the security measures put in place in and around the building than it does on the configuration of the building itself. Answer d is incorrect because secure areas must allow for the transit of materials and the vehicles delivering those materials.

Domain Physical Security

Reference ISO/IEC 17799:2000, Section 7.1.3 Securing Offices, Rooms and Facilities — B.[44]

66. The efficient use of resources when attempting to mitigate a business risk is often described as a positive:

    a. Operating expense ratio.
    b. Return on investment.
    c. Risk assessment.
    d. Security analysis.

Explanation Answer b is the correct answer and can be found in the cited reference. Answer a is a method used to measure management's ability to control operating expenses. Answer c is a term that represents the assignment of value to assets, threat frequency, and other elements of chance. Answer d is a method to review security controls.

Domain Security Management Practices

Reference Parker (2000), pages 38–39.[62]

67. How many layers are in the TCP/IP protocol stack?

   a. One
   b. Seven
   c. Five
   d. Four

Explanation Answer c is the correct answer. The TCP/IP protocol stack has five layers: physical, data-link, network, transport, and application.

Domain Telecommunications and Network Security

Reference Tipton and Krause (2000), Vol. 2, page 66.[73]

68. The computer controlling automatic access control devices must be:

   a. Remote from the secured area.
   b. Protected as well as the other computers in the secure area.
   c. Isolated from the remainder of the network.
   d. Running a hardened operating system.

Explanation The correct answer is b; if the computer controlling the automatic access control devices is as well protected as the other computers in the secure area, then it should meet the criteria of being protected to a degree commensurate with its value. Answer a is incorrect because it is not necessary to have the access control computer in a remote location. Answer c is also incorrect because the access control computer will almost certainly need to be accessed from another point in the network for maintenance and diagnostic purposes. Answer d is incorrect because the standard protection afforded other computers on the network must be adequate for the access control computer or it will be inadequate for the assets the access control computer is helping protect.

Domain Physical Security

Reference Carroll (1996).[43]

69. Which is *not* a component of public key infrastructure?

    a. Certificate authority
    b. Symmetric encryption
    c. Digital certificate
    d. Certificate revocation

Explanation   Answer b is correct; the public key infrastructure uses asymmetric encryption. Answers a, c, and d are all components of public key infrastructure.

Domain   Cryptography

Reference   Fites and Kratz (1996), page 25.[20]

70. In the seven-layer OSI model, what does each layer depend on from the layers below it?

    a. Protocols
    b. Services
    c. Entities
    d. Data

Explanation   Answer b is correct. Each layer of the OSI model, along with all the layers below it, provides a service to the layer immediately above. Answer a is incorrect because different protocols can be used at each layer. Answers c and d are incorrect because they are general and nonspecific terms that are not considered to be the best answer.

Domain   Security Architecture and Models

Reference   Summers (1997), page 470.[49]

71. Accountability is defined as:

    a. Meeting schedules and budgets in a fiscally secure manner.
    b. Gathering and retaining records pertaining to financial matters.
    c. Performing actions within a job role that are governed by security policy.
    d. Ensuring that access to information is consistent and correct.

Explanation   Answer c is the correct answer. Accountability is the concept of making employees directly responsible for actions taken during their daily job assignments. Answer a is incorrect because meeting fiscal requirements is within the financial policy, not the security policy. Answer b is incorrect because record retention is a legal or internal requirement. Answer d is consistent with the concept of availability.

Domain   Access Control Systems and Methodology

Reference   Ford and Baum (1997), pages 94–95.[2]

72. Which of the following do not need to be a part of the TCB?

a. Operating system kernels
b. Protected subsystems
c. Trusted applications
d. Untrusted applications

Explanation Answer d is the correct answer and is taken from the cited reference. Answers a, b, and c are all elements of an effective TCB. Keeping the TCB as small and simple as possible is the key to making it amenable to detailed analysis.

Domain Operations Security

Reference National Research Council (1991), chapter 3.[36]

73. The method for separating a process from other processes that relies on using different hardware facilities is known as:

a. Logical separation.
b. Isolation.
c. Temporal separation.
d. Physical separation.

Explanation Answer d is the correct answer. Answers a and b are synonymous terms that refer to separation based on the application of a reference monitor to separate objects of one user from those of another. Answer c is incorrect because temporal separation relies on separating processes by when they are run.

Domain Security Architecture and Models

Reference Pfleeger (1996), page 297.[48]

74. Which of the following is *not* an active telecommunications attack (by definition, attack on the data in the network is altered)?

a. Playback
b. Denial-of-service
c. Sniffing
d. Spoofing

Explanation Answer c is the correct answer. Sniffers collect the data going across the network but do not alter it. Answer a is incorrect; playback occurs when something is recorded and then played back into the process for which it was intended. Answer b is incorrect; denial-of-service could be software or physical problems. Answer d is incorrect; spoofing is taking over someone's ID.

Domain Telecommunications and Network Security

Reference Fites and Kratz (1996), page 195.[70]

75. Digital signatures used in combination with e-mail do *not* provide:

    a. Integrity.
    b. Confidentiality.
    c. Authentication.
    d. Non-repudiation.

Explanation   Answer b is the correct answer. Digital signatures do not provide confidentiality; the sender can send the document to many people. Answer a is incorrect; a digital signature allows the recipient of a given file or message to detect whether that file or message has been modified. Answer c is incorrect; a digital signature makes it possible to cryptographically verify the identity of the person who signed the message. Answer d is incorrect; a digital signature prevents the sender of a message from later claiming that he or she never sent it.

Domain   Telecommunications and Network Security

Reference   Tipton and Krause (2000), Vol. 2, page 75.[73]

76. When using e-mail, which of the following is the *best* way to secure a message?

    a. Send the message only to the person you want to see it.
    b. Write the message assuming that someone is listening in.
    c. Encrypt the message before sending it.
    d. Sign the message using a digital signature.

Explanation   Answer c is the correct answer. Encrypting on your side will require the receiver to decrypt the message with your public key or a private key given to them. Answer a is incorrect; the message can be intercepted and read. Answer b is incorrect; no protection is assumed and the message can be read by anyone. Answer d is incorrect; the sender is verified but the data is not necessarily secure.

Domain   Telecommunications and Network Security

Reference   Tipton and Krause (2000), Vol. 2, page 73.[73]

77. Fallback equipment and backup media should be sited at a safe distance to avoid:

    a. Theft.
    b. Damage from an incident that affects the main site.
    c. Mistaken use as "production version" equipment and media.
    d. Corruption from constant handling.

Explanation   Answer b is correct; fallback equipment and media need to be far enough away from the main site to avoid being affected by the very event that would require their use. Answer a is incorrect because wherever the equipment and media are stored, they should be protected against theft. Likewise, answers c and d are incorrect because procedures should exist to ensure that fallback equipment and media are never used as production versions and thus are not subject to constant handling.

Domain Physical Security

Reference ISO/IEC 17799:2000, Section 7.1.3, Security Offices, Rooms And Facilities — I.[44]

78. Responsible senior management should formalize decisions and next-step actions following their concurrence with business impact analysis results to:
   a. Satisfy shareholder concerns.
   b. Satisfy audit requirements.
   c. Communicate precise recovery time objectives for prioritized business processes and supporting resources within the enterprise.
   d. Provide vendors with guidelines for providing recovery services to the enterprise.

Explanation Answer c is the correct answer and is taken from the cited reference. Answer a is incorrect because it is too narrow an audience and should not be relevant to shareholders at this time. Answer b is incorrect because the BIA should have nothing to do with satisfying audit criticisms. Answer d is incorrect because it only focuses on one narrow definition of what the BIA results should be used for.

Domain Business Continuity Planning and Disaster Recovery Planning

Reference Tipton and Krause (2000), Vol. 2, page 504.[17]

79. When considering operations security, controls should be placed on system software commensurate with the risk, including:
   a. Authorization for system changes. A combination of logical and physical access controls can be used to protect software and backup copies.
   b. Use of powerful system utilities that can potentially compromise the integrity of operating systems and logical access controls.
   c. Policies for loading and executing new software on a system.
   d. All of the above.

Explanation Answer d is the correct answer and is taken from the cited reference.

Domain Operations Security

Reference National Institute of Standards and Technology (1996), Section 3.9.[35]

80. Which best describes the definition of protocol?

    a. Multiple communications networks
    b. A set of rules for how information is exchanged over a communications network
    c. Layering of networks
    d. Layering of suites

Explanation Answer b is the correct answer; answer b dictates the formats and the sequences of the messages passed between the sender and the receiver. Answers a, c, and d do not define how the communications take place and are therefore incorrect.

Domain Telecommunications and Network Security

Reference Russell and Gangemi (1991), page 209.[71]

81. One of the primary reasons that computer systems have bugs is:

    a. Malicious code.
    b. Faulty system design.
    c. Programming errors.
    d. Program specifications.

Explanation Answer d is the correct answer. Computer systems have program errors (or bugs) because the specifications are either incorrect or they are implemented incorrectly. Answer a is incorrect because it relates to an intentional threat not caused by an error. Answer c is only partially correct because it does not include bugs caused by programming errors, while answer b is incorrect because it addresses only bugs caused by faulty implementation and does not take into account faulty program specifications.

Domain Applications and System Development Security

Reference Fites and Kratz (1996), page 317.[7]

82. The *principle of least privilege* supports which domain implementation method?

    a. Providing protected entry points into a network
    b. Providing privilege checking within a system or application access
    c. Providing hardware that allows access to certain functions
    d. Providing many small domains

Explanation Answer d is correct. Access permissions change within each domain as different information is required. The other answers are related in that they provide support within the domain. The overall question is asking about the principle, not the supporting functions of the principle.

Domain   Access Control Systems and Methodology

Reference   Summers (1997), pages 298–302.[4]

83. What application does PGP help protect?

   a. E-mail
   b. Web browsing
   c. File transfers (FTP)
   d. Telnet

Explanation   Answer a is correct. Answer b is incorrect because SSL encrypts Web traffic. Answer c is incorrect because FTP encryption takes place inside an encrypted tunnel, not with an application. Answer d is incorrect; SSH replaces Telnet and adds encryption.

Domain   Cryptography

Reference   Schneier (1996), page 436.[26]

84. A time bomb is a type of what form of malicious software?

   a. Virus
   b. Trojan horse
   c. Logic bomb
   d. Worm

Explanation   Answer c is the correct answer. A logic bomb is a type of malicious code that is activated when a specific condition is met. A time bomb is a logic bomb that is triggered by a time or date. Answers a, b, and d are incorrect because they are examples of malicious code that is activated upon the occurrence of a specific condition.

Domain   Applications and System Development Security

Reference   Pfleeger (1996), page 179.[10]

85. Robert T. Morris designed the Internet Worm to do all of the following except

   a. Determine where it could spread.
   b. Spread its infection.
   c. Exhaust Internet resources.
   d. Remain undiscovered and undiscoverable.

Explanation   Answer c is the correct answer. Morris' original intent was to find out the extent to which the worm could spread, and to actually spread without being detected. However, because of a flaw in its logic, copies of the worm did not terminate as Morris intended, resulting in severe degradation of system performance and exhaustion of network resources.

Domain   Applications and System Development Security

Reference   Pfleeger (1996), page 193.[10]

86. Personnel should be aware of the activities within a secured area:
    a. If the activities constitute a hazard to the employees' health.
    b. Where the nearest accessible fire exit is through the secured area.
    c. Only on a need-to-know basis.
    d. When those activities create input to the personnel's jobs.

Explanation   Answer c is correct — only those personnel who have a reason (related to the performance of their duties) should be aware of what goes on in a secure area. Answer b is incorrect because a general fire exit should never be situated within a secure area (fire exit only for employees working in the secure area), and answer a is incorrect because no activity that constitutes a hazard to the health of the general employee population should take place where it can affect the general employee population. Answer d is incorrect because personnel need only be aware of where the input comes from and not what processes occur in that area.

Domain   Physical Security

Reference   ISO/IEC 17799:2000, Section 7.1.4 Working in Secure Areas — A.[44]

87. According to Eugene Spafford, computer break-ins are ethical only:
    a. To catch a person committing fraud.
    b. To prove the security of a computer network system.
    c. In extreme situations, such as a life-critical emergency.
    d. Whenever corporate management has been forewarned of the break-in attempts.

Explanation   Answer c is the correct answer and is taken verbatim from the cited reference. The other answers are incorrect because they were not cited by Spafford.

Domain   Law, Investigations, and Ethics

Reference   Ermann, Williams, and Shauf (1997), page 125.[27]

88. Cryptography addresses which of the following security issues?
    a. Confidentiality and availability
    b. Integrity and availability

c. Fault tolerance and integrity

d. Confidentiality and integrity

Explanation   Answer d is correct. Answers a, b, and c are all incorrect because they contain availability or fault tolerance.

Domain   Cryptography

Reference   Atkinson (1995).[19]

89. Visitors to restricted areas should be:

a. Only technical staff.

b. Made to wear badges.

c. Kept to designated areas.

d. Allowed in only at particular times.

Explanation   Answer c is correct according to the cited reference. Answer a is incorrect because owners of data centers, etc. frequently want to show their data centers to many types of visitors. Answer b is incorrect because badges simply designate someone as a visitor and do not necessarily control that person's access to a restricted area. Answer d is incorrect because the times visitors may enter is a matter of policy for individual organizations.

Domain   Physical Security

Reference   Carroll (1996).[43]

90. The objective of secure areas is:

a. To lower insurance costs.

b. To keep traffic to a minimum.

c. To prevent unauthorized access to business premises.

d. To prevent the unauthorized removal of equipment.

Explanation   Answer c is correct according to the cited reference. Answer a is incorrect because having secure areas does not necessarily result in lower insurance premiums. Likewise, answer b is incorrect because secure areas must allow authorized access and that may not be the same as keeping traffic to a minimum. Answer d is incorrect because equipment removal will be governed by procedures rather than just the existence of a secure area.

Domain   Physical Security

Reference   ISO/IEC 17799:2000, Section 7.1, page 33.[44]

91. *Access control* supports the principles of:

    a. Ownership, need-to-know, and data classification.
    b. Authorization, least privilege, and separation of duty.
    c. Connectivity, password controls, and session controls.
    d. Privacy, monitoring, and compliance.

Explanation Answer b is the correct answer. Users of computing resources must be properly authorized, have the minimum access allowed to perform necessary job functions, and be controlled within their job function (e.g., not doing accounts payable and receivable functions within the same job role). Answer a is incorrect because these are attributes of the information being accessed. Answer c, although important, addresses policy surrounding processes used to control access, not the access control principle. Answer d is incorrect because the privacy of the user accessing data is not connected to the action of accessing information in an authorized manner.

Domain Access Control Systems and Methodology

Reference Summers (1997), pages 10–11.[4]

92. A program that moves through an address space by making a copy of itself in a new location is known as a:

    a. Virus.
    b. Worm.
    c. Trojan horse.
    d. Logic bomb.

Explanation Answer b is the correct answer. A worm is an independent program that moves through an address space by making a copy of itself in a new location. Answers a, c, and d are incorrect because viruses, Trojan horses, and logic bombs are not independent programs, and spread by copying themselves onto another program.

Domain Applications and System Development Security

Reference Fites and Kratz (1996), page 446.[7]

93. The primary reasons that each aspect of computer support and operations should be documented include all but one of the following. Which one is *not* included?

    a. To ensure continuity and consistency
    b. To eliminate security lapses and oversights
    c. To provide new personnel with sufficiently detailed instructions
    d. To satisfy audit requirements

Explanation Answer d is the most correct answer, as taken from the cited reference. The other answers are reasons why computer support and operations should be documented.

Domain Operations Security

Reference Vallabhaneni (2000), page 319.[42]

94. The files required to perform a batch update are:

    a. Master file and transaction file.
    b. Batch file and record file.
    c. Update file and production file.
    d. Sequential file and master file.

Explanation Answer a is the correct answer. The process of updating a batch file uses information from the records in a transaction file to update information in some or all of the records in the master file. Answers b, c, and d are distracters.

Domain Applications and System Development Security

Reference Hutt, Bosworth, and Hoyt (1995), page 14-14.[8]

95. SHA1 and MD5 are two examples of:

    a. Key exchange mechanisms.
    b. Hashing algorithms.
    c. Certificate authorities.
    d. Symmetric encryption algorithms.

Explanation Answer b is the correct answer. Answer a is incorrect because common key exchange mechanisms are private or public key distribution. Answer c is incorrect because certificate authorities are a component of the key exchange for public key cryptography. Answer d is incorrect because it is too broad in focus.

Domain Cryptography

Reference Krawczyk, Bellare, and Canette (1997).[23]

96. A possible danger to a system, whether it be a person, thing, or event, that might exploit a vulnerability of the system is termed a:

    a. Problem.
    b. Danger.
    c. Concern.
    d. Threat.

Explanation Answer d is the correct answer and is taken from the cited reference. Answers a, b, and c are incorrect in that they fail to reflect the level of severity that a threat poses to a system.

Domain Security Management Practices

Reference Russell and Gangemi (1991), page 11.[66]

97. According to Orange Book criteria, which of the following is required for C1 security?

a. Labels
b. Trusted recovery
c. System architecture (software engineering)
d. Object reuse

Explanation Answer d is the correct answer and is taken from the cited references. The other answers are elements of Mandatory (B) Protection. Just for clarification on answer c, Discretionary (C) Protection does require system architecture, but only for process isolation, not software engineering.

Domain Operations Security

Reference Summers (1997), chapter 6;[37] The Orange Book.[40]

98. Which term relates to a cryptographic key exchange?

a. Diffie–Hellman
b. Cipher block chaining
c. Elliptical curve cryptography
d. Steam cipher encryption

Explanation Answer a is correct. Answer b is incorrect because it is a term that relates to how an algorithm encrypts chunks of data. Answer c is incorrect because it deals with how an asymmetric algorithm uses discrete logarithms to encrypt the data. Answer d is incorrect because it is the opposite of answer b, which is also incorrect.

Domain Cryptography

Reference Schneier (1996), page 275.[26]

99. The characteristic of information being disclosed only to authorized persons, entities, and processes at authorized times and in the authorized manner is known as:

a. Integrity.
b. Availability.

c. Accountability.
d. Confidentiality.

Explanation   Answer d is the correct answer and is found in the cited reference. Answer a is the characteristic of being accurate; answer b is the characteristic of information being accessible; and answer c is the ability to audit.

Domain   Security Management Practices

Reference   International Information Security Foundation, *GASSP*, Version 1.0, page 14 (see Reference 57).

100.   If the recovery-time objective for an enterprise's IT computer operations is 24 hours or less, the most appropriate recovery alternative would be a:

a. Cold site.
b. Warm site.
c. Hot site.
d. Drop-ship arrangement with an appropriate IT equipment manufacturer.

Explanation   Answer c is the best answer, given the amount of information in the question. Answers a and b are considered incorrect because the time requirement for recovery tends to be past the 24-hour mark. Answer d is incorrect for the same reason.

Domain   Business Continuity Planning and Disaster Recovery Planning

References   Vallabhaneni (2000), page 341;[18] Hutt, Bosworth, and Hoyt (1995), page 7-19.[15]

101.   Which of the following is *not* a defined mode of access in the Bell–LaPadula model?

a. Read-only
b. Write-only
c. Read-and-write
d. Execute

Explanation   Answer d is correct because Bell–LaPadula has only three modes, as in a, b, and c above. Answers a, b, and c are valid and are therefore incorrect answers.

Domain   Security Architecture and Models

Reference   Fites and Kratz (1996), page 411.[46]

102. Digital certificates are based on what international standard?

   a. X.25
   b. X.400
   c. 802.3
   d. X.509

Explanation   Answer d is the correct answer. Answer a is incorrect because X.25 is a WAN protocol. Answer b is incorrect because X.400 is an e-mail directory database standard. Answer c is incorrect because 802.3 is an IPX standard.

Domain   Cryptography

Reference   Housley, Ford, Polk and Solo (1999).[22]

103. There are generally two types of denial-of-service attacks that are the most prevalent. They are:

   a. Planting and Trojan horses.
   b. TCP hijacking and IP address spoofing.
   c. TCP SYN attack and ICMP Ping flood.
   d. Buffer overflow and sniffing.

Explanation   Answer c is correct. All the other answers are relevant to types of attacks (the closest being buffer overflow), but not specific to denial-of-service attacks.

Domain   Access Control Systems and Methodology

Reference   Tipton and Krause (2000), pages 128–130.[5]

104. The concept of *least privilege*, as it pertains to operations security, means that:

   a. An operator needs access to documentation about operating system internals.
   b. An operator must have full access to the media library.
   c. An operator must be able to adjust resource quotas.
   d. Both a and c are correct.

Explanation   Answer c is the correct answer and is taken from the cited reference. Answer a is incorrect because this is a system programmer responsibility. Answer b is incorrect with regard to sensitive data, in that the media need only be released to the operator at the job's scheduled time.

Domain   Operations Security

Reference   Summers (1997), chapter 12.[37]

105. An enterprisewide approach to BCP/DRP should include the development of several types of plans that together comprise a strong BCP/DRP function. The different types of plans are:

a. Business continuity plans for business operations; disaster recovery plans for IT and communications; and off-site data storage plans.
b. Business continuity plans for business operations; disaster recovery plans for IT and communications; and emergency response/crisis management plans for reacting to an emergency prior to recovery.
c. Business continuity plans for business operations; disaster recovery plans for IT and communications; and building evacuation plans.
d. Business continuity plans for business operations; disaster recovery plans for IT and communications; and media kits and communications plans.

Explanation   Answer b is the correct answer. The others present types of plans that are really subcomponents of the emergency response/crisis management plan.

Domain   Business Continuity Planning and Disaster Recovery Planning

Reference   Tipton and Krause (2000), Vol. 2, page 511.[17]

106. The acronym ITSEC represents:

a. Information Technology Security Evaluation Criteria.
b. Information Transfer Systems Evaluation Criteria.
c. Internationally Tested Security Evaluation Certificate.
d. Information Technology Systems Evaluation Certificate.

Explanation   Answer a is the correct answer. Answers b, c, and d are merely fictitious terms.

Domain   Security Architecture and Models

Reference   Fites and Kratz (1996), page 166.[46]

107. On a DOS disk, the space taken up by the "real" file when you erase it is called:

a. Slack space.
b. Unallocated space.
c. Swap files.
d. Cache files.

Explanation   Answer b is the correct answer and is taken verbatim from the cited reference. The other answers are incorrect. Answers a, c, and d all describe other types of space on a DOS disk, but they do not fit the definition.

Domain   Law, Investigations, and Ethics

Reference   Stephenson (2000), page 101.[29]

108. The objective of separation of duties is to protect each of the following from compromise, except for:

a. Applications.
b. Activities.
c. Controls.
d. Vendors.

Explanation   Answer d is the correct answer because it is the least likely of the four answers to be the objective of separation of duties. Applications, activities, and controls are subject to compromise by individuals acting alone, and therefore separation of duties can be effective in protecting them.

Domain   Operations Security

Reference   Vallabhaneni (2000), page 311.[42]

109. The best technique to identify and authenticate a person to a system is to:

a. Establish biometric access through a secured server or Web site.
b. Make sure the person knows something to identify and authenticate him/herself, and has something to do the same.
c. Maintain correct and accurate ACLs (access control lists) to allow access to applications.
d. Allow access only through user ID and password.

Explanation   Although all are acceptable, answer b is *most* correct. "Something you know" and "something you have" is a widely accepted best practice for identification and authentication. This could be a combination of a PIN and a smart card or other token. The other answers are misleading; answer a indicates biometrics only; answer c assumes that a client has already accessed a host system; and answer d is a weak, yet common security design.

Domain   Access Control Systems and Methodology

Reference   King, Dalton, and Osmanoglu (2001), pages 119–121.[3]

110. A change control board is intended to evaluate all proposed changes on the basis of:

a. Cost-effectiveness and impact.
b. Desirability and correctness.

c. Privacy and security.

d. Timeliness and comprehensiveness.

Explanation Answer b is the correct answer. The primary purpose of the change control board is to evaluate proposed changes on the basis of how desirable and correct they are. Although answers a, c, and d may be considered by the change control board as part of its evaluation for desirability and correctness, these three answers are too limited in scope to be correct.

Domain Applications and System Development Security

Reference Pfleeger (1996), page 211.[10]

111. "...to prove the content of a writing, recording, or photograph, the original writing, recording, or photograph is required, except as otherwise provided in these rules or by Act of Congress" is taken from the:

a. Chain of Custody Rule.

b. Hearsay Rule.

c. Best Evidence Rule.

d. Distinctive Evidence Rule.

Explanation Answer c is the correct answer and is taken verbatim from the cited reference. The other answers are incorrect because they all are distracters.

Domain Law, Investigations, and Ethics

Reference Stephenson (2000), page 129.[29]

112. Which one of the following is a major component of the Common Criteria Standard?

a. User Profile

b. Protection Profile

c. Desktop Profile

d. Network Profile

Explanation Answers a and c are system specific; answer b is correct; and answer d is a fictitious term.

Domain Security Architecture and Models

Reference (1999), page 9.[45]

113. Which of the following are generally not characteristic of biometric systems?

a. Accuracy, speed, and throughput rate

b. Uniqueness of the biometric organ and action

c. Subject and system contact requirements

d. Increased overhead of administration and support time

Explanation Answer d is correct. If implemented in a structured design, biometric authentication can be cost-effective because token inventories and token maintenance functions can be decreased. Answers a, b, and c are all characteristics of biometric systems.

Domain Access Control Systems and Methodology

Reference Tipton and Krause (2000), pages 5–26.[5]

114. Following a disruption, the purpose of the recovery team management organization outlined within the BCPs/DRPs is to:

a. Develop recovery procedures to address the specific situation.

b. Arrange for the press to visit the damaged location.

c. Protect human life and to facilitate timely recovery of time-critical operational components in order to protect enterprise assets.

d. Go to the backup site and recover operations.

Explanation Answer c is the *most* correct answer. Answers a and b are totally inappropriate, and answer d is only partially correct. Development of recovery procedures after the disaster is the incorrect thing to do; they should have been developed prior to the event. Communication with the press must be centralized and controlled; it is not a job for individual recovery team personnel.

Domain Business Continuity Planning and Disaster Recovery Planning

Reference Devlin and Emerson (1999), page I-6-1.[13]

115. *Spoofing*, or *masquerading*, is a means of tampering with communications by:

a. Changing data fields in financial transactions.

b. Convincing a user to submit information to an alias system.

c. Pretending to be someone in order to access specific information.

d. Allowing packets to be sent from one host to another trusted host.

Explanation Answer c is the best definition. Spoofing can be done be a variety of methods. Answer a is true once a person has obtained access to a system through falsifying the credentials needed to access that system. Answer b is also somewhat true, but would happen to a user unbeknown to that user. Answer d is true of an IP spoofing technique, but is not specifically asked in this question.

Domain Access Control Systems and Methodology

Reference Ford and Baum (1997);[2] Summers (1997), pages 81–82.[4]

116. Reciprocal/mutual agreements for off-site backup are normally considered a poor recovery alternative because:

    a. Auditors do not like this practice.
    b. Of a slow response to requests to recover operations.
    c. Network incompatibilities.
    d. Of difficulties in keeping agreements, plans, and configurations managed and up-to-date.

Explanation   Answer d is the best answer, given the amount of information in the question. Answer a is simply not true. Answers b and c are potentially partially correct but too narrow in focus.

Domain   Business Continuity Planning and Disaster Recovery Planning

Reference   Vallabhaneni (2000), page 341;[18] Hutt, Bosworth, and Hoyt (1995), page 7-19.[15]

117. Discretionary access control (DAC) refers to what common configuration requirement of TCSEC levels C2 through D?

    a. Objects in a computer system must meet minimum security requirements.
    b. Owners of objects in a computer system can determine the ability of users to access the objects.
    c. Object access control lists can be modified, depending on the criticality of the object.
    d. Objects in a computer system must be secured using the strictest method possible.

Explanation   Answer c is correct. The concept of DAC is that every object has an owner, and that owner alone can determine or modify access to that object. Answer a is incorrect because it is too broad a statement for this issue. Answer b is somewhat correct, but the owner holds final control over object access rights. Answer d is more attuned to the concept of mandatory access control.

Domain   Access Control Systems and Methodology

Reference   Tudor (2001), pages 126–127.[6]

118. The U.S. Economic Espionage Act of 1996 defines someone as undertaking economic espionage if they knowingly perform any of five activities. One of these activities includes:

    a. Intentionally, without authorization, accessing any non-public computer of a department or agency of the United States, accessing such a computer of that department or agency that is exclusively for the use of the U.S. Government.

b. Not obtaining consent for the collection, use, or disclosure of personal information.
c. Causing loss aggregating at least $5000 in value during any one-year period to one or more individuals.
d. Receiving, buying, or possessing a trade secret, knowing the same to have been stolen or appropriated, obtained, or converted without authorization.

Explanation   Answer d is the correct answer, and is taken verbatim from the cited reference. The other answers are incorrect. Answer a is incorrect; it is taken from the Computer Fraud and Misuse Act. Answer b is incorrect; it is taken from the Online Privacy Protection Act of 1999. Answer c is incorrect; it is taken from the Computer Fraud and Misuse Act.

Domain   Law, Investigations, and Ethics

Reference   U.S. Congressional Record of 1996; http://cybercrime.gov/ EEAleghist.htm.[31]

119.   The *custodian* of information has the primary responsibility for:

a. Logically ensuring that information is properly safeguarded from unauthorized access, modification, or disclosure.
b. Implementing safeguards such as ACLs to protect information.
c. Accessing information in a manner controlled by ACL safeguards and supported by policy.
d. Physically ensuring that information is safeguarded and maintained in a secure manner.

Explanation   Answer b is correct. The custodian is generally an application administrator or system administrator. Answer a is incorrect because it is the best-practice definition of information ownership. Answer c is more typical of a user or client than a custodian. Answer d, although it could be part of a custodial function, refers more to an infrastructure support service, such as a data center operations function.

Domain   Access Control Systems and Methodology

Reference   Tudor (2001), pages 41–42.[6]

120.   The process of investigating a target environment and the relationships of dangers to the target is known in information security circles as:

a. Value analysis.
b. Risk analysis.
c. Risk assessment.
d. Safeguard checking.

Explanation   Answer b is correct and is found in the cited reference. Answer a is another form of qualitative risk analysis and answer c is a process to assign a value to assets. Answer d is a post-risk analysis process usually found in a vulnerability assessment.

Domain   Security Management Practices

Reference   Tipton and Krause (2000), page 429.[67]

121.   The concept of non-repudiation means that:

  a. The sender can verify that the receiver read the message.
  b. The receiver can prove that the sender sent the message.
  c. The sender can verify the receiver's private key.
  d. The receiver can verify that the certificate authority has not been compromised.

Explanation   Answer b is the correct answer. Answer a is incorrect because it is a feature of an e-mail client and not encryption. Answer c is incorrect because private keys are not sent out in encryption. Answer d is incorrect because there is no mechanism in any standard to ensure a secure certificate authority.

Domain   Cryptography

Reference   Atkinson (1995).[19]

122.   The concepts of due care and due diligence are key to operations security undertakings. Examples of due diligence include all but one of the following. Which one is *not* included?

  a. Good housekeeping
  b. Requesting that employees acknowledge and sign off on computer security requirements
  c. Issuing appropriate formalized security policies and procedures
  d. Allowing unrestricted access to both public and private spaces

Explanation   Answer d is the correct answer. Answers a, b, and c are all examples of due diligence and are taken directly from the cited reference.

Domain   Operations Security

Reference   Vallabhaneni (2000), page 325.[42]

123.   The NSA (National Security Agency) has published the TCSEC, often referred to as the Orange Book. What does the acronym TCSEC stand for?

  a. Total Computer Security Enhancement Conventions
  b. Trusted Compliant Security Evaluation Classification

c. Total Confidential System Examination Considerations

d. Trusted Computer System Evaluation Criteria

Explanation The correct answer is d. The TCSEC, as published by the U.S. Department of Defense, is commonly accepted as the standard in the United States for system certification in a number of classes (A1 through D). The other answers are simply different acronyms.

Domain Access Control Systems and Methodology

Reference Tudor (2001), pages 126–127.[6]

124. The absence or weakness of a risk-reducing safeguard is known as:

a. An uncertainty.

b. Detection.

c. Exposure.

d. A vulnerability.

Explanation Answer d is the correct answer and can be found in the cited reference. Answer a is the degree to which there is less than complete confidence in the value of any element of the risk assessment. Answer b is the process of identifying the occurrence of an event and the possible agent involved. Answer c is the specific instance of the condition of being unduly exposed to losses.

Domain Security Management Practices

Reference Tipton and Krause (2000), page 430.[67]

125. A shared resource matrix is a technique commonly used to locate:

a. Malicious code.

b. Security flaws.

c. Trap doors.

d. Covert channels.

Explanation Answer d is the correct answer. Analyzing resources of a system is one standard for locating covert channels because the basis of a covert channel is a shared resource. Answers a, b, and c are incorrect because a shared resource matrix will not normally lead to the identification of malicious code, security flaws, or trap doors.

Domain Applications and System Development Security

Reference Pfleeger (1996), page 204.[10]

126. What is the definition of cryptography?

a. The art or science of secret writing

b. The practice of defeating attempts to hide information

c. The study of secret writing and defeating the science of secret writing
d. The secure exchange of information over a local area network

Explanation   Answer a is correct. Answer b is incorrect because it is the definition of cryptanalysis. Answer c is incorrect because it is the definition of cryptology. Answer d is incorrect because cryptography is not restricted to a local area network.

Domain   Cryptography

Reference   Schneier (1996), page 1.[26]

127. To protect audit trails, the audit database must be protected. Which of the following techniques can help counter attacks on the audit database?

a. Write-once optical disks
b. Cryptographic protection
c. Remote storage of audit trails
d. All of the above

Explanation   Answer d is the correct answer and is taken from the cited reference. In addition to establishing accountability, an audit trail may also reveal suspicious patterns of access and thus enable detection of improper behavior by both legitimate users and masqueraders. Limitations to this use of audit information often restrict its use to detecting unsophisticated intruders because sophisticated intruders have been known to circumvent audit trails in the course of penetrating systems. Techniques, such as those listed above in a, b, and c, can help counter some of those attacks on the audit database itself, although these measures do not address all the vulnerabilities of audit mechanisms.

Domain   Operations Security

Reference   National Research Council (1991), chapter 3.[36]

128. What is one drawback to using authentication headers?

a. Single-factor authentication
b. Increased packet size
c. Authentication headers are proprietary
d. Only 56-bit encryption algorithms support authentication headers

Explanation   Answer b is the correct answer. Answer a is incorrect because single-factor authentication is a password for access control. Answer c is incorrect because authentication headers are written into the IPSec standard. Answer d is incorrect because many protocols specified in the IPSec standard can use authentication headers.

Domain   Cryptography

Reference   Atkinson (1995).[19]

129. What does the acronym DES represent?

    a. Dual Encryption Standard
    b. Data Encryption Standard
    c. Data Encryption Scheme
    d. Dual Encryption Scheme

Explanation   Answer b is the correct answer and is taken from the cited reference. While answers a, c, and d all look correct at first glance, they all have a misrepresented word.

Domain   Cryptography

Reference   Fites and Kratz (1996), page 33.[20]

130. Hazardous or combustible materials should be:

    a. Taken to a local landfill.
    b. Inventoried.
    c. Stored a safe distance from secure areas.
    d. Handled and disposed of only by a licensed vendor.

Explanation   Answer c is correct because the point here is physical protection of a secure area. Answers a and d — where appropriate — are concerned with the disposal (not storage) of hazardous materials. Answer b has to do with the management of materials and not with the protection of secure areas.

Domain   Physical Security

Reference   ISO/IEC 17799:2000, Section 7.1.3, Security Offices, Rooms and Facilities — H.[44]

131. U.S. criminal law identifies a crime as being a wrong against:

    a. A private citizen.
    b. Society.
    c. The U.S. Government.
    d. Taxpayers.

Explanation   Answer b is the correct answer and is taken verbatim from the cited reference. The other answers are incorrect because they are not specifically addressed within any U.S. criminal law definitions. However, they are sometimes specifically addressed within specific state and local laws.

Domain   Law, Investigations, and Ethics

Reference   Tipton and Krause (2000), page 602.[30]

132. Under ITSEC evaluation, what assurance class represents inadequate assurance that the target of evaluation has met its requirements?

  a. E0
  b. E1
  c. E2
  d. E3

Explanation   Answer a is the correct answer. Answer b meets requirements to the minimum assurance level. Answers c and d meet requirements to higher assurance levels.

Domain   Security Architecture and Models

Reference   Fites and Kratz (1996), page 166.[46]

133. What kinds of cases are much easier to convict because the burden of proof required for a conviction is much less?

  a. Misdemeanor
  b. Civil
  c. Criminal
  d. Domestic

Explanation   Answer b is the correct answer and is taken verbatim from the cited reference. The other answers are incorrect because a criminal case requires a preponderance of evidence beyond a reasonable doubt. *Misdemeanor* and *domestic* are not considered case classifications.

Domain   Law, Investigations, and Ethics

Reference   Tipton and Krause (2000), page 606.[30]

134. The traditional five phases of the BCP/DRP development methodology are:

  a. Project scope and planning, business impact analysis, recovery alternative strategy development, recovery plan development, recovery plan testing, and maintenance strategy development.
  b. Project scope and planning, risk management review, recovery plan development, plan testing, and maintenance strategy development.
  c. Project scope and planning, recovery strategy development, recovery plan development, recovery plan testing, and maintenance strategy development.

d. Project scope and planning, business impact analysis, recovery plan development, and risk management review.

Explanation   Answer a is the correct answer. Answers b, c, and d are all methodology steps that are either out of order, not primary methodology phase activities, or sub-phase activities.

Domain   Business Continuity Planning and Disaster Recovery Planning

Reference   Tipton and Krause 1996–97 Yearbook Edition, page S-75.[16]

135.   A non-interference access control model is best suited for:

   a. Systems that require strict access flow and do not easily accommodate flexibility in information flow.
   b. Systems that are stand-alone and do not communicate with others in a networking capacity.
   c. Systems that do not require classification schemes and have all public information.
   d. Systems that rely on state machine architectures and capabilities.

Explanation   The concept of non-interference is that one group of users is non-interfering with another group if the actions of the first group have no effect on what the second group can see. Therefore, answer a is correct. Answer b is incorrect because it illustrates the concept of a decidedly trusted system. Answer c is incorrect because principles of data classification contribute to access control definition, but are not applicable to this question. Answer d is incorrect because a state machine model is another form of access control model.

Domain   Access Control Systems and Methodology

Reference   Summers (1997), pages 137–140.[4]

136.   U.S. criminal law falls under two main jurisdictions; they are:

   a. Federal and local.
   b. County and local.
   c. Federal and state.
   d. National and international.

Explanation   Answer c is the correct answer and is taken verbatim from the cited reference. The other answers are incorrect because local and county jurisdictions do not address criminal law because they are addressed by federal and state laws. There is not formal terminology with regard to national or international jurisdictions.

Domain   Law, Investigations, and Ethics

Reference   Tipton and Krause (2000), page 603.[30]

137. Real evidence is:

    a. Things such as tools used in the crime.
    b. Made up of tangible objects that prove or disprove guilt.
    c. Evidence used to aid the jury in the form of a model, experiment, chart, or an illustration offered as proof.
    d. Oral testimony, whereby the knowledge is obtained from any of the witness' five senses.

Explanation   Answer b is the correct answer and is taken verbatim from the cited reference. Answer a is an example of physical evidence; answer c is an example of demonstrative evidence; and answer d is an example of direct evidence.

Domain   Law, Investigations, and Ethics

Reference   Tipton and Krause (2000), page 607.[30]

138. Which of the following applies to the notion of a specific security policy maintaining a *secure state* as defined by Bell–LaPadula?

    a. The policy must define the hierarchy of integrity levels.
    b. The policy must prevent unauthorized users from making modifications.
    c. The policy must define logging of subject activity.
    d. The policy must define the permitted modes of access between subjects and objects.

Explanation   Answer d is the correct answer. Answer a relates to integrity; Bell–LaPadula relates to confidentiality. Answer b relates to integrity; Bell–LaPadula relates to confidentiality. Answer c is not contained within the Bell–LaPadula model.

Domain   Security Architecture and Models

Reference   Fites and Kratz (1996), page 411.[46]

139. According to RFC 1087, any activity is characterized as unethical and unacceptable that purposely:

    a. Destroys the integrity of computer-based information.
    b. Results in fraud.
    c. Threatens e-mail message delivery.
    d. Participates in gambling.

Explanation   Answer a is the correct answer and is taken verbatim from the cited reference. The other activities that also fit this definition include:

- Seeks to gain unauthorized access to the resources of the Internet
- Disrupts the intended use of the Internet
- Wastes resources (people, capacity, computers) through such actions
- Compromises the privacy of users
- Involves negligence in the conduct of Internet-wide experiments

The other answers are incorrect.

Domain   Law, Investigations, and Ethics

Reference   Tipton and Krause (2000), page 651.[30]

140. The process in which an independent security evaluation team checks on compliance with software development standards on an unannounced basis is known as:

   a. Independent evaluation.
   b. Security audit.
   c. Validation.
   d. Certification.

   Explanation   Answer b is the correct answer. A security audit is the process used to ensure that standards are being effectively followed in the development of software. The security audit includes a review of designs, documentation, and code to ensure that standards have been followed. Answers a, c, and d are incorrect because they are processes used to provide assurance for a specific project, and are too narrow.

   Domain   Applications and System Development Security

   Reference   Pfleeger (1996), page 223.[10]

141. Which of the following is *not* one of the three integrity goals addressed by the Clark–Wilson model?

   a. Prevent unauthorized users from making modifications.
   b. Prevent unauthorized users from viewing classified objects.
   c. Prevent authorized users from making improper modifications.
   d. Maintain internal and external consistency.

   Explanation   Answer a is a valid integrity goal under the model. Answer b is the correct answer because it is a goal of *confidentiality*. Answers c and d are valid integrity goals under the model.

   Domain   Security Architecture and Models

   Reference   Fites and Kratz (1996), page 334.[46]

142. The basic phases of a system life cycle are:

  a. Design, programming, installation, operation, and retirement.
  b. Planning, development, testing, operation, and disposal.
  c. Initiation, development/acquisition, implementation, operation, and disposal.
  d. Planning, programming, testing, installation, operation, and retirement.

Explanation Answer c is the correct answer. The system life cycle begins with project initiation, followed by development or acquisition of the system, implementation of the system, system operation, and then system disposal. Answer a does not include the initiation phase and system design takes place during the development/acquisition phase. Answer b is incorrect because planning is merely a part of the initiation phase. Answer d is incorrect because planning is merely a part of the initiation phase, and testing and installation are each sub-elements of the implementation phase.

Domain Applications and System Development Security

Reference National Institute of Standards and Technology (1995), page 75.[9]

143. In distributed systems, the basic security problem is knowing:

  a. Who to trust.
  b. When to reconnect.
  c. How to name resources.
  d. The order of transactions.

Explanation Answer a is the correct answer. Who to trust is the basic problem; the incorrect answer can wreak havoc on your systems. Typically, you do not have physical access to all the systems so the authentication of each is essential for trust. Answers b, c, and d are not security problems in distributed systems.

Domain Telecommunications and Network Security

Reference Russell and Gangemi (1991), page 221.[71]

144. Which of the following is a generally accepted implementation of a role-based authentication model?

  a. People are assigned access to an application through certain communications paths.
  b. People are assigned access to an application by group identifiers, not individual accounts.

    c. People are assigned access to an application through groups by job function or location.

    d. People are assigned access to an application directly by their own account.

Explanation Answer c is correct. People are assigned to roles that are assigned to application access rights. This simplifies administration and maintenance when people change job roles. Answer a is incorrect because the access is not controlled through a role, although access control can certainly support a role-based model. Answers b and d are incorrect because they infer generic or personal accounts, not assignment by job function.

Domain Access Control Systems and Methodology

Reference Summers (1997), pages 128–129.[4]

145. Which of the following should clients consider *best practice* for password selection?

    a. Use randomly generated passwords during a log-in sequence.

    b. Do not re-use passwords when expiration is indicated.

    c. Select six-character passwords with special characters included.

    d. Use the same eight-character password on all systems to which access is allowed.

Explanation Answer c is considered the *best practice* for clients selecting their password (the keyword here being *select*). Answer a is incorrect because randomly generated passwords are not selected by clients, but by software. Answer b is incorrect because that is a system parameter that is set by an administrator. Answer d is a more secure implementation of passwords, simply because of the length of characters, but should not be used on all systems unless risks on those systems have been clearly identified.

Domain Access Control Systems and Methodology

Reference ISO/IEC 17799:2000:E, page 36.[1]

146. Photographic, video, or audio recording equipment should be allowed in secure areas:

    a. Only in specific, highly exceptional circumstances.

    b. Only when accompanied by physical security personnel.

    c. Only for the purpose of company publicity.

    d. Only when the normal staff complement is not present.

Explanation Answer a is the correct answer because the number of times that recording devices are allowed in secure areas should be strictly limited, and the purpose for which they are used should be strictly monitored — to avoid an organization's secure processes being recorded and shown or played for a competitor. Answer b once again may be impractical but, where it is practical, will increase the control. Answer c is incorrect because it is not possible to predict the purpose for which this may be necessary. Answer d is a distracter.

Domain   Physical Security

Reference   ISO/IEC 17799:2000, Section 7.1.4 Working in Secure Areas — E.[44]

147. Vacant secure areas should be:

   a. Locked and periodically checked.
   b. Cleared of all equipment.
   c. Made ready to be used as non-secure areas.
   d. Kept open.

Explanation   Answer a is correct; secure areas that are not being used should be kept locked and should be checked periodically to ensure that no breach of security has taken place. Answers b and c are incorrect because they assume that the secure area is being "decommissioned" and that may not necessarily be true. Answer d is incorrect for the same reason.

Domain   Physical Security

Reference   ISO/IEC 17799:2000, Section 7.1.4 Working in Secure Areas — C.[44]

148. Physical evidence is:

   a. Things such as tools used in the crime.
   b. Evidence presented to the court in the form of business records, manuals, printouts, etc.
   c. Evidence used to aid the jury in the form of a model, experiment, chart, or an illustration offered as proof.
   d. Oral testimony, whereby the knowledge is obtained from any of the witness' five senses.

Explanation   Answer a is the correct answer and is taken verbatim from the cited reference. Answer b is an example of documentary evidence and is incorrect. Answer c is incorrect because it is an example of demonstrative evidence. Answer d is also incorrect because it is an example of direct evidence.

Domain   Law, Investigations, and Ethics

Reference   Tipton and Krause (2000), page 607.[30]

149. The portion of risk that remains due to management decisions, unconsidered factors, or incorrect conclusions is termed:

   a. Loss.
   b. Residual risk.
   c. Insurance.
   d. A threat factor.

Explanation Answer b is the correct answer and can be found in the cited reference. Answer a is what occurs if corrective actions are inadequate, and answer c is a policy one buys to transfer the cost to a third party. Answer d is a factor that can impact an asset.

Domain Security Management Practices

Reference National Security Agency (1997).[61]

150. Within an access control model, the *subject* is:

   a. The entity that performs an action.
   b. The entity that is acted upon.
   c. The user account.
   d. The program.

Explanation Answer a is the correct answer. Answer b is the object. Answer c may be true but subjects are not limited to user entities. Answer d may be true but subjects are not limited to program entities.

Domain Security Architecture and Models

Reference Fites and Kratz (1996), page 152.[46]

151. A secure area might be:

   a. In the basement of the building.
   b. A locked office or offices inside a security perimeter.
   c. Made up of several different buildings in several locations.
   d. Close to neighboring premises.

Explanation Answer b is the correct answer; a secured area can be almost any configuration as long as it all lies within the same security perimeter. Answer a is incorrect because it is inadvisable to place a secure area in an area that is prone to flooding — such as a basement. Answer c is incorrect because it would be difficult-to-impossible to extend the same security perimeter around several buildings in different locations. Answer d is incorrect for much the same reason as answer a — neighboring premises pose the threat of leakage or flooding.

Domain Physical Security

Reference ISO/IEC 17799:2000, Section 7.1.3, Securing Offices, Rooms, and Facilities.[44]

152. Record retention programs are important so that both paper and computer records are maintained to satisfy all but one of the following management requirements.

    a. Legal requirements
    b. Audit requirements
    c. Tax guidelines
    d. ACLU requirements

Explanation Answer d is the correct answer because ACLU requirements play little if any role in records retention. Answers a, b, and c are all management requirements.

Domain Operations Security

Reference Vallabhaneni (2000), page 319.[42]

153. What is the definition of cryptanalysis?

    a. The art or science of secret writing
    b. The practice of defeating attempts to hide information
    c. The study of secret writing and defeating the science of secret writing
    d. The exchange of information securely over a local area network

Explanation Answer b is the correct answer. Answer a is the definition of cryptography. Answer c is incorrect because it is the definition of cryptanalysis. Answer d is incorrect because local area networking is never a restriction on cryptography.

Domain Cryptography

Reference Schneier (1996), page 1.[26]

154. What is the greatest challenge to the security of private key cryptographic systems?

    a. Keeping the key secure
    b. Authenticating the user
    c. Export restrictions
    d. The security of the certificate authority

Explanation Answer a is the correct answer and is taken from the cited reference. Answer b is incorrect because no user authentication is required for symmetric encryption. Answer c is incorrect because export restrictions have been relaxed, and the restriction was based on key length, not if the encryption used a private or public key. Answer d is incorrect because a certificate authority is used in public key encryption, not in private key.

Domain Cryptography

Reference Fites and Kratz (1996), pages 25–26.[20]

155. The two basic principles that underlie most well-constructed software are:

    a. Data hiding and abstraction.
    b. Segmentation and accountability.
    c. Layering and modularity.
    d. Isolation and separation of duties.

Explanation Answer c is the correct answer; layering and modularity are the two basic principles used in developing secure software. Layering refers to constructing processes in layers so that each layer deals with a specific kind of activity; modularity refers to breaking activities into segments that are small enough that individual pieces are easily understood and facilitate testing. Answers a, b, and d are incorrect because each relates to various techniques used in software development, and in the case of separation of duties, to computer operations.

Domain Applications and System Development Security

Reference Fites and Kratz (1996), page 317.[7]

156. What is one advantage to using 3-DES over DES?

    a. 3-DES supports digital signatures and DES does not.
    b. IPSec standards allow the use of 3-DES only.
    c. 3-DES is standards based, and DES is proprietary.
    d. 3-DES is based on a longer encryption key than DES.

Explanation Answer d is correct. Answer a is incorrect because DES supports digital signatures. Answers b and c are incorrect because IPSec specifies that any encryption algorithm can be used, but DES is mentioned by name.

Domain Cryptography

Reference Schneier (1996), page 241.[26]

157. Configuration management is another important component of operations security and is defined as:

    a. Controlling modification to system hardware, firmware, software, and documentation against improper modification.
    b. Security safeguards designed to detect and prevent unauthorized access.
    c. Ensuring availability of critical systems components.
    d. Maintenance of essential DP services after a major outage.

Explanation Answer a is the correct answer. Answers b, c, and d are either two narrow or describe the definitions of another component of the access control environment.

Domain   Operations Security

Reference   Depuis (2001), August 23, 2001, page 3.[32]

158. Direct evidence is:

a. Things such as tools used in the crime.
b. Evidence presented to the court in the form of business records, manuals, printouts, etc.
c. Evidence used to aid the jury in the form of a model, experiment, chart, or an illustration offered as proof.
d. Oral testimony, whereby the knowledge is obtained from any of the witness' five senses.

Explanation   Answer d is the correct answer and is taken verbatim from the cited reference. Answer a is incorrect because it is an example of physical evidence. Answer b is incorrect because it is an example of documentary evidence. Answer c is also incorrect because it is an example of demonstrative evidence.

Domain   Law, Investigations, and Ethics

Reference   Tipton and Krause (2000), page 607.[30]

159. Any action, device, procedure, technique, or other process that reduces the vulnerability of a system or asset to an acceptable level is best identified as a:

a. Safeguard.
b. Precaution.
c. Safety measure.
d. Countermeasure.

Explanation   Answer d is the correct answer and is found in the cited reference. Answer a is another form of countermeasure; answer b is a reason why countermeasures might be installed; and answer c is a combination of answers a and d.

Domain   Security Management Practices

Reference   Fites and Kratz (1996), page 151.[54]

160. Which of the following is *not* one of the Ten Commandments of Computer Ethics published by the Computer Ethics Institute?

a. Thou shalt not use a computer to harm other people.
b. Thou shalt not use a computer to steal.
c. Thou shalt not use a computer to perform a denial-of-service attack.
d. Thou shalt not use use other people's computer resources without authorization or proper compensation.

Explanation Answer c is the correct answer and is taken verbatim from the published Ten Commandments of Computer Ethics published by the Computer Ethics Institute (see reference). The other answers are incorrect because they all appear in the Ten Commandments.

Domain Law, Investigations, and Ethics

Reference Ermann, Williams, and Shauf (1997), page 313.[27]

161. In the system development life cycle, when should security requirements be developed?

a. During the initiation phase
b. At the same time that other requirements for the system are developed
c. During system testing
d. As part of the sensitivity assessment

Explanation Answer b is the correct answer. The identification of security requirements should be integrated into the overall process for identifying system requirements in general. Answer a is incorrect because security requirements are defined during the development/acquisition phase. Answer c is incorrect because system testing occurs after requirements definition, during the implementation phase. Answer d is incorrect because security requirements are developed after the sensitivity assessment is conducted, not as part of the sensitivity assessment.

Domain Applications and System Development Security

Reference National Institute of Standards and Technology (1995), page 80.[9]

162. What is the proper definition of a lattice-based access control environment?

a. A lattice security structure is mathematically based and represents the meaning of security levels within a flow model.
b. A lattice security structure defines access control lists needed for TCSEC compliance.
c. A lattice security model does not change once requirements have been defined.
d. Lattice models support military definitions of clearance and need-to-know processes.

Explanation Answer a is correct. The lattice-based access control model was established in 1976 by Dorothy Denning, and refers to business process flow and identification as opposed to specific access controls. Answer b is incorrect because information flow helps build the access control list and has nothing to do with TCSEC. Answer c is incorrect because security requirements are continually changing, and all models must take that into account. Answer d is nonapplicable in this instance.

Domain   Access Control Systems and Methodology

Reference   Summers (1997), pages 134–137.[4]

163. The formal authorization by a management official for a system to operate and an explicit acceptance of risk is known as:

    a. Certification.
    b. Acceptance.
    c. Quality control statement.
    d. Accreditation.

Explanation   Answer d is the correct answer. Accreditation is the process in which an accrediting management authority formally authorizes a system to operate in a particular environment based on an explicit acceptance of risks. Answer a is incorrect because certification is the process for formally testing the security safeguards implemented in a computer system and is a preliminary step to accreditation. Answer b is incorrect because acceptance is a phase in the system development life cycle. Answer c is a distracter.

Domain   Applications and System Development Security

Reference   National Institute of Standards and Technoloy (1995), page 84.[9]

164. Which of the following is *not* used for sending information securely over the Internet?

    a. SSL
    b. S-HTTP
    c. HTML
    d. SET

Explanation   Answer c is the the correct answer. HTML stands for Hypertext Markup Language and controls how Web pages are formatted and displayed. Answer a is incorrect; SSL (Secure Socket Layer) is a protocol developed by Netscape for transmitting private documents via the Internet. Answer b is incorrect; S-HTTP (Secure Hypertext Transfer Protocol) creates a secure connection between a client and a server. Answer d is incorrect; Secure Electronic Transaction (SET) was designed to provide a complete system for secure electronic transactions.

Domain   Telecommunications and Network Security

Reference   Tipton and Krause (2000), Vol. 2, page 77.[73]

165. The characteristic of a resource or an asset that implies its value or importance, and may include its vulnerability, is known as:

a. Public data.
b. Sensitivity.
c. Internal use.
d. A threat.

Explanation   Answer b is the correct answer and can be found in the cited reference. Answers a and c are levels usually found in an information classification system. Answer d is an element in a risk analysis process.

Domain   Security Management Practices

Reference   Fites and Kratz (1996), page 52.[59]

166. Which of the following is *not* a communication threat?

a. Masquerade
b. Playback
c. Repudiation
d. Proxy

Explanation   Answer d is the correct answer; a proxy is a type of firewall and helps provide secure communications. Answer a is incorrect and occurs when an imposter pretends to be an authorized user. Answer b is incorrect and occurs when someone records a legitimate message and later sends it again (a funds transfer). Answer c is incorrect; someone may deny that they ever received a message, although they did receive it.

Domain   Telecommunications and Network Security

Reference   Russell and Gangemi (1991), page 204.[71]

167. What makes up a security association?

a. The security parameter index and the source address
b. The security parameter index and the MD5 hash
c. The MD5 hash and the source address
d. The security parameter index and the destination address

Explanation   Answer d is the correct answer. Answer a is incorrect because the source address is not included in the security association. Answers b and c are incorrect because they both contain the MD5 hash.

Domain   Cryptography

Reference   Atkinson (1995).[19]

168. The primary purpose of the Business Impact Analysis is to:

  a. Create management awareness and support.
  b. Satisfy audit requirements.
  c. Identify and prioritize time-critical business processes and recovery-time objectives.
  d. Provide a route map for resources that support business functions.

Explanation Answer c is the correct answer and is taken from the cited reference. Answer a is incorrect because it is only one narrow definition of what the BIA should accomplish. Answer b is incorrect because the BIA should have nothing to do with satisfying audit criticisms. Answer d is incorrect because it only focuses on one narrow definition of what the BIA should accomplish.

Domain Business Continuity Planning and Disaster Recovery Planning

Reference Tipton and Krause (2000), Vol. 2, page 502.[17]

169. In public key cryptography, which key does the sender use to encrypt the data?

  a. Sender's public key
  b. Sender's private key
  c. Recipient's public key
  d. Recipient's private key

Explanation Answer c is correct, since the sender needs to have the recipient's public key to send an encrypted message to him. Answer a is incorrect because the sender's public key would be used when others want to encrypt a message to the sender. Answer b is incorrect because the sender's private key generates the public key but does not encrypt messages. Answer d is incorrect because it is the key used to decrypt the data.

Domain Cryptography

Reference Fites and Kratz (1996), page 43.[20]

170. The security of a system should also be documented and would typically include all but one of the following. Which is *not* included?

  a. IT facilities telephone books
  b. Security plans
  c. Risk analysis
  d. Security policies and procedures

Explanation Answer a is the correct answer, taken from the cited reference. Answers b, c, and d would typically be included while answer a has nothing to do with operations security.

Domain   Operations Security

Reference   Vallabhaneni (2000), page 319.[42]

171. What is the most commonly employed network protocol for remote access systems?

  a. DECNet
  b. SNA
  c. IPX/NetBIOS
  d. TCP/IP

Explanation   Answer d is the correct answer. Most corporations either use TCP/IP as their network protocol or allow their traffic to be encapsulated over TCP/IP networks. Answers a, b, and c are older protocols that are not widely supported.

Domain   Telecommunications and Network Security

Reference   Tipton and Krause (2000), Vol. 2, page 104.[73]

172. The formal testing of the security safeguards implemented in a computer system to determine whether they meet applicable requirements and specifications is known as:

  a. Certification.
  b. Accreditation.
  c. Security testing.
  d. Acceptance.

Explanation   Answer a is the correct answer. Certification is the process for producing a statement that specifies the extent to which security measures meet specifications. Answer b is incorrect because accreditation is the process in which an accrediting management authority formally authorizes a system to operate in a particular environment based on an explicit acceptance of risks. Although generically correct, answer c is not correct here because it is less precise than answer a. Answer d is incorrect because acceptance is a phase in the system development life cycle.

Domain   Applications and System Development Security

Reference   National Institute of Standards and Technology (1995), page 84.[9]

173. A security perimeter is:

  a. Always manned by a security guard.
  b. Something that builds a barrier.

c. A wall with a locked door.
d. A necessary part of a data center.

Explanation   Answer b is the correct answer according to the cited reference. Answer a is incorrect because the controlled openings in a security perimeter can be under electronic control. Answer c is not correct because there are many different means of crossing a security perimeter — including a gate with a security guard; and answer d is inaccurate because data centers do not always have security perimeters and security perimeters are not limited only to data centers.

Domain   Physical Security

Reference   ISO/IEC 17799:2000, Section 7.1, Secure Areas, page 33.[44]

174.   Which of the following represents a Star Property in the Bell–LaPadula model?

   a. Subject cannot read upward to an object of higher secrecy classification.
   b. Subject cannot write upward to an object of higher secrecy classification.
   c. Subject cannot write downward to an object of lower secrecy classification.
   d. Subject cannot read or write upward or downwards to an object outside of their own secrecy classification.

Explanation   Answer a would represent a *Simple Security Property*. Answer b would represent a *Strong Star Property*. Answer c is correct — "No Write Down." Answer d would represent a *Strong Star Property*.

Domain   Security Architecture and Models

Reference   Fites and Kratz (1996), page 411.

175.   Third-party access to secure areas should be:

   a. Restricted and granted only when required.
   b. Denied.
   c. Granted on the same basis as other employees.
   d. Granted only with a physical escort.

Explanation   Answer a is correct. Third-party personnel — unlike regular employees — need to be authorized each time they require access to secure areas, as failure to do so leads to lax security controls and can allow for misuse of the access. Answer b is incorrect because third-party personnel (such as cleaning staff) will need access to the area. Answer c is not correct because third-party personnel do not need access on the same basis as other employees. Answer d is incorrect because it is often impractical — but where it is practical, it can be a useful additional control.

Domain   Physical Security

Reference   ISO/IEC 17799:2000, Section 7.1.4, Working in Secure Areas.[44]

176. Which is the *most* secure type of modem?

    a. Dial-back modems
    b. Password modems
    c. Encryption modems
    d. Silent modems

Explanation   Answer c is the correct answer. All information sent via the modem is encrypted when sent and decrypted at reception; encryption modems protect against wire tapping and unauthorized users. Answer a is incorrect; dial-back modems can be defeated by call-forwarding. Answer b is incorrect; password modems rely on the strength of the password, which is often weak. Answer c is incorrect; silent modems will not signal that the connection has been made until you begin the log-on session, and do not secure the data.

Domain   Telecommunications and Network Security

Reference   Russell and Gangemi (1991), page 206.[71]

177. U.S. criminal conduct is broken down into two classifications, depending upon severity. They are:

    a. First offence and repeat offence.
    b. Juvenile and adult.
    c. Tort and felony.
    d. Felony and misdemeanor.

Explanation   Answer d is the correct answer and is taken verbatim from the cited reference. The other answers are incorrect because they are not classifications of criminal conduct, but rather general terminology used within criminal cases; a tort is another name for civil law.

Domain   Law, Investigations, and Ethics

Reference   Tipton and Krause (2000), page 603.[30]

178. A sniffer attack has which of the following characteristics?

    a. It uses hardware called a sniffer to intercept packets being transferred in a telecommunications session.
    b. It uses pen test capabilities to access a system and then gather passwords for continued access.

c. It uses a technique called tunneling to get under a certain safeguard within a system.
d. It uses transportation procedures to convert information within an application.

Explanation   Answer b is correct. Vulnerabilities are exploited from the outside into a network by a sniffer attack. Answer a is incorrect, although a sniffer is a commonly used tool for network diagnostics. Answer c is incorrect because tunneling is another form of intrusion technique. Answer d is incorrect because the term "transportation procedures" pertains to a process within a specific integrity model (Clark–Wilson).

Domain   Access Control Systems and Methodology

Reference   Summers (1997), pages 84–85.[4]

179. The closest definition of the *principle of least privilege* is:

a. People should perform job roles based on clearly written job descriptions.
b. People should know how to execute all functions in an application or department.
c. People should be authorized only to the resources they need to do their jobs.
d. People performing increasingly more responsible job functions should have increased system access rights.

Explanation   Answer c is correct. Keeping access restricted to a minimum results in less opportunity for misuse (accidental or intentional), but also assists with access rights administration. Answer a is incorrect because job roles do not necessarily constitute access rights. Answer b is incorrect because it refers to nonadherence of the separation of duty principle. Answer d is incorrect because job or grade advancement does not necessarily mean additional access rights to systems or applications.

Domain   Access Control Systems and Methodology

Reference   Summers (1997), pages 583–584.[4]

180. Salami attacks are effective because:

a. The amount of funds diverted is so small that it is not easily noticed.
b. The number of affected transactions is so limited that they are not noticeable.
c. They involve electronic funds transfers.
d. They are committed by individuals with detailed knowledge of the system.

Explanation   Answer a is the correct answer. In a salami attack, small amounts of money are shaved from each computation through rounding or truncation, and the amount shaved is so small that it may fall within the acceptable range.

Domain   Applications and System Development Security

Reference   Pfleeger (1996), page 211.[10]

181.   General non-mandatory recommendations designed to achieve the policy objectives by providing a framework within which to implement procedures are known as:

   a. Guidelines.
   b. Policies.
   c. Laws.
   d. Procedures.

Explanation   The correct answer is a and can be found in the cited reference. Answer b is the management statement of direction. Answer c is what generally starts the cycle of policy, standard, and guideline development. Answer d is the mandatory step-by-step process to complete a task.

Domain   Security Management Practices

Reference   Peltier (2001a), Section 3.4.1.[64]

182.   Which of the following telecommunications media is *most* resistant to tapping?

   a. Microwave
   b. Twisted pair
   c. Fiber optic
   d. Coaxial cable

Explanation   Answer c is the correct answer. Because signals in fiber-optic cabling are in the form of laser light pulses, electromagnetic emissions that might be used to tap the line are essentially nonexistent. Answer a is incorrect; you only have to have access to the path of the microwave to intercept it. Answer b is incorrect; you only have to lop a wire around the twisted pair to pick up emissions. Answer d is incorrect; coaxial cable is more secure than either microwave or twisted pair media, but can be tapped with inexpensive equipment.

Domain   Telecommunications and Network Security

Reference   Fites and Kratz (1996), page 193.[70]

183. Something of value or what security professionals are trying to protect. This can include data, information, personnel, facilities, applications, hardware, software, or transmission devices. This item of value is known in information security as:

   a. A asset.
   b. A program.
   c. A code.
   d. Top secret.

Explanation Answer a is correct, and can be found in the cited reference. Answer b is a type of asset, as is answer c. Answer d is a classification level for information.

Domain Security Management Practices

Reference Peltier (2001b), page 250.[65]

184. In a policy on employee responsibilities for handling organization information, this individual — the creator of the information or the primary user of the information — is classified as the:

   a. Custodian.
   b. Steward.
   c. User.
   d. Owner.

Explanation Answer d is the correct answer and is found in the cited reference. Answers a and b refer to the individual or entity charged with keeping and protecting the information based on the requirements identified by the owner. Answer c is the party granted the right to use the information.

Domain Security Management Practices

Reference Fites and Kratz (1996), pages 183–184.[54]

185. Access rights to secure areas should be:

   a. Given only to the people who work there.
   b. Given by the manager of the area.
   c. Reviewed regularly and updated regularly.
   d. Given to emergency services personnel.

Explanation Answer c is correct. Like any other access right, access to a secure area needs to be maintained and can only be done so through regular reviews and updates. Answer a is incorrect because other staff — who do not work in the secured area — and visitors have valid reasons for entering the area (such as troubleshooting problems or collecting sensitive material from the secured area). Answer b is not correct because a higher authority might retain the right to grant access or the manager of the area may delegate that authority to someone in his or her organization. Answer d is incorrect because emergency services personnel will be given access on an exception basis and not granted regular access rights.

Domain   Physical Security

Reference   ISO/IEC 17799:2000, Section 7.1.2, Physical Security Controls.[44]

186. Business Continuity Plans must focus primarily on:

   a. Recovery of all business functionality.
   b. Recovery of telecommunications circuits.
   c. Recovery of time-critical business processes and supporting resources.
   d. Recovery of IT department off-site data files.

Explanation   Answer c is the correct answer and is taken from the cited reference. The other answers are incorrect because they are each too narrow. Answer a is incorrect because it defines business continuity plans as recovering too wide a scope of business functions. Answers c and d are incorrect because they focus on IT (DRP) recovery planning specifics.

Domain   Business Continuity Planning and Disaster Recovery Planning

Reference   Tipton and Krause (2000), Vol. 2, page 502;[17] Tipton and Krause, chapter 26, starting on page 563.

187. Bulk supplies, such as stationery, should:

   a. Be stored in a cool, dark, dry space.
   b. Be delivered only to designated bulk-handling facilities.
   c. Be stored somewhere other than a secure facility.
   d. Be examined regularly for wastage.

Explanation   Answer c is correct; bulk supplies are space-consuming and often constitute hazardous material, and thus should be stored at a separate site. Answer a is a materials-handling preference, not a physical security one. Answer b is also a materials-handling preference, while answer c is about materials management.

Domain   Physical Security

Reference   ISO/IEC 17799:2000, Section 7.1.3, Security Offices, Rooms and Facilities.[44]

188. Visitors to a restricted area should be:

a. Supervised.
b. Granted access for only a specific date and time.
c. Issued instructions on security procedures.
d. All of the above.

Explanation   Answer d is the correct answer. Visitors should be supervised or escorted at all times while in a secure area. Their access should be restricted to only the day(s) and time(s) necessary to complete the business of their visit, and they should be made aware of prevailing security procedures so that they do not inadvertently break them.

Domain   Physical Security

Reference   ISO/IEC 17799:2000, Section 7.1.2, Physical Security Controls.[44]

189. Layer 4 of the OSI (Open System Integration) stack is known as:

a. The data-link layer.
b. The transport layer.
c. The network layer.
d. The presentation layer.

Explanation   Answer b is the correct answer, per the OSI Model.

Domain   Telecommunications and Network Security

Reference   Russell and Gangemi (1991), page 215.[71]

190. What is the most widely used standard for digital certificates?

a. X.17799
b. X.509
c. POP3
d. X.25

Explanation   Answer b is the correct answer. X.509 is an ITU recommendation, which means it has not yet been defined or approved and may be implemented in different ways. Answer a is incorrect; there is no standard X.17799. Answer c is incorrect; POP3 stands for Post Office Protocol version 3. Answer d is incorrect; X.25 is CCITT's (Comité Consultatif Internationale Telegraphique et Telephonique) protocol for packet-switching networks.

Domain   Telecommunications and Network Security

Reference   Tipton and Krause (2000), Vol. 2, page 76.[73]

191. Which of the following *best* describes the principle of hardware segmentation as it relates to systems architecture?

    a. Machines are stored in different physical locations.
    b. Disks are split into multiple logical drive letters.
    c. Virtual memory is divided into segments.
    d. Computers are given unique IP addresses.

Explanation Answer c is the correct answer because user processes cannot access segments restricted to system use. Answers a, b, and d are not relevant to operating systems architecture.

Domain Security Architecture and Models

Reference Fites and Kratz (1996), page 169.[46]

192. A Vital Records program is an essential prerequisite to a well-rounded BCP/DRP process implementation. All but one of the following should be considered for an effective Vital Records program. Which one should *not* be considered?

    a. Assignment of responsibility for identifying and backing up critical information
    b. Maintenance of current inventories of information needed to recreate data
    c. Storing critical data/information at an off-site backup location an appropriate distance from the primary site
    d. Ensuring that all employees store critical vital records necessary for the execution of their job function at an off-site location such as their residence or in the trunk of their car

Explanation Answer d is obviously the correct answer; under no circumstances should critical information be stored at a residence or in a private automobile as a matter of policy or practice of the enterprise. Answers a, b, and c are all part of a Vital Records program.

Domain Business Continuity Planning and Disaster Recovery Planning

Reference Hutt, Bosworth, and Hoyt (1995), page 7-8.[15]

193. The employee, department, or third-party entity entrusted with ensuring that information assets or resources are appropriately maintained, secured, processed, archived, and available as directed by the owner is:

    a. The custodian.
    b. The user.
    c. Management.
    d. The ISSO.

Explanation   Answer a is correct and is found in the cited reference. Answer b is the entity authorized by the owner to user the resource as approved. Answer c is the group required to have policies and to support them. Answer d is the group or individual (Information Systems Security Officer) charged with creating a security architecture to support the business objectives.

Domain   Security Management Practices

Reference   Fites and Kratz (1996), page 423.[54]

194.   Mandatory activities, actions, rules, or regulations designed to provide policies with the support structure and specific direction are:

   a. Guidelines.
   b. Processes.
   c. Practices.
   d. Standards.

Explanation   Answer d is the correct answer and is taken verbatim from the cited reference. Answer a is incorrect because guidelines are not mandatory. Answers b and c are spell out specific steps that must be taken to complete a process.

Domain   Security Management Practices

Reference   Fites and Kratz (1996), page 49.[54]

195.   Which of the following is covered by U.S. Title 18 of the U.S. Code, Section 1030, also known as the Computer Fraud and Abuse Act?

   a. Obtaining free telephone service by fraud
   b. Disrupting computer services
   c. Monitoring employee communications
   d. Trafficking in passwords

Explanation   Answer d is the correct answer and is taken verbatim from the cited reference. Answers a and b are covered by various state and local laws and are incorrect. Answer c is covered by the Electronic Communications Privacy Act and is also incorrect.

Domain   Law, Investigations, and Ethics

Reference   Stephenson (2000), page 239.[29]

196.   Information hiding is a design principle whereby:

   a. The program module operates as if surrounded by a shield.
   b. A program module is isolated from the negative effects of other modules.

c. How a program module does its task is concealed.
d. The data processed by a program module is concealed.

Explanation   Answer c is the correct answer. Data hiding is a method used to conceal the manner in which a program module does its task. Answers a and b are incorrect because they describe encapsulation. Answer d is incorrect because information hiding does not result in the concealment of data input or output from the module.

Domain   Applications and Systems Development Security

Reference   Pfleeger (1996), page 211.[10]

197.   Authentication protocols can combine certain elements that can be effective against "man-in-the-middle" attacks. What is the definition of such an attack?

a. Active sniffers are used to inspect packets being transmitted from one system to another.
b. Active spoofing is used to masquerade an intruder's whereabouts on a system.
c. Active session hijacking moves the destination of one session to another location.
d. Active attackers intercede in protocol exchange that modifies data moving in both directions.

Explanation   Answer d is the correct answer. The concept that there is active modification of data in lateral directions is key. Answer a refers to the use of physical devices used to inspect data transfer. Answer b is relevant to another form of attack method. Answer c is incorrect because the definition is inaccurate and pertains to another form of attack.

Domain   Access Control Systems and Methodology

Reference   Ford and Baum (1997), pages 129–130.[2]

198.   The security of the physical security perimeter is:

a. Consistent with the value of the assets being protected.
b. The outer doors to the building.
c. Constantly monitored.
d. The responsibility of information security.

Explanation   Answer a is the correct answer and is taken from the cited reference. Answer b is incorrect because the perimeter can be internal to the building. Answer c is also incorrect because the perimeter can be "spot monitored" (i.e., not constant but periodic); and answer d is incorrect because the responsibility for perimeter security can be assigned to other functions.

Domain   Physical Security

Reference   ISO/IEC 17799:2000, page 33.[44]

199. There are several types of detection methods for finding viruses. The most common is the:

a. Heuristic scanner.
b. Pattern scanner.
c. Integrity checker.
d. Behavior blocker.

Explanation   Answer b is the correct answer and is taken verbatim from the cited reference. Pattern scanners work based on the *dissection* of the virus, isolation of a string of code thought to be unique to the virus, and comparison of the suspected virus with a database of those known signatures. Answer a, heuristic scanner, is incorrect because it does a behavior-based analysis. Such scanners often cause false alarms. Answer c, integrity checker, produces a database of signatures of files on a PC that represent the files in the uninfected state. Answer d, behavior blocker, looks for combinations of disallowed events to occur, stops program execution, and warns the user.

Domain   Law, Investigations, and Ethics

Reference   Stephenson (2000), page 35.[29]

200. To update anti-virus software the quickest, which location is best to update first?

a. Mail server (Notes, Exchange)
b. Network server
c. PC
d. Internet gateway virus server

Explanation   Answer d is the correct answer. With most viruses being spread via the Internet or e-mail, the best location to update anti-virus software first is at the Internet gateway virus server. One update will stop any new viruses from entering the network. Answers a, b, and c, all may/will require multiple updates, which will allow the virus to spread while the machines are being updated.

Domain   Telecommunications and Network Security

Reference   Scambray, McClure, and Kurtz (2001), page 651.[72]

201. What is the definition of cryptology?

    a. The art or science of secret writing
    b. The practice of defeating attempts to hide information
    c. The study of secret writing and defeating the science of secret writing
    d. The exchange of information securely over a local area network

Explanation Answer c is the correct answer. Answer a is incorrect because it is the definition of cryptography. Answer b is incorrect because it is the definition of cryptanalysis. Answer d is incorrect because a local area network is not necessary for crypto-anything.

Domain Cryptography

Reference Schneier (1996), page 1.[26]

202. Mandatory access control is related to which of the following?

    a. Permanent and irreversible access rules defined within an operating system
    b. Controls defined by the security administrator, or within his or her policy, that are classified as mandatory
    c. Control capability defined within an operating system that the security administrator, or his or her policy may opt to utilize
    d. Controls enforced by the reference monitor

Explanation Answer a is correct; controls are built in and cannot be overridden. Answer b is incorrect because mandatory controls must be hard-coded into the operating system, not defined by user policy. Answer c is discretionary access control. Answer d is incorrect because both discretionary and mandatory access controls are enforced within a system by the reference monitor.

Domain Security Architecture and Models

Reference Fites and Kratz (1996), page 155.[46]

203. Every program or system component must operate with the minimum set of privileges it needs to accomplish its task. This is the definition of:

    a. Least privilege.
    b. Open design.
    c. Separation of privilege.
    d. Economy of mechanism.

Explanation Answer a is the correct answer and is taken from the cited reference. Answer b is defined as: the design itself should not be a secret, and an open design can be reviewed by many experts and potential users, so deficiencies are more likely to be found and corrected.

Passwords and encryption keys must be kept secret, but not designs. Answer c is defined as: two or more keys are needed to unlock a protection mechanism or if two independent mechanisms must agree before an action is allowed. Answer d is defined as: keeping the design as simple and small as possible.

Domain   Operations Security

Reference   Summers (1997), chapter 6.[37]

204.   Understanding the breadth and scope of enterprise insurance coverage relative to potential recovery of losses sustained as the result of a disaster is an important component of the BCP/DRP equation. All but one of the following types of insurance coverage are relevant to BCP/DRP planning. Which one is *not* relevant?

   a. Business interruption
   b. Media reconstruction
   c. Medical
   d. Extra-expense

Explanation   Answer c is the correct answer; medical insurance coverage is really of no concern to the BCP/DRP program. The others types of insurance coverage are and should be understood.

Domain   Business Continuity Planning and Disaster Recovery Planning

Reference   Hutt, Bosworth, and Hoyt (1995), page 8-2.[15]

205.   "Processes have no more privilege than is required to perform authorized functions" is a definition of which system architecture principle?

   a. Enforcement of greatest access
   b. Execution of lowest rights
   c. Implementation of highest privilege
   d. Enforcement of least privilege

Explanation   Answers a and c are the opposite of the correct answer. Answer b is the correct principle but using the incorrect terminology. Answer d is the correct principle using the documented terminology.

Domain   Security Architecture and Models

Reference   Fites and Kratz (1996), page 156.[46]

206.   One major difference between the ITSEC and TCSEC is that the ITSEC:

   a. Does not address networking.
   b. Includes availability and integrity as security goals.

c. Provides for bundled ratings for functionality and assurance.
d. Addresses only commercial requirements.

Explanation Answer b is the correct answer. The ITSEC establishes integrity and availability as security goals, along with confidentiality. Answer a is incorrect because the ITSEC does address network security requirements. Answer c is incorrect because ITSEC provides for separate ratings for functionality and assurance, unlike the TCSEC. Answer d is incorrect in that the ITSEC addresses both commercial and government requirements.

Domain Security Architecture and Models

Reference Summers (1997), pages 262–264.[49]

207. Behavior that is unexpected is referred to as an anomaly. An example of an anomaly detection system would be:

a. Using statistical profiles to measure behavior.
b. Using misuse signatures to measure activity.
c. Using checksums to measure quantity.
d. Using probes to measure traffic.

Explanation Answer a is correct. Statistical profiles will determine if clients are accessing resources at the proper time, in the correct volume, and with predictable frequency. Answer b is applicable to misuse detection systems, another type of IDS configuration. Answers c and d are IDS terms interchanged and irrelevant to the question.

Domain Access Control Systems and Methodology

Reference Tipton and Krause (2000), page 686.[5]

208. Which of the following ITSEC functionality and assurance class ratings corresponds most closely to a C2 rating under TCSEC criteria?

a. F-B3, E6
b. F-B3, E5
c. F-C2, E2
d. F-C1, E1

Explanation Answer a: the E assurance level is not relevant, so FB-3 roughly equates to B3. Answer b: the E assurance level is not relevant, so FB-3 roughly equates to B3. Answer c is correct. Answer d: the E assurance level is not relevant, so FC1 roughly equates to C1.

Domain Security Architecture and Models

Reference Fites and Kratz (1996), page 166.[46]

209. The information flow model is also known as:

a. The non-interference model.
b. The lattice-based access control model.
c. The risk-acceptance model.
d. The discrete model.

Explanation   Answer b is correct. The lattice-based access control model was established in 1976 by Dorothy Denning, and refers to business process flow and identification as opposed to specific access controls. Answer a is incorrect because it is an alternative model. Answers c and d are intentionally misleading answers and have no relevance.

Domain   Access Control Systems and Methodology

Reference   Summers (1997), pages 134–139.[4]

210. The process applied when transactions fail to complete after making some updates to an online file is known as a:

a. Checkpoint.
b. Recovery.
c. Restart.
d. Back-out.

Explanation   Answer d is the correct answer. Back-out is the process that uses a transaction log file to correct the results of incomplete updates when transactions fail to complete after making some updates to an online file. Answer a is incorrect because a checkpoint is the process for writing a program's results to secondary storage to minimize the risk of work loss. Answer b is incorrect because recovery is the process for reconstituting a database following a processing error or failure. Answer c is incorrect because a restart is the resumption of program execution using data recorded at a checkpoint.

Domain   Applications and System Development Security

Reference   Hutt, Bosworth, and Hoyt (1995), page 14-13.[8]

211. Before evidence can be presented in a U.S. case, it must be competent, relevant, and material to the issue, and it must be:

a. Presented in compliance with the rules of evidence.
b. Returned to the owner following case closure.
c. Reliable.
d. Relevant.

Explanation   Answer a is the correct answer and is taken verbatim from the cited reference. The other answers are incorrect. Answer b is incorrect because evidence does not necessarily have to be returned to the owner; it depends on the situation. Answer c is not correct because reliability is not a specifically stated requirement for evidence within U.S. cases; again, it depends on the case and the quality or availability of other evidence. Answer d is a restatement of a requirement from the question.

Domain   Law, Investigations, and Ethics

Reference   Tipton and Krause (2000), page 607.[30]

212.   Which of the following represents a *Simple Security Property* in the Bell–LaPadula model?

   a. Subject cannot read upward to an object of higher secrecy classification.
   b. Subject cannot read downward to an object of lower secrecy classification.
   c. Subject cannot write upward to an object of higher secrecy classification.
   d. Subject cannot write downward to an object of lower secrecy classification.

Explanation   Answer a is correct — "No Read Up." Answer b would represent a *Strong Star Property*. Answer c would represent a *Strong Star Property*. Answer d would represent a *Star Property*.

Domain   Security Architecture and Models

Reference   Fites and Kratz (1996), page 411.[46]

213.   The goal of the System Security Engineering Capability Maturity Model (SSE CMM) is to lead to the development of software that performs computing tasks as well as:

   a. Follows a structured system development life cycle.
   b. Employs modularity and encapsulation.
   c. Meets ISO 9000 standards.
   d. Enforces security requirements.

Explanation   Answer d is the correct answer. The purpose of the SSE CMM is to provide a structure for developing software that not only performs computing tasks it is designed to do, but also enforces security specifications while doing so. Answer a is incorrect because the SSE CMM does not prescribe a system development life cycle. Answer b is incorrect because it does not specifically require the use of modularity and encapsulation. Answer c is incorrect because ISO 9000 standards are not a part of the SSE CMM.

Domain   Applications and System Development Security

Reference   Pfleeger (1996), page 218.[10]

214.   There are four types of computer-generated evidence. They are visual output on the monitor, film recorder (includes magnetic representation on disk, tape, or cartridge, and optical representation on CD), printed evidence on a plotter, and:

a. Voice mail messages.
b. Scanned images.
c. Generated business files.
d. Printed evidence on a printer.

Explanation   Answer d is the correct answer and is taken verbatim from the cited reference. The other answers are incorrect because they are not necessarily generated by computers. Answer a is considered real evidence; answer b is considered physical evidence; and answer c is considered documentary evidence.

Domain   Law, Investigations, and Ethics

Reference   Tipton and Krause (2000), page 608.[30]

215.   Which algorithms does PGP support?

a. DES and El Gamal
b. IDEA and DES
c. DES and PPTP
d. PPTP and IDEA

Explanation   Answer b is correct. Answers c and d are incorrect because PPTP is an older version of encryption developed by Microsoft. Answer a is incorrect because PGP does not support El Gamal.

Domain   Cryptography

Reference   Schneier (1996), page 436.[26]

216.   The benefit of regularly testing business continuity plans and disaster recovery plans include all but one of the following. Which one is *not* included?

a. To ascertain the level of discomfort recovery team members will sustain without complaint
b. To assess whether the written plans are accurate and up-to-date
c. To train recovery planning personnel in their roles and responsibilities
d. To satisfy audit criticisms or to ensure compliance with applicable laws or regulations

Explanation Answer a is the *most* correct answer; this obviously should not be a goal of testing, although it sometimes does occur. The other answers are benefits of testing recovery plans.

Domain Business Continuity Planning and Disaster Recovery Planning

References Devlin and Emerson (1999), chapter I-8 page I-8-1;[13] Hutt, Bosworth and Hoyt (1995), page 7-31.[15]

217. To best protect the network from viruses, where should anti-virus software be placed?

    a. On the firewall
    b. On the PC
    c. On the router
    d. On the server

Explanation Answer d is the correct answer. Server anti-virus software will detect and eradicate viruses at the network level. Answer a is incorrect. Anti-virus software should never be placed on the firewall; it slows down the firewall. Answer b is incorrect; anti-virus software on the PC will detect and eradicate viruses on the PC, but not the network. Answer c is incorrect because there is no anti-virus software developed for routers.

Domain Telecommunications and Network Security

Reference Scambray, McClure, and Kurtz (2001), page 650.[72]

218. The following statement describes what information security tenet? For management to be able to rely on information that is as intended and is not contaminated or corrupted by malicious acts, uncorrected error conditions, or other failures.

    a. Accountability
    b. Authenticity
    c. Access control
    d. Integrity

Explanation Answer d is the correct answer and can be found in the cited reference. Answer a is part of the audit process; answer b is the process to ensure system users are who they claim to be; and answer c is a process to allow authorized users to access information, transactions, or other system functions.

Domain Security Management Practices

Reference International Information Security Foundation (1997), Section 2.2.7, page 26.[57]

219. Protecting the integrity of programs and documentation is the main security motivation for using:

a. Configuration management.
b. Separation of duties.
c. Modular programming.
d. System development controls.

Explanation Answer a is the correct answer because configuration management is concerned with applying controls to maintain software and documentation integrity. Answers b and c are incorrect because separation of duties and modular programming do not fully address program/documentation integrity. Answer d is incorrect because the main security motivation for using system development controls is much broader than maintaining the integrity of programs and documentation.

Domain Applications and System Development Security

Reference Pfleeger (1996), page 212.[10]

220. In public key cryptography, which key does the recipient use to decrypt the data?

a. Sender's public key
b. Sender's private key
c. Recipient's public key
d. Recipient's private key

Explanation Answer d is correct. Answer a is incorrect because it is the key used to encrypt the data. Answer b is incorrect because it will generate the sender's public key, which is used to encrypt the data. Answer c is incorrect because it is the key used when the recipient sends an encrypted message.

Domain Cryptography

Reference Fites and Kratz (1996), page 43.[20]

221. All vehicles entering or leaving a restricted area should be:

a. Stopped.
b. Clearly marked as to their reason for being there.
c. Accompanied by a security person.
d. Subject to search.

Explanation As a condition of entry, all vehicles — upon entry or exit — should be subject to search; thus answer d is the correct one. Answer a is incorrect because many vehicles routinely and frequently visit restricted areas and are allowed through without stopping if they display appropriate credentials (however, the owner of the restricted area retains the right to demand that they stop and be searched —

randomly). Answer b is incorrect because displaying the reason for the visit on a vehicle is costly, time-consuming, and unnecessary. Similarly, it is highly impractical for all vehicles to be accompanied by a security person and therefore answer c is also incorrect.

Domain Physical Security

Reference Carroll (1996).[43]

222. Another component of operations security is the logging of media for inventory purposes. The information contained in media logs includes all but one of the following. Whcih one is *not* included?

a. Control or tracking numbers
b. Times and dates of transfers
c. Names and signatures of the individuals involved
d. Number of bytes of information contained on the media

Explanation Answer d is the *most* correct answer. The other answers are the types of information one would expect to see on the log.

Domain Operations Security

Reference National Institute of Standards and Technology (1995) chapter 14, page 161 (Logging).[34]

223. The Business Impact Analysis is also used as the primary input into the next phase of the BCP/DRP development methodology, which is:

a. Identifying recovery team members.
b. Developing testing and maintenance objectives.
c. Document recovery plans.
d. Determining appropriate recovery strategies and resource needs.

Explanation Answer d is the correct answer and is taken from the cited reference. Answer a is incorrect because this activity takes place as part of the plan development phase. Answers b and c are incorrect because they are part of the development methodology to be addressed following this phase.

Domain Business Continuity Planning and Disaster Recovery Planning

Reference Tipton and Krause (2000), Vol. 2, page 519.[17]

224. For BCP purposes, when determining business operations recovery strategies, all but one of the following should be considered. Which one should *not* be considered?

a. Distance to the backup facility
b. Time-critical business processes to be recovered

c. Recovery team members roles and responsibilities
d. Insurance coverage for replacement of the primary site equipment

Explanation   Answer d is the *best* answer because insurance coverage considerations should be postponed until after life safety issues and critical business operations have been recovered. Answers a, b, and c are all considerations when determining appropriate recovery strategies.

Domain   Business Continuity Planning and Disaster Recovery Planning

Reference   Vallabhaneni (2000), page 343.[18]

225.   Computer operators should be able to:

a. Authorize users to access the system.
b. Set the time and date on the system.
c. Maintain and manage the audit log files.
d. Run tools to format, compress, and analyze data.

Explanation   Answer b is the correct answer and is taken from the cited reference. Answer a is the role of a security administrator; and answers c and d are the roles of an auditor.

Domain   Operations Security

Reference   Summers (1997), chapter 8.[37]

226.   A classic form of risk analysis was presented to the information security profession when it was included in the FIPS PUB 65 in 1979. This process requires the use of the formula of *Loss = Impact × Frequency of Occurrence.* The results will give the user:

a. A threat analysis.
b. A quantitative risk analysis.
c. The annual loss exposure.
d. The frequency of threat.

Explanation   Answer c is correct and is found in the cited reference. Answer a is another form of risk analysis created by FEMA. Answer b is one of the two major classifications of risk analysis, and answer d is an element in ALE.

Domain   Security Management Practices

Reference   Tipton and Krause (2000), pages 91–94.[67]

227.   *Secondary storage,* as it relates to systems architecture, is.

a. Memory directly accessible to the CPU.
b. Extending the apparent size of RAM by using part of the hard disk.

c. A storage location in memory with direct access to peripherals.

d. A nonvolatile medium to store data even after power-off.

Explanation   Answer a is *primary storage*. Answer b is *virtual storage*. Answer c is *real storage*. Answer d is correct (e.g., a disk drive).

Domain   Security Architecture and Models

Reference   Fites and Kratz (1996), page 147.[54]

228. The technique in which an operating system strictly limits what system resources a program can access is known as:

a. Segmentation.

b. Segregation.

c. Confinement.

d. Isolation.

Explanation   Answer c is the correct answer. Confinement is the technique that is used to strictly limit what system resources an untrusted program can use. Answers a, b, and d are terms that express similar security concepts but are incorrect because they are not a function of an operating system.

Domain   Applications and System Development Security

Reference   Pfleeger (1996), page 222.[10]

229. The process of identifying, controlling, and minimizing or eliminating security risks that may affect information systems, for an acceptable cost, is known as:

a. A vulnerability assessment.

b. Risk management.

c. An information security policy.

d. A safeguard review.

Explanation   Answer b is the correct answer and is taken from the cited reference. Answers a and c are similar in that both address the process of reviewing controls after they have been implemented. Answer d relates to assessment of controls or safeguards and is part of the risk management process.

Domain   Security Management Practices

Reference   ISO/IEC 17799:2000, Section 2.3, page 5.[58]

230. Off-site storage is another important component of the overall BCP/DRP process. Controls relative to storing data off-site include all but one of the following. Which control is *not* included?

a. The off-site storage location is physically and environmentally secure.
b. Record-keeping of the movement of data/media to and from the off-site storage location provides an adequate audit trail.
c. Data storage location(s) must be within three miles of the primary site.
d. Only authorized personnel are allowed access to the off-site storage facility or have the ability to request transfer of data/media.

Explanation Answer c is the correct answer; there are no precise guidelines on how far the data/media must be stored relative to the primary location. Answers a, b, and d are all part of an effective plan to control off-site backup.

Domain Business Continuity Planning and Disaster Recovery Planning

Reference Vallabhaneni (2000), page 345.[18]

231. Which of the following is *not* an attribute of an open system?

a. It provides a standard interface.
b. It provides a non-standard interface.
c. It permits interoperability with other systems.
d. It permits use of non-proprietary languages.

Explanation Answer b is the correct answer; it is a feature of a *closed system*. Answers a, c, and d are attributes of an *open system*.

Domain Security Architecture and Models

Reference Fites and Kratz (1996), page 168.[46]

232. Operations security is:

a. Used to identify and define the physical security of computer facilities and media.
b. Used to define and control access to software.
c. Used to identify the controls over hardware, media, and the operations with access privileges to any of these resources.
d. Used to define and control access to computer systems.

Explanation Answer c is the correct answer and is taken verbatim from the cited reference. The other answers are incorrect because they are each too narrow.

Domain Operations Security

Reference Vallabhaneni (2000), page 310.[42]

233. Which one of the following mechanisms do manual key exchanges use?

 a. PKI
 b. Kerberos
 c. Shared secrets
 d. Diffie–Hellman

Explanation Answer c is correct. Answers a, b, and d are all incorrect because they are all functions of asymmetric encryption.

Domain Cryptography

Reference Fites and Kratz (1996), page 27.[20]

234. The Business Impact Assessment quantifies and qualifies loss potential in terms of:

 a. People, processes, and technology.
 b. Financial (monetary) loss and operational (customer service related) loss impact potentials.
 c. Communications network downtime.
 d. Overtime hour estimates.

Explanation Answer b is the correct answer and is taken from the cited reference. Answer a is partially correct but is too broad in definition; management and selected employees will be in the audience, but not all employees. Answers b and d are partially correct but only focus on narrow definitions of what information the BIA should present.

Domain Business Continuity Planning and Disaster Recovery Planning

Reference Hare (1999), page 27.[14]

235. One reason why intellectual property is a special ethical issue when applied to software is because:

 a. Computer software is expensive to create.
 b. Computer software typically has many features.
 c. Computer software is easy to reproduce and distribute.
 d. Computer software takes a long time to program.

Explanation Answer c is the correct answer and is taken verbatim from the cited reference. The other answers, while possibly applicable, are incorrect because they are not the best answer to the question.

Domain Law, Investigations, and Ethics

Reference Ermann, Williams, and Shauf (1997), page 153.[27]

236. The mandatory, step-by-step processes that must be done to complete a task or assignment are known as:

 a. Policies.
 b. Standards.
 c. Guidelines.
 d. Procedures.

Explanation Answer d is the correct answer and can be found in the reference cited. Answer a addresses high-level management directives and the general means for their completion. Answer b relates to the mandatory actions or requirements that support policies, and answer c relates to the non-mandatory actions that can be used to support a policy.

Domain Security Management Practices

Reference D'Agenais and Carruthers (1985), page 39.[53]

237. Configuration management normally addresses:

 a. Hardware and software.
 b. Networking.
 c. Tape library management.
 d. Both a and b.

Explanation Answer d is the correct answer and is taken from the cited reference. Answer c is incorrect because it is an element of media controls.

Domain Operations Security

Reference National Institute of Standards and Technology (1995), chapter 14.[34]

238. During the recovery alternative strategy development phase of the BCP/ DRP development methodology, all activities except this one should be performed. Which activity should *not* be performed?

 a. Utilize BIA business process priorities to map to both IT and business operations support resources.
 b. Prepare cost estimates for acquisition of the recovery resources required.
 c. Obtain senior management concurrence on acquiring appropriate recovery resources.
 d. Document recovery plans.

Explanation Answer d is the *most* correct answer, meaning that during this phase of the methodology, recovery plan development should not be performed, but should be postponed until all arrangements have been made and management agreement and funding have been obtained. Answers a, b, and c are activities that should take place during this phase.

Domain   Business Continuity Planning and Disaster Recovery Planning

Reference   Devlin and emerson (1999), chapter I-7 page I-7-5;[13] Tipton and Krause (2000), Vol. 2, page 503.[17]

239. A virus scanner works on all the following principles, except for:

   a. Viruses must be in memory to execute.
   b. Viruses can be completely invisible.
   c. Viruses execute in a particular way.
   d. Viruses use certain methods to spread.

Explanation   Answer b is the correct answer. Because code must be stored somewhere and must be in memory to execute, it cannot be completely invisible. Answers a, c, and d are incorrect because they each express a principle for how a virus scanner functions.

Domain   Applications and System Development Security

Reference   Pfleeger (1996), page 186.[10]

240. A *single state* computer:

   a. Simultaneously processes the data of two or more security levels.
   b. Executes only non-privileged instructions.
   c. Processes data of a single security level at one time.
   d. Contains the data of only one security level or classification.

Explanation   Answer c is correct. Answer a is multi-state computer. Answer b is a feature of problem state. Answer d may be true but refers to the stored contents, not the state of operation.

Domain   Security Architecture and Models

Reference   Fites and Kratz (1996), page 169.[46]

241. Which of the following is a requirement for a system operating in system-high security mode?

   a. Each user has a valid personnel clearance for the least sensitive information processed on the system.
   b. Each user has a valid personnel clearance for the most restricted information processed by the system.

c. Each user has a valid need-to-know for *all* the information contained within the system.
d. Each user has a valid need-to-know for *some* of the information contained within the system.

Explanation   Answer d is correct because system-high security mode requires that each user have a need for access to some system information, but not all. Answer a is incorrect because a valid personnel clearance for the most sensitive system information is required in system-high mode. Answer b is incorrect because it pertains to a requirement of the compartmented security mode, and not system-high security mode. Answer c is incorrect in that need-to-know for all information contained within a system pertains to dedicated security mode rather than system-high security mode.

Domain   Security Architecture and Models

Reference   Vallabhaneni (2000), page 304.[51]

242.   What does the acronym ESP represent?

a. Encrypted secure packet
b. Encrypted secure payload
c. Encapsulated secure packet
d. Encapsulated secure payload

Explanation   Answer d is the correct answer. While answers a, b, and c all look correct at first glance, they all have a misrepresented word.

Domain   Cryptography

Reference   Atkinson (1995).[19]

243.   In what field of an IPSec packet might one find the MD5 message digest?

a. In the data field
b. In the encapsulated secure payload
c. In the authentication header
d. In the destination field

Explanation   Answer c is the correct answer. Answers a, b, and d are incorrect because they all have other packet information and not the MD5 message digest.

Domain   Cryptography

Reference   Atkinson (1995).[19]

244. One of the key processes used in a personnel security program is a method that allows organizations to assess threats presented to them by individuals. This process is normally conducted prior to hiring and is termed:

 a. Background investigation.
 b. Resumé skimming.
 c. Reference checking.
 d. Credential verification.

Explanation Answer a is the correct answer and is taken from the cited reference. Answers b, c, and d are all part of the employee hiring process, handled by the human resources department.

Domain Security Management Practices

Reference Icove, Seger, and VonStorch (1995), page 24.[56]

245. Another important element of a well-rounded BCP/DRP process implementation is the development, testing, and maintenance of emergency response procedures. All but one of the following should be considered for inclusion in an effective emergency response procedure. Which one should *not* be included?

 a. Building evacuation plans
 b. Bomb threat procedures
 c. Earthquake evacuation plans and procedures
 d. Detailed business impact analysis information on time-critical IT applications

Explanation Answer d is the obvious correct answer. BIA information does not belong in emergency response procedures that should streamlined and posted throughout the enterprise facility(s). Answers a, b, and c are all part of a emergency response procedure document.

Domain Business Continuity Planning and Disaster Recovery Planning

Reference Hutt, Bosworth, and Hoyt (1995), page 7-9; Devlin and Emerson (1999), page II-14-1.[13]

246. Which of the following is *incorrect* when access to an application or process is changed?

 a. Revocation of rights to an application or process should be automatic when a role changes within an ACL.
 b. Revocation of rights to an application or process should be automatic when an employee leaves the company.

    c. Revocation of rights to an application or process should be automatic when a security breach is observed.

    d. Revocation of rights to an application or process should be automatic, based on job rotation.

Explanation Answer c is the correct answer. When a security breach is observed, certain controlled processes and investigations are initiated. Revoking access rights is always done in a controlled manner, as reflected in the other answers.

Domain Access Control Systems and Methodology

Reference ISO/IEC 17799:2000(E), page 34.[1]

247. The written recovery plan (either BCP or DRP) should *most* correctly contain all of the following sections:

    a. Recovery team structure; detailed activities and tasks for recovery of time-critical operations; EOC location; reporting structure; inventory information (hardware, software, data, space, communications, transportation, people, etc.)

    b. Plan scope, assumption, approach; recovery team structure; detailed activities and tasks for recovery of time-critical operations; EOC location; reporting structure; inventory information (hardware, software, data, space, communications, transportation, people, etc.)

    c. Plan scope, assumption, approach; recovery team structure; detailed activities and tasks for recovery of time-critical operations; EOC location; reporting structure; emergency response procedures

    d. Plan scope, assumption, approach; recovery team structure; off-site backup location; EOC location; reporting structure; inventory information (hardware, software, data, space, communications, transportation, people, etc.)

Explanation Answer b is the correct answer. Answers a, c, and d present types of plans that are really sub-components of the BCP/DRP formalized plans.

Domain Business Continuity Planning and Disaster Recovery Planning

Reference Hutt, Bosworth, and Hoyt (1995), page 7-29.[15]

248. Unsupervised working in secure areas should be avoided:

    a. Because it allows for employee wastage of company time.

    b. To prevent opportunities for malicious activities.

    c. Because it is against OSHA regulations.

    d. Because mistakes can be missed and can cause production outages.

Explanation   Answer b is the correct answer; unsupervised working in secure areas creates opportunities for malicious activities and should thus be avoided. Answer a is an employee management issue and not a physical security issue. Answer c is incorrect — unsupervised working in a secure area is not against OSHA regulations. Answer d is a quality-control issue, not a physical security issue, and is thus incorrect.

Domain   Physical Security

Reference   ISO/IEC 17799:2000, Section 7.1.4, Working in Secure Areas.[44]

249.   Mandatory access control (MAC) techniques are usually used for highly secured, noncommercial computing systems. What are the characteristics of a MAC-compliant system?

    a. Internal and external controls (physical and software) must be employed to be certified as a MAC-compliant system.
    b. MAC-implemented systems enforce policy about which computers connect to one another and what data can pass on a connection.
    c. Access control lists (ACLs) and user authentication constitute a MAC environment.
    d. Mandatory access is only permitted if allowed by mandatory rules and discretionary rights.

Explanation   Answer b is correct. Answer a is incorrect because physical controls are not normally employed in a MAC-designed environment. Answer c is incorrect because user authentication is not a factor in the MAC definition. Answer d is partially correct in this context, but is too detailed for the purposes of the question.

Domain   Access Control Systems and Methodology

Reference   Summers, (1997), pages 11, 356–357.[4]

250.   The statement "Subject cannot modify objects of higher integrity" represents which property of the Biba Access Control Model?

    a. Simple Integrity Property
    b. Simple Security Property
    c. Star Property
    d. Integrity Star Property

Explanation   Answer a is "cannot read down," and answer b is "cannot read up" in Bell–LaPadula. Answer c is "cannot write down" in Bell–LaPadula. Answer d is correct: "no write up."

Domain   Security Architecture and Models

Reference   Fites and Kratz (1996), page 411.[46]

Index

T - #0636 - 101024 - C0 - 254/178/17 - PB - 9780849313509 - Gloss Lamination